Bedlam in the Back Seat

BOOKS BY JANET GILLESPIE

Bedlam in the Backseat

The Joy of a Small Garden

Peacock Manure and Marigolds

A Joyful Noise

With A Merry Heart

Bedlam in
the Back Seat

JANET GILLESPIE

Drawings by Alden Wicks

PARTNERS VILLAGE PRESS
Westport, Massachusetts

BEDLAM IN THE BACKSEAT

Janet Gillespie

This edition printed in 2001
by Partners Village Press
A division of Partners Village Store
999 Main Road, P.O. Box 3051
Westport, Massachusetts 02790
(508) 636-2572
http://www.partnersvillagestore.com

Library of Congress Catalog Card No. 61-5954

ISBN 0-9668225-1-X

Printed in the United States of America

10 9 8 7 6 5 4 3 2 1

To Ernie, Hilly, Chippy, Peggy, and Timmy with love

Contents

Bedlam in the Back Seat

We Leave Home

Bob and I had been married for sixteen years and had acquired four children, a house full of furniture, half an acre of land, and 832 old *New Yorkers*. There were wasps in the attic, a hamster named Mrs. Tittlemouse in the kitchen, two seed-spitting parakeets in the living room, and the two dogs, Mollie and Cluny, who slept in the downstairs bathroom.

There was every reason why we should not go abroad. First of all, the children. Kathy was at the time fifteen, Pete was thirteen, Margie ten, and Billy seven. The two oldest were about to change from public school into private so it was vital that their education should be uninterrupted. The two smallest, people said, were not old enough to get anything out of Europe. In any case four children plus two parents makes six people and it's even expensive for us all to go to a movie.

Then there was the house. It is a nice house which we built when young and ignorant. It has bow windows but hardly any closet space. The cellar floods but we have apple blossoms in the spring and an old stone wall. At intervals pieces of the kitchen ceiling fall onto the floor. Nobody minds. It's our house and we love it. Every time we leave we expect it to burn to the ground and every time we come back one of us always says, "Well, it's still there," in a tone of surprise. If we went abroad we would either have to leave it all alone to burn down or rent it and let strangers live in it.

The garden could not be left at any time without disaster. If we went away in the spring we missed the daffodils and the spring planting; if we went away in the summer we missed the lettuce and peas and everything would die of drought, weeds, or bugs. If we went away in the fall we missed the late corn and the tomatoes and if we went away in the winter the ice storms would wreck the trees and there would be nobody to knock the snow off the evergreens.

There was, too, the problem of the dogs. After infinite pains, involving all varieties of puppies, thoroughbred and otherwise, we had found a perfect female—a mongrel, naturally—and from her haphazard litters of puppies selected the perfect male. Good family dogs are hard to come by and our line, just established, was almost flawless. The dogs were relaxed, well-mannered, and tolerant. They apparently held down steady jobs outside, as they were off all day and reeled in just in time for dinner. They asked for nothing but love and food and were otherwise self-sufficient. We couldn't possibly give them away and if we boarded them for a year it would cost $730.

That summer we had driven 699 miles to our island in Canada, and on the way up two of the children were car-sick, three on the way back. We arrived home in the middle of hurricane Carol, hub-deep in torn leaves and branches. After heating a can of stew over the wood fire we sat for a while, speechless, in the light of three candle stumps. Finally Bob said that never again as long as we lived would we drive anywhere with the children.

One of the most valid reasons why we couldn't go abroad was

that we overdrew our account every month at the bank. "No more checks until after the 20th," Bob would say, and then I would go up in the attic and dig up some wedding presents and Bob would polish and glue together old ski boots which we would sell to the junk man.

There was really only one good reason for going abroad and that was that in the beginning we wanted to. First I wanted to, especially on rainy Sunday afternoons or on days when I was carrying the woolens up to the attic. Then I would tell Bob that our lives were practically over and we had done nothing, seen nothing, gone nowhere.

It is true that I had been to Europe twice before our marriage and that he had been to Bermuda to play rugby and spent ten months on an air-strip in Greenland at the expense of the U.S. Government. However, we had never gone anywhere together except to Canada in the summers and once to New York when he had a week's leave from the Navy during the War.

As long as Bob was against me I could give hundreds of reasons why we should go abroad. I used to lecture him at breakfast and tell him that my father had never had any money and he had taken all seven of us abroad. I quoted his advice to his children: Leap before you look or you'll never do anything. Bob was a teacher of the classics in a large school, I said, and he had never seen Greece and Rome. Everybody else on the Academy faculty took sabbatical leave and he had passed up two.

Although Bob countered all my arguments he must have wanted to go abroad, too, at first. One day he came home and said that he had applied for a Fulbright fellowship and a sabbatical leave for the following year. The sabbatical had already been granted by the Principal. We would take a villa in Italy and send the children to the American School in Florence.

I was absolutely appalled and gave him a hundred reasons why it was impossible for us to go. He had an answer to all of them. We would receive our full salary. We would rent the

3

house and sell the new station wagon. We would get a Fulbright. We would buy a Volkswagen bus to travel in.

"Rent the house!" I cried. "Sell the car!"

"Of course," he said, "it will be easy."

"We don't want people in our house," I said, "and how can I pack enough clothes for six people for a year? I can't, that's all."

Then it was settled and we were going. We sent for steamer listings and Italian linguaphone records and learned how to say "Behold the bedroom of the baby," "Here is the armchair of the grandfather," and other useful everyday remarks. By the time we had made tourist class reservations on a ship sailing in September, we were both panic-stricken. Bob, after spending an evening gluing canceled checks into the checkbook and adding up figures, groaned and said we were ruined.

"You mean we can't go?" I asked hopefully.

"I mean we can't even live in this house. We'll have to sell it and move into a dormitory at the school," he said.

I suggested that we have a drink and he said we could no longer live like millionaires.

The next day the Fulbright Committee regretted to inform him that they could not give him a fellowship. The effect was instantaneous.

"That settles it," said Bob. "We're going no matter what happens. Who do they think they are?"

By evening he was saying, "Thank God I didn't get a Fulbright. Now we can go anywhere we want to."

The next day we told the children that we were really going abroad. On one of the fastest steamers in the world, I added nervously. The girls looked apprehensive.

"What about school?" said Kathy.

"You mean leave all our friends for a *whole year?*" asked Margie.

Billy and Pete were excited but cautious about the ship and wanted to know how lifeboats worked and were there any sub-

4

marines? Billy several times asked me privately whether ships ever ran into each other any more and whether they could sink. I said no, this was absolutely impossible because of radar, radio, and air compartments but I was by no means convinced myself. One night before going to bed Margie asked me whether ships ever ran into icebergs any more like that one in the book. I said "Certainly not." As a matter of fact, I had just read *A Night to Remember,* which described the sinking of the *Titanic,* and had seen a vision of Bob standing on the deck, his hand raised in farewell while the band played "Nearer My God to Thee."

Billy also asked me if we would ride on those teensy little trains in Italy and see all those little weentsy black goats.

"Goats?" I said.

"Yah, you know. Beside the tracks."

"Oh," I said.

Margie asked if we would see those candy stores on the corners in Paris.

"What candy stores?" I asked.

"Oh, those ones on corners with candy and stuff in glass jars," she said.

"Oh, those," I said. "Yes, I guess so."

Aside from these remarks the children acted as though going abroad were something we did every day; they spent their time playing with their friends and eating in the usual way.

I, myself, felt exactly as though I were going to die in six months and did everything possible to avoid packing or preparing the house for renters. I was able to rationalize this behavior by telling myself that I had to plan the route. Bob spent all his time writing his book on Vergil and said that as long as we got to Italy and a place called Alesia in France, he didn't care where else we went.

One day in the spring he wrote and changed our sailings from September to January.

"We may have to go abroad," he said, "but we don't have to stay *that* long."

"Nobody will rent the house for only five months," I said happily.

"Well, we didn't want to rent it anyway," he said.

The man at the garage said, "Now I'll be honest with you, lady. The bottom has dropped out of the used-car market. That car will probably be here when you get back." This made me feel quite optimistic.

We found a place that would take $169 to board the dogs for five months.

"Maybe we'll be thrown in jail for debt and won't have to go," I said.

"We could go to New York and hide for a while and then sneak back here," said Bob.

By the first of September I was convinced that our departure for Europe would coincide with, if not actually insure, the outbreak of World War III. The school year started and the class bells rang without Bob. All the familiar machinery of the fall term went into motion and we were outside it. This added to the sense of doom which hung over me and it hardly seemed worth while doing anything. I couldn't find any guidebook which dealt with taking children abroad. The assumption seemed to be that all travelers are childless.

Once I found a guidebook written, it said, for Women, but apparently, mothers aren't really women. To the authors of this fascinating work a Woman is single and on the prowl and Europe in the last analysis simply a giant hunting ground where herds of men await capture. "You will find," I read, "that the monuments, cathedrals, equestrian statues, and medieval churches of Europe are extremely interesting and beautiful, but the men of Europe, if you know how to look at them and if you understand what you see, are a hundred times more interesting and worth exploring."

I would say that if you know how to look at men it couldn't matter less whether or not you understand what you see, as you will be too busy fighting them off. Anyway, all that stuff about catching men was no help to me, although I wasted a good many hours glued to the pages of this guide. After reading a chapter called, "Looking for the Bluebird—or How European Women Find Happiness," I angrily discarded it and read a book about a man who went to Italy *alone*. On the first page he had a slipped disc in his back and on page 35, I had a slipped disc, too.

After the slipped disc I developed virus pneumonia, thus filling in the time until Christmas. All I had done in preparation for five months abroad was to buy three folders. In the one marked *Steamer* I had a lot of typed sheets and pink blanks that proved we had ordered one Volkswagen Kleinbus to be delivered to us on the dock at Le Havre. I had another folder marked *Italy* containing a letter from a friend of ours explaining how they had exceeded their budget and had to return from Italy two months early. Then I had a folder marked *Route* which held an old envelope with "Ferme d'Augustin, St. Tropez" on it and the words "2 doz. eggs pnut butter, bird seed." Somehow this array made me feel completely hopeless and it seemed easier to do nothing and wait for the end.

As I lay in my hospital bed the people who had had slipped discs came in and said they had never been out of pain until they had a "fusion operation." The people who had had virus pneumonia came in and said they had "felt like death" for three months and were a year "getting their strength back." Those who had been abroad came and told me that (a) Europe in winter was colder than the Arctic and they never had a comfortable moment, (b) the food in Europe was so rich that everybody got ulcers and it was pure madness to eat fresh vegetables because they were fertilized with You-Know-What, (c) the water in Europe was lethal, so was the milk, and everybody got dysentery, (d) the people in Europe hated Americans, cheated them all the time, and in some cases murdered them, (e) Latin men were so insane over blondes that it was dangerous to appear on the street without a male escort or bodyguard.

7

Other people with a more relaxed viewpoint said blithely that (a) it was unnecessary to take along anything but the most basic items as most things could be bought over there, (b) that everybody in Europe adored Americans, (c) that they never had a cold or anything else all winter, (d) that you could live in Austria for $1.49 a day if you rode a bicycle and slept in a tent.

These conversations reduced me to a state of extreme depression and I wept while eating a revolting hospital supper at the terrible hour of 4:30 P.M.

Bob, who knows a last straw when he sees it, took a firm line and said I was to stop worrying. Everything was going to be all right.

"But what about packing?" I quavered, mopping my eyes.

"It will get done," he said with authority. He went on to say that there had been some slight changes in the Master Plan. The Volkswagen would not meet us at the boat but in Paris. We would then drive across Europe to the Austrian Tyrol where I could be warm. The mountains, he said, were the only place in Europe that had heat in winter because of the electric power. I didn't really understand this, but Bob explained that the mountains were warm since the people understood and expected cold and so were prepared. There seemed to be a flaw in this reasoning somewhere but I couldn't put my finger on it.

I wrote all the way across Europe and made reservations in a small inn near the Brenner Pass where some friends of ours had stayed. This gave me a slight, but only slight, feeling of hope; there was something definite to look forward to. Also memories of skiing in the White Mountains combined with a romantic movie of Vivian Leigh falling into sin in Davos gave the whole prospect a glamorous touch. Bob produced a photographer, and he took a passport picture of me wearing my coat over a nightgown. I consulted the mirror afterwards and decided that I looked exactly like a spy.

The doctor let me go home the day before Christmas, and after a week spent making lists and tearing them up I became suddenly perfectly calm. I went to Boston and bought four large canvas containers called Car-pacs and six small zipper bags. I bought a black silk suit at a sale, some English walking shoes, a lot of children's underwear, three drip-dry shirts, a ruffled nightgown, and an album of Handel organ concertos. Then I went home and packed with inhuman ferocity. For two days I did nothing but pack, and the upstairs rooms were waist deep in clothing, rolls of toilet paper, boxes of Kleenex, and plastic bags. Finally it was all done and every single item was entered, with its location, in a black notebook.

I solved very simply the problem of what clothes to take for the children. I just took everything they owned and stuffed socks and underwear into all the empty spaces. If there was a corner left anywhere I filled it with a roll of toilet paper or a wad of Kleenex. I forced all that was left over into four duffel bags and loaded my old suitcase with games until it was immovable.

Every time a child took off a piece of clothing, I washed it, and as soon as it came out of the dryer I packed it. Each morning after they had gone to school I unpacked all the stuffed animals, trucks, shells, and dolls clothes from their zipper bags and every night they put them back. Presently nobody had anything to wear but what he stood up in, and whenever I left the house someone would root around in the Car-pacs to get a sweater or a pair of socks. In the end nobody knew where anything was, but by that time nobody cared.

One minute I would be scrubbing out the icebox and Bob would be driving to the dump and the next minute we would be out at a dinner party eating pheasant and drinking champagne.

I don't remember anything about the last day. It has sunk without a trace into my subconscious. There is probably a scientific word for this phenomenon. I do remember that the hotel in New York wouldn't let us in because the people in our rooms were still there. As we went across town to the Great Northern Hotel, Margie said she thought she was going to up-chuck. On that note we went to bed.

9

The next morning we drove down to the docks in a taxi and saw the steamer looming up against a gray, rainy sky. The great sheds were full of cold wind and noise. We stood in lines like cattle waiting at the barn gate and eventually went aboard and through a labyrinth of red and gray corridors to our staterooms. Margie said she thought she might up-chuck any minute and some people asked us to a champagne party in First Class which we had to refuse.

We sailed in a drizzle. I stood on the boat deck and tried to stop the boys from crawling under the rail to get more paper streamers. Kathy wandered gloomily in the distance and Margie lay, the color of cheese, on the deck behind us. Bob was standing in line for Dining Room tables the entire time but did emerge just as we passed the Statue of Liberty. From the river New York looked magnificent and unreal, and I kept trying to whip up some enthusiasm for the sight but nobody cared. I did drag Margie to the rail to watch the Statue of Liberty go by, but she merely lay down there.

We were still in the river and the boat was steady as a church but suddenly all the children were seasick.

During this nightmare period, while Bob and I were constantly in attendance, the steward came staggering in with a pile of florists' boxes, champagne bottles, and telegrams, some of which were for a man called Hugh Selvidge. All the things for H. Selvidge were from a female called Susan, although the telegram was from Susan and The Crowd. We ourselves had a great many telegrams of our own which made me wonder why on earth we had ever left home.

Down in the bowels of the ship we lost all track of time and only the gong for meals distinguished night from day. We had signed up for the first sitting because of our children, so we ate in a forest of highchairs, a kind of Lilliputian Tower of Babel where food was refused or thrown around in ten different languages. Babies screamed and every few minutes some desperate parent led out a green child.

10

The rest of the time we sat on the edges of lower berths and drank champagne out of tumblers. As a result I existed in a dreamlike state, staring at my spray of butterfly orchids without a thought in my head.

The sight of Bob crouched morosely on the edge of the other berth added the final touch to the paranoid, prison-cell atmosphere of A47. Salvador Dali would have screamed for joy. White orchids lay among toothbrushes, camellias and Kleenex slid about on the window sill. At intervals we fell over the champagne bucket to reach the seasick cartons and reeled back to hold the head of a child wearing a rosebud corsage. The same horrid surrealistic atmosphere obtained in A46, where Kathy was immobile in the upper berth and there were more orchids, also a plate containing unripe bananas and deflated balloons.

There were two push buttons by the door, one green labeled Stewardess, and a red one called Steward. If you pressed the green one nothing happened. If you pressed the red one nothing usually happened but sometimes, hours later, one of the several Puerto Rican bellboys would appear. It was very, very difficult to get anything done, however, as the bellboys wouldn't deal with the seasick cartons, although they would, if given the right change, go to the bar and get ginger ale. The steward would cope with seasick cartons but wouldn't buy ginger ale. He sometimes brought apples, though, and bowls of ice or saltines. The stewardess would do hardly anything.

Day after day the dark blue Homeric sea rolled to the horizon in great toppling waves laced with whitecaps. The ship, knifing steadily through the brilliant circle of the horizon, hardly lifted her bow. Only below decks in the tilting stairways or in the berths could you feel the strong rise and fall of the sea breathing and the heartbeat of the engines.

The children finally emerged into the daylight, wan and big-eyed.

"Boy," they said, "this is neat. Wish we could stay on this boat all the time."

11

They then took to the elevators and we hardly saw them. Not that we didn't try. Looking for children was practically all I did until we landed.

The passenger list was like all Tourist Class lists. There were a great many nuns who sat in the Ping-pong room telling their beads and whispering. There were priests who murmured to one another in unknown tongues. There was a pair of beady-eyed East Indians with a beady-eyed baby and a dismal, but less beady-eyed, grandfather who looked like the Walrus in *Alice*. There was the usual sepia-colored gentleman in a pink turban, black sunglasses, and black beard who was attended by a troupe of patent-leather young men with butterfly wives in saris. Pete picked up a synthetic Humphrey Bogart who was, we thought, Dutch and who communicated by galvanic winks and gestures. I picked up a fake Laurence Olivier who told me all about deep-sea diving, and Billy made friends with a Persian or Hittite, more like a burst horsehair sofa than anything human. John Wayne (real) was in First Class and was also in the Tourist Movie once, a fact which confused Billy so much that he nearly drove us mad with questions.

On the sunny days we watched the scarlet funnels rocking against the sky while we lay like cocoons in our deck chairs. Pete played shuffleboard with the synthetic Humphrey Bogart and Billy conversed with his Hittite who used to twiddle on some unknown flutelike instrument (piccolo?). The fake Laurence Olivier introduced us to his friend, a very nice young man who was rebelling against the advertising business and had taken the trip to decide whether or not to abandon it and write, just like somebody in Marquand.

At intervals I did some valuable research on nuns in the Ping-pong room. Most of the nuns were formidable characters but one was very young and as pretty as a peach and with her I had some half-French, half-English conversations. In the convent, she said, they were allowed no private property; all their letters were opened by the Mother Superior and they were not permitted to ask questions about each others' previous experiences or to indulge in *idle or purposeless conversation*. It was easy to see that I would make a rotten nun, but the chances of my having to be one are remote.

Our last day on board was as perfect as possible, the sea a calm brilliant blue, scintillating in the sunlight, and the ship at last steady beneath our feet. Except for the hushed, seething whisper of foam there was no sound under the enormous sky.

I got up early and watched the sunrise from the top deck in company with the pretty nun. She was leaning against the rail facing the golden furnace of the east and I saw that she was praying so I didn't disturb her. The ocean was like boiling copper and clouds of rose and orange shredded upward from the horizon.

Late on the final afternoon, off the coast of England, we stood on the open promenade deck as we passed through the Breton fishing fleet. In the hot level sunlight the sea was a floor of diamonds, an enormous silver and blue silence through which the ship moved without a sound, light as a floating feather. It seemed pure magic, this peace, after nearly a week of tossing and creaking, of howling winds and all the multiple screaming, thumping, whistling voices of a ship at sea. I stood by the rail and looked down on the toy fishing boats spread out over the brilliant water like a flock of ducks. The men on them waved and cried up to us with tiny voices, French voices, barely audible. There were gulls riding the blue air over us, the sun snow-white on their breasts. A nice change from those peculiar mid-ocean birds (petrels?) that skitter down the troughs of waves in such a seasick manner.

After dinner we all went up on the top deck and under a sky of a thousand stars watched the lights of the Scilly Isles slide by. There was a crescent moon, the wind blew gently, bringing with it a faint warmth and sweetness from the land. The horrors of the voyage might never have been. It was wonderful to be back near the comforting earth where trees were

13

and grass and the lighted windows of houses. After the lonely emptiness of mid-ocean the land itself was home and Europe was no longer Abroad because *we* were there. Now it was America, far away across the impersonal sea that was laid open to the dangers and uncertainties of remote places.

Paris, Mon Coeur

The next morning when we woke the stillness was complete. The pulse that had hummed and quivered in the mattress, in the steel bulkheads, in the deck, and had set the water glass chattering on its stand—this pulse had stopped. Outside, voices shouting in French rang full and clear in the silence. Gulls clamored and down below there were mysterious thumps and rumbles.

France.

I crawled over to the porthole and saw part of a wall, a roof with gulls on it. Then there was a thunderous bang on the door.

"Get up!" shouted Pete, "Jeeze, they've come for the bags. Hurry, Daddy says."

I pounded on the bottom of Kathy's berth and she sat up with a cry, hitting her head against the ceiling.

We stumbled out of the two cabins and there were the

stewards and bellboys waiting for tips. Even the stewardess turned up. We edged by her coldly. Her contribution to our week's martyrdom had been one plate of crackers. To George, the colored waiter, who had been friend, doctor, and stewardess rolled into one, we dealt out all our tip money.

At 6 A.M. Le Havre had the gray skeletal outline of all large ports, and our little family, shepherded by Olivier and Marquand, straggled off the gangplank into cavernous sheds echoing with the cries of porters. With my Berlitz phrase book in hand I was able to communicate after a fashion with one of these. However, even now I have only the most confused memory of darkness, berets, trains, noise, and handfuls of French money.

In our compartment on the Paris train we were joined by Marquand, our last link with home, to whom we clung feverishly. The train ran through Normandy, where rows of tall narrow poplars stood against a silvery sky, and red-tiled roofs and medieval looking farm yards reminded me of Breughel. Enormous wood pigeons flapped out of unfamiliar trees, and men in earth-colored clothes and berets stared at us from neat little vegetable gardens. The Frenchness of everything, the signs, the gray-shuttered towns filled me with delight, but as far as I could see our children simply ignored France and argued about who should sit where. Finally a customs official came and sat gloomily by the door. He discussed something in somber tones with another official, absent-mindedly scribbled on our bags with pink chalk, and left.

We had a second breakfast in the dining car at vast expense, and, hours later, the first of Paris began to slip past the windows. At the Gare Saint Lazare, Marquand and Bob established contact with a porter on the platform and our luggage was handed out the window over the heads of the crowd. Our porter, in his blue coverall and beret, built a kind of beaver dam across the stream of traffic, so that by the time we had fought our way out of the train he had trapped a seething maelstrom of passengers, luggage-carriers, and porters. Into this we threw ourselves. Bob and Marquand and the porter were swallowed up together,

16

and I, organizing a human chain of children, forced my way after them. Pete went ahead as a scout, returning at intervals to report. Bob kept appearing downstream and waving, then disappearing again. Marquand drifted by on his way out, carrying his skis. The pretty nun waved farewell as she climbed into a taxi. Humphrey Bogart made a last signal of good fellowship in our direction and I saw the Hittite borne away on a kind of tidal wave of beards and black hats. When Bob finally joined us he looked drawn.

"Explain to this bird where we're going," he said.

The porter gave me a gay and conspiratorial smile. His hands rose to his shoulders in a gesture of mock despair. I thought how much I loved the French and told him the address of our hotel. He bowed and smiled as though I had given him a rose.

We drove through Paris in two taxis, the luggage following us in a blue van guarded by the porter.

Every time the traffic slowed down, our drivers got out and argued violently in the street. During one of these exchanges our taxi began to roll down hill and I was forced to climb over the front seat and take the controls, causing great consternation among the bystanders. Cries of *"Tiens!"* *"Mon Dieu!"* and *"Holà, la madame!"* rang through the street. We passed a shop called "Tits" and a sign advertising a soft drink called "Pschitt." Both these items gave intense pleasure to the children.

As in New York, we were greeted at the hotel by the news that there were people in our rooms. For a while we attempted to argue about this with the concierge and were soon the center of an interested crowd. Two boys in caps, the taxi drivers, and a man with a twig broom sided with us and reviled the concierge. The porter, also on our side, complimented me on my French and my children. We all glared at the concierge. Fortunately, my long sessions with the incomparable Michelin guide to France had provided us with an ace in the hole and we found a hotel in the next block. Its name was the Franklin Roosevelt, not as French as we would have liked, but the hotel itself was perfect.

17

It stood on a narrow side street where tall narrow houses faced each other. The austerity of their shuttered façades was relieved by the frivolity of the iron railings that edged the balconies. They were like those strips of black lace worn on the throats of elegant old ladies.

"*Bonjour, mademoiselle,*" I said to the pretty girl at the desk.

"Good morning, madame," she said in exquisite English. "The *valet de chambre* will take up your bags."

Our rooms were large and high-ceilinged, with the garlands, rosebuds, chintzes, and paneling I have always imagined to be characteristic of a good bawdy house. (Bob was, he said, unable to verify this.) There were tall French windows opening onto tiny balconies with rococco iron railings. Heavy metal shutters folded back on each side, and long draperies of gold and red velvet gave an air of great elegance which was eminently satisfying. One corner of each room was fenced off by flowered screens to hide the basin and bidet, an article which naturally aroused much interest among the young.

"I don't get it," said Billy, who holds all washing in deep contempt.

"Some people like to be clean, that's all," I said firmly.

There was no one else visible in the hotel but we saw a tray with a teapot on it outside No. 10, and sounds of coughing issued hollowly from No. 6. Down the hall was a narrow cell with a toilet in it but so far as we could see no light. However, Billy, with the male's natural instinct for gadgets, discovered that the lock controlled the light and spent some time demonstrating this to those willing to join him inside the cell.

Back in our room I read all those framed signs that are such a feature of French hotels and found that *Lavage* in the wash basin was *Absolument Interdit;* that baths cost so many francs apiece and that the chambermaid would provide towels. The problems of cleanliness depressed me momentarily until I figured out that if we locked our door nobody would see the *Lavage* hanging on our plastic line. After investing in all that drip-dry stuff and carefully decanting detergents into pliofilm bags, I would not be foiled by a mere sign. Bob said that women were a lawless, immoral lot but I said that if everybody obeyed the law we'd still be living in caves.

The emotional tensions of French life had reduced Bob and myself almost to ashes so we went out to look for a place to eat. Across from the hotel on the corner was a restaurant called Chez André and outside the door was a kind of shrine dedicated to food where a curly-haired man in a beret was opening oysters. On shelves under an arch strung with lemons were all the delicacies of land and sea arranged like works of art. On beds of seaweed lay the spiny rosettes of sea urchins, coral, arabesques of shrimp, blue mussels, and the tiny oysters of France. There were mushrooms nested in dried ferns, delicate as Valentines, and the famous *escargots,* the snails of Burgundy, already plugged with butter and herbs.

André wore a red cardigan and established us at a table with those wide sweeping bows and whiskings of napkins that are a specialty of his countrymen. The menus hadn't changed in twenty years—they were still written in illegible purple ink.

I ordered *escargots* and something with mushrooms in it. Bob ordered oysters and a bottle of white wine.

"Hamburger," said Billy, "and Coke."

"No, no," we said, "try something French."

"Tuna-fish salad," said Margie, "and Coke."

In the end they all ordered steak, French fried potatoes, and peas. Also Cokes.

This meal renewed us wonderfully and we suggested to the children that they come with us and explore Paris.

"No," they said, "we want to stay in the hotel and have fun."

"But what will you do?" I asked.

"Oh, have fun," they said.

Feeling guilty but relieved, we left them in Kathy's care and walked over to the Champs Élysées, down through the gardens, and over to the Opéra. Nothing was ever so enchanting as this city—shuttered, silvery, mysterious, and at the same time as

19

gay and effervescent as a light opera. In the park the trees were etched in black upon violet, misty air. The brilliant grass was like spring; hollies and boxwood shone with a dark luster, and under them in the soft, velvety earth were crocuses, primroses, and violas already in bloom. I saw a tiny European robin and a thrush running upon the grass. Pigeons as large as ducks weighed down the bushes and crashed about in the chestnuts overhead.

On returning to the hotel, my exalted state of mind was somewhat shaken by Kathy's report that the boys had spent all their time riding up and down in the automatic elevator and that they had locked themselves out of their room. Also, she said, there was an old, old man who had been trying to go up to the next floor and the boys had brought him back down to the lobby twice.

Pete said that (a) Kathy had been a grouch every minute and wouldn't let them do anything, (b) what were elevators for anyway? and (c) how were they to know that the old man practically lived in it?

Overcome with guilt at having left them, I suggested to Bob that we take them out for a treat. On pushing the elevator button to go down I was horrified to see a very tall man of immense age descend to our level glaring malevolently through the glass door like an exhibit in a museum.

"See, there he is," said Billy. "Gosh, he *never* gets out of it."

We walked down the stairs but were unable to avoid meeting the old gentleman emerging from the elevator at the bottom. His basilisk eye raked us.

We escaped into the street and asked the children what they wanted to do.

"Buy comic books," they said, "and get some Coke."

We compromised by taking them to a candy shop where we had to buy some very expensive lollypops. Then we went to a cafeteria to save money. Bob and I ate omelets. The children ate steaks, French fried potatoes, peas, and Cokes.

Bob cursed the Volkswagen garage who had said, when he telephoned, that our car was "somewhere between Munich and the border." Since they had promised to have it waiting on the dock for us, he had been reasonably angry when they said that it would meet us in Paris. Was it here? No. Was it even in France? No. As I had never really expected it to be, I wasn't particularly upset by this. Also I wanted to stay in Paris as long as possible. If we stayed here the whole five months it would be all right with me.

We returned to the hotel and put the children in their rooms. Then we locked our door and washed out all our dacron, hanging it up to drip into the bidet and basin. We were just crawling into bed when Margie came in and said, "Guess what, Billy never takes off his underwear *or* his T shirt *or* his socks when he goes to bed but just puts his pajamas on *over* them. Then," she said, "when he gets up he puts his clothes on *over* everything, even the pajamas."

"You go to bed," I said, "and I'll tend to Billy."

"He *smells*," said Margie, following me toward the boys' door, "and you should see his *feet*. He never washes, never brushes his teeth and he's just *filthy*."

"You don't know anything about it," I said, realizing that for some days I had forgotten to check the boys' lingerie.

I sent her back to her own room and opened the boys' door. They both had underwear on *over* their pajama pants and were grappling in the middle of the floor.

"What do you think you're doing?" I asked.

"Wrestling," said Pete briefly, unwrapping himself.

"Why do you wear your underwear outside like that?" I asked.

"We're Superman," said Billy, hitching up his garments. "I got some underneath, too."

"Do you wear your underwear to bed?" I asked, coming straight to the point.

"Sure he does," said Pete traitorously. "Never takes it off.

21

You ought to see it. He's had that one on for about a week."

Billy grinned happily.

"Do you do that?" I said.

"Yah," he replied. "I like to."

"Why?"

"Because it's easier to get dressed," he answered.

"Where's your toothbrush?" I asked and ordered him to the washbasin while I picked up dirty clothes from the piles of junk around the floor. Then I scrubbed him violently with soap and water, even making him put his feet in the basin. When he was pink and damp and in clean pajamas I kissed his bullet head and tucked him in bed, feeling strongly that little boys are heavenly creatures.

"Now you," I said to Pete, "I suppose you haven't washed either?"

"Oh, no you don't," said he. "I'll do it. Get out of here, Maw, Jeeze!"

I departed, holding Billy's underwear in my finger tips and went into the girls' room to say good night. Margie was sitting up in bed, brushed and rosy in her blue pajamas, reading *Mary Poppins*. Raggedy Ann and Raggedy Andy sat on each side of her, her baby doll was in bed in the armchair, covered with a pink blanket; all her books and treasures lined up and squared off on her table. She always builds her nest before going to bed, no matter where she is.

Kathy was sitting cross-legged on the other bed putting her freshly washed hair up in pin curls. Her shirt and slip were hanging up to dry and the room smelled of soap and Yardley's lavender powder.

I kissed them good night and went out thinking what heavenly creatures little girls are. Bob was reading in bed and I said I thought all our mice were divine.

"Hmmmm?" he said.

"Don't you?" I said.

"Don't I what?"

22

"Think they are divine?"

"Who?" etc. etc.

I climbed into bed and lay there looking up at the plaster garlands on the ceiling and thinking, "We're in Paris. We're in *Paris.*" However, I was so tired that I couldn't make it register. I then tried to read the book I'd been trying to read on the boat, and fell asleep at once.

Togetherness, Parisian Style

Waking in the darkness of our shuttered room, I lay for a while listening to the sounds of the street, the clatter of shutters being folded back, voices calling in French, the whish of small cars going by, and footsteps tap-tapping like flocks of woodpeckers. Below and beyond these close crisp notes rolled the full ground bass of sound, the deep resonant voice of Paris beginning a day.

When I stood up, the carpeted floor swayed under me in memory of the steamer. I folded back our shutters and looked out over the curly iron balcony to the little market across the street. A black-aproned cheerful man was piling oranges outside the door; a child in a pinafore trotted by with a small covered milk can, and there was a whistling man in a beret pushing a wicker barrow stacked with long loaves of bread. I saw an old gentleman with a goatee carrying a string bag of oranges, then a lady airing a poodle.

The day seemed to be sunless as a white light shone up from the curved lines of paving stones in the street. When I leaned out I could see the chimney pots, each with its plume of smoke. The sky was silvery, with a look of light shining through mist. The smell of Paris was of ground coffee, fresh bread, coal smoke, and exhausts.

I was so delighted with everything that I wanted all my family to wake up and enjoy it. The first impressions of a foreign country are as clean and new as a horse chestnut just out of its husk, but it's wiser on the whole to savor these impressions alone. Men don't seem to want to be chivvied out of bed to see other men going to work.

Having ordered breakfast, I went to wake the children, who had locked themselves in. The smaller in each room was awake and after some difficulty I was admitted. No one seemed interested in looking out the window and all said that they would have bacon and eggs for breakfast. Also grapefruit. I explained several times that their only choice was between coffee and chocolate. When I returned to our bedroom I found Bob hiding coyly behind the screen in the corner while a maid set forth our *petit déjeuner.* After she left I made Bob move the table over near the window so that we could see out, thereby compressing as many sensations as possible into the fleeting moment.

We had hardly begun buttering our *croissants* when Margie came in to report that there was skin on her cocoa and that Kathy wouldn't get up. After this both boys came in carrying *croissants* and asked whether they had to eat them. Bob and I traded our small loaves of bread for the *croissants,* a deal which became part of each day's routine. Eventually we all got out in the hall dressed for sight-seeing but by some mysterious process our key had disappeared. (We never saw it again but found that the key to No. 4 worked just as well in our door.)

That morning we walked down the Champs Élysées to the

25

Place de la Concorde, and the children were in a state of perpetual amazement at the small size of the cars, the sight of men
in berets, and the incredible number of poodles clipped like
toys. Peter was considerably revolted by the boys his own age
wearing shorts, long socks, and berets.

"Jeeze," he said disgustedly, "whatta buncha fairies."

"They're not," I said. "That's how French boys dress."

This argument was brought to an abrupt close by the vision
of a handsome officer's head grinning at us over the shutters of
one of those conveniences seen only in Latin countries.

"What's *he* doing?" hissed Margie.

I explained what he was doing.

"But how come right out in the *street?*"

I said that the French were different about these things.

"Jeeze," said Pete.

Another thing that caused the children a great deal of pleas-
urable horror was the amount of love about. Couples holding
hands or walking with their arms around each other seemed to
shock them deeply.

"Hey, look," Billy kept saying. "They're *lovers.*"

"Don't say that," I said. "It doesn't mean what you think."

"What does it mean?" inquired Margie, interested.

"Nothing," said Bob. "Now watch where you're going or
we'll all be killed."

We crossed over to the Seine at the Place de la Concorde,
a feat of some skill, because the whole place was like a merry-
go-round. It was very misty down on the quays; the sun shone
like a silver dollar and the sycamore trees with their network of
twigs and dangling seed-capsules made exquisite patterns in the
fog. We walked in what seemed like silence after the rush of
traffic above. Barges slid past on the river without a ripple; the
water was smooth as oil, reflecting the arches of bridges in exact
reverse. Lonely fishermen sat in classic attitudes of patience,
holding bamboo poles. Sometimes we met a woman with a dog
or a man with a twig broom sweeping the pavement. Under the
arches of one bridge floated little boats painted scarlet and blue.

Once we passed an old man cooking over a fire of sticks while another man kneeled by the water shaving.

The boys ran ahead of us, leaned over the water at dangerous angles, balanced on slimy ledges, fished for nameless flotsam with sticks and hung upside down from the iron rings in the walls. Margie, who for some reason had insisted on wearing her rubber boots over bedroom slippers, ran after her brothers clumping heavily, but Kathy walked with dignity beside Bob, looking very elegant in her polo coat.

When I saw Billy teetering up the outside railing of a stone stairway, I decided that the law of diminishing returns had set in. They might not get run over on the quays but they would soon fall in the river. I expect Gesell would have said to let them and then they'd Learn, but Gesell isn't a mother who had to wash all those clothes in a room where *Lavage,* even of dacron, was *Interdit. Absolument Interdit.* Therefore we took a bus and boarded one of those big green ones, as cowboys leap onto galloping horses in the movies. Everyone in the bus regarded us fixedly and a large woman with a moustache explained to me where the bus went, in a sort of pig-English.

When we got off at the Châtelet, Kathy informed us that a man had tried to pick her up. I wondered whether to issue a warning against white slavers, that legend of my youth, but decided against it and instead told them all that they must walk around the block so as to come on Notre Dame from the most dramatic angle.

"Now look!" I said as we turned into the square.

The marvelous cathedral rose against the moving sky, its stone the crumbly silvery color of wasp nests. A nun was standing in front of the door and the wind blew her enormous white coif around as though it were a slatting jib. Pigeons rose from the pavement, whirled like dry leaves, and settled again. There were the old four-branched street lamps tilting against the clouds.

"Hey, there's one of those bathroom places!" cried Billy rapturously, sighting a *pissoir.*

27

"Jeeze," said Pete. "I'm going to try it!"

If, at that moment, we had grasped the significance of this episode, much needless suffering would have been averted. Instead of realizing that excitement over the *pissoir* and indifference to Notre Dame were logical and natural at their age, I was outraged. I threw up my hands.

"Oh, God," I said to the girls, who out of necessity had remained with me, "all the way across the ocean and for what?"

"Now, Mum," said Kathy, "relax."

"Why can't *we* go in there?" Margie asked plaintively.

A similar thing happened at Sainte Chapelle. Outside the gates was one of those stands selling artificial dog messes and other Gallic inventions of a similar character. We had been having a rather rough passage through the streets with people stepping on each other, some shoving, and sporadic arguments about buying Disney comic books. However, all differences dissolved in the delighted speculations aroused by this revolting display and for nearly an hour peace and good will reigned among us. Even Bob and myself suggested certain enemies of humanity who might benefit by gifts of this kind and we all reeled along, united in laughter. To the children, looking at Sainte Chapelle was apparently like going to school. The dog messes were part of real life.

This proved to be true of any expedition which called only for staring at buildings, pictures, or historical sites. Anything, however, about which or to which it was possible to *do* something tended to be a success. For this reason everybody was happy in the Flower and Bird Markets where the atmosphere was that of a country village.

In the nursery-garden stalls, stoves burned cosily and the smoking chimneys gave a domestic touch to the neat wattled shelters. Primroses and tulips in pots were set out in rows, and the proprietors took their ease in deck chairs or on the curbstone smoking pipes or reading papers.

In the Bird Market, finches and parakeets kept up an inces-

28

sant chatter, canaries sang piercingly, and there was an enormous parrot croaking French to himself. Chickens crooned in rough wicker cages and big gray rabbits pressed twitching noses against their prisons.

In front of a seed store an old gentleman with a goatee was examining gladiolus bulbs through his eyeglass. Little trees in leaf stood out on the sidewalk. There was a sound of trickling water from the tanks of goldfish and a smell of loam and moss, chickens, puppies, shavings, and manure.

We spent a long time in this area: the children poked their fingers in cages, watched fish swimming in tanks, and examined piles of shells, sponges, corals, cork, and other curiosities set forth for sale. Bob lit his pipe and he and I went across the street and looked at the prints and old books in the stalls. Then, as it was lunch time, we went to the Bouteille d'Or, near Notre Dame, and ate one of those French meals. From copper casseroles rose the fragrance of herbs and garlic; the butter was in pale fluted whorls; the bread warm and crusty. They had trout in a tank and an old dog wandered among the tables.

Bob had chicken livers in wine, I had Poulet Provençal, the children had *entrecôtes, pommes frites, petit pois,* and *quatre Coca-Colàs* (steak, french fries, peas, and Cokes). We argued with them but they were adamant and in any case steak is cheap in Paris. However, the bill at the end of this orgy was so enormous that Bob nearly turned to stone before our eyes.

After any French meal except breakfast one should rest quietly, preferably on one's back under a tree but, if this is not practical, in a sunny café where the mood of gentle philosophy can be indulged. Obviously Bob and I had no chance to do either of these things, both because it was winter and because we were always being urged by the children to get out of places and *do* something.

On this first day, though, we had not given up the conventional notion that we should take advantage of every moment even when completely exhausted. It was a kind of noble martyrdom painful for all. Bob finally deserted us—men have a lower

29

threshold of pain—and went off to hunt for obscure classical books. I straggled after him with my brood, letting the tide take me where it would.

The bookstalls, confetti-colored and gay along the silvery quays, were wonderful but exhausting. What with being dragged one way to look at a picture of a naked woman and dragged another way to see a print of cats being Rabelaisian, I was almost torn to shreds. Luckily Pete found a case full of old medals and Kathy a music stall, so for a while we haggled over an old *Croix de Guerre* and obscure medals from the Boer War. I was absolutely convinced that it was wrong for Pete to wear the *Légion d'Honneur* or Billy to have a *Croix de Guerre,* but as usual was outargued and feebly bought them on the condition that they must *never* be worn.

After this Pete became interested, heaven knows why, in a series of pictures of monks eating, so we combed the print stalls for those and bought several for him. This necessitated buying some for Billy and Margie as well, although I told them that just because Pete collected pictures of monks eating was no reason for them to be copy cats.

"But we *love* them!" they said.

I felt definitely that things were getting beyond me and knew that Bob would be unsympathetic with every one of our recent purchases. However, Kathy bought some sheet music for the equivalent of one cent, which seemed, at the time, to justify everything.

It began to get very chilly, with mist rising and a slow drizzle falling. Between the sagging dark sky and the slate-gray river ran the wet streets, the wet sidewalks, the wet cars and umbrellas—all shining greasily in the failing light. The only bright colors in all the world were the fluttering prints on the bookstalls, the kiosks, and a child in a scarlet jacket. Duffel coats, blue jeans, black overcoats, and berets jostled each other ahead of us. Once two bearded painters went by, carrying enormous abstract canvases covered with pinwheels of blue and crimson.

A flock of nuns, their veils flying, was crossing the Pont du Carrousel. Upon us all the plane trees dripped and the light rain frosted everyones' hair and clothing. It was the lonely hour of the day when people go home.

When Bob finally joined us he said that he had bought a copy of some rare classical book for *less* than we paid for one French comic book. There seemed no real answer to this, but I said I was too tired even to think about the subway so we took a taxi. All the way back to the hotel I thought about home and the look of New England stone walls, our apple trees, the big white farm houses, and the sound of snowplows bumbling through a blizzard at 2 A.M. (I think the last made me most homesick.) The thought of New England in the midst of Paris has a peculiar piquancy, like thinking of spring in the middle of winter, or of Christmas on a scorching day in July.

I knew that everybody else was homesick, too, so I pulled myself together and after dinner built a kind of spiritual home in our room. We talked about funny things that the children had done as babies—the more peculiar, the prouder they were —a process which taxed the memory to its utmost, it being necessary to dole out an equal number of memorable, and if possible, disgraceful exploits to each child. The worst part of it was not being able to remember which one had done what. One very popular anecdote of a child who drank kerosene was the cause of much dispute.

"I think I did that," said Billy, hopefully.

"No, you didn't," I said. "You weren't even born. It was Pete, I'm sure, unless it was Kathy."

"Why wasn't it me?" asked Margie.

"Because Daddy was in Greenland," I said, "and you weren't born."

After they went to bed I subjected our day to a merciless analysis. What of value, I asked myself, had the children absorbed from it? Instead of helping them to sense the magnificent pageantry of French history, what had we done? We had discussed the *pissoir*, bought religious medals in which we did not really believe, eaten gluttonously, abetted them in looking at indecent pictures and laughing about the dog messes, bought illegally medals probably stripped from dead heroes, and supplied them with Disney comic books at double home prices. On the other side of the room Bob added up our expenses and said that we had spent roughly three times the amount he had allowed per day.

"We'll have about two weeks over here," he said. "Then all our money will be gone."

These thoughts, combined with extreme weariness, depressed me a good deal.

The next morning everything was different. We had slept soundly, and I opened the shutters on a day brilliant with sun. Color from the sky dyed the paving stones as blue as mussel shells. The chimney-pots smoked in gold, royally; the air was frosty, peppermint-cold. Nothing, we felt sure, could go wrong on such a day. That was the day we went to the Louvre. When I say that we spent one out of our two hours there waiting for Bob by the Winged Victory while he waited for us by a small reproduction of same downstairs, I have said enough. Even after this hideous experience, we would be deceived by the blue and gold of a new day and set forth, six-strong with pitiful optimism.

On those mornings, the whole world seemed to be in motion: the merry and busy crowds, the swiftly rushing traffic, the flashing river. We used to take a bus which rattled down the Seine, and through its windows we could see the Eiffel Tower like a ghost in the violet haze across the river. The lovely patterns of bare chestnut branches repeated themselves against sky and clouds. The bookstalls were as gay as window boxes; the flower-sellers' barrows exploded with color. Under its gold and ivory bridges the Seine had a hot, sequined glitter like spring, like summer. Notre Dame riding there on its island seemed to draw all into focus—trees, boats, palaces, flowers, people, clouds, cars—all flowed toward that central magnificence.

Then—it seemed like the next minute—Margie would be sitting on the curb moaning that she couldn't walk any more, Kathy would say why didn't we go back to the hotel, and the boys would start chasing each other across streets.

"I can't stand this much longer," I said to Bob one day. "What shall we do?"

Bob said gloomily that we soon would be penniless and have to return home, which would solve everything.

The next day he went to the travel agency and put our sailings back a month. The fact is—any resemblance between traveling with children and traveling without them is purely coincidental. If you have been abroad before that means nothing. Any parent embarking on a family journey to Europe should, therefore, be aware of certain basic truths.

One truth, which you would think would be self-evident, is that going *abroad with children* means that you will not only be away from home in a foreign country but that you will be *with children*. All the time. We are a fairly normal family and naturally avoid going about together in a herd. Whoever invented the word Togetherness has obviously never traveled with children. When we were at large in Paris, stumbling and lurching against each other in order to keep together and out of the traffic, it was almost impossible for anyone to see anything. Like a pair of inefficient shepherd dogs, Bob and I grabbed and pushed at our flock who alternately walked up the backs of our heels or broke into a gallop ahead of us.

After a whole day of this we would come shuffling into the hotel and realize all over again that there was *no refuge,* no sinking into a favorite chair by a new fire, nothing but more Togetherness, this time in one room. At first we simply huddled there under the central light, being homesick. Then I discovered the mother's role. It was that of creator of homes-away-from-home. No matter how tired I might be, it was up to me to pro-

33

duce an atmosphere of coziness and security. If I was cross everybody was cross. Sometimes it took an almost superhuman effort to face serenely another evening in that room where there was never a peaceful moment. Someone would accuse someone else of cheating at Double Canfield and I would find that I had read the same sentence ten times over. It was simplest not to try to read at all.

The second important truth, which it took Bob and me a long time to accept, is that from a child's standpoint a foreign country is simply a place where it is more difficult to carry on his usual activities. Kathy, being sixteen, was more or less adult but the other three were fourteen, eleven, and eight respectively, and people that age are interested primarily in doing something. By doing something they mean running, chasing things, hunting for things, making things, breaking things, and pretending to be somebody else—say Wild Bill Hickok or a Bad Guy.

In the hotel they were forced to do the best they could with door keys and the elevator. It was possible to lock each other both in and out of three different rooms. Sometimes the boys locked the girls in, sometimes the girls locked the boys in, sometimes the boys locked the girls out or one boy would lock the other *out* or one girl would lock everybody *in*—well, you can see the infinite combinations open to creative minds.

Then there was the elevator, which involved the dangerous element of the old man who might be brought up or down by mistake. There were also all the variations on bringing each other up and down either on purpose to frustrate, or simply to see who could dominate whom by pushing which button. You could also race the elevator on the staircase which wound around its cage.

In theory the resourcefulness of our children was admirable but in fact these activities were intolerable in a hotel and also fatal to the delicate nervous equilibrium of Bob and myself.

One day I saw Billy standing alone on the sidewalk outside the entrance. He was backed up against the wall and was wearing his dungarees and a cowboy holster. Lying on the pavement nearby was a little French boy pretending to shoot a cat under a car. After a bit Billy took his pistol out of its holster. The little boy watched him guardedly. Presently they were face to face and were exchanging weapons.

"Zing!" shouted the little French boy.

"Kah-kah-kahhhh!" yelled Billy.

They rushed at the cat. I could see them scrambling around in the gutter chattering excitedly.

Then a woman stepped out of a shop and summoned the little boy. He went off reluctantly and she dragged him angrily into the shop.

On Bill's face as he stood once more alone by the wall was a look that nearly undid me, so forlorn was it.

"Oh, damn!" I said to Bob. "That does it."

"What happened?" he asked, startled. I told him. Then said, "They need to get away from us. They need to play."

"So do we," he said.

We sat in gloomy silence. Suddenly it came to me in all its heavenly simplicity—the solution to our problems.

"Baby-sitter," I said. "Then we can separate."

I rushed down to the lobby and there was the concierge.

"Certainly," he said, "I know a very fine baby-sitter. The telephone number is this."

After Madame LeRoux had taken the small ones to ride donkeys once or twice, we never minded being together. She was like a sleeping pill that you know is there if you need it.

The Fifth Freedom:
Freedom from Responsibility

Everyone has his own values, and Responsibility, that fighting word, is interpreted in almost as many ways as there are human beings. I have no intention of balancing the various interpretations against each other but when you are abroad you realize with amazement that the life of the average parent involves an incredible number of gadfly interruptions which are known as responsibilities but which are in reality just a damned nuisance.

In *Walden* Thoreau cries, "Simplify, simplify!" and throws out a piece of rock because he can't bother to dust it. There are times when I get enraged with Thoreau because I feel that he really simplified his life not by living in that shack at Walden Pond but by avoiding marriage and a family. Anybody can simplify his own life, but how do you simplify the combined life of six people and two dogs, one of which is constantly having puppies in the downstairs bathroom?

In Paris we discovered how you do this. You leave home. The best way to simplify a mother's life is to spend a fortune and live abroad in hotels. For the first time since Kathy's birth I was free from the labors of maintenance, from the tyranny of the car, the telephone, and the doorbell. There were no dishes to wash, no beds to make, no wet towels to hang up, no dogs to feed, no *people* to feed. Nobody called to ask if I would mind picking up the children at dancing school. No one wanted to know if I would make a cake for the food sale or buy Fuller brushes. I didn't have to hear those piping voices asking, "Is Billy there?" nor did I have to stumble through piles of boots, wet snow suits, and pools of melting snow in the kitchen.

It is true I still had to pick up from the floor the clothes of my four children, but I did not have to pick up the clothes of half the children in the neighborhood as well. I didn't have to go look at finger-painting exhibits at 7 P.M., or take dogs to have shots or hunt for hot lunch money or find a nickel for Banking on Tuesdays or clean up puppy puddles or shift the clothes from the Bendix to the dryer or taxi the children to the movies at 1 P.M. I didn't have to iron dresses for Sunday school at nine o'clock on Sunday morning or remember to get a space gun by 3 P.M. for somebody's birthday party or drive the cleaning lady home on the way to pick up Margie at her music lesson. Nobody had to eat early to go to a pack meeting nor did I have to go to pack meetings and be told that my son hadn't done the project on Family Fun.

Not only was I free from all these destroyers of time but I was free from guilt. At home I am absolutely eaten up with guilt. If I stay in the garden and plant primroses instead of going to a Unit Meeting on Water Pollution I feel that I am a real failure as a member of the community. (I like working in the garden so I can claim no credit for doing so.) This guilt

37

complex doesn't make me go to the next meeting either; it just corrodes my character. I have nothing but admiration for women who run committees, organize PTA meetings and church suppers, and become Den Mothers, but I can't do these things myself. It isn't so much that I can't as that I simply know that I won't.

I once read a book called *Wake Up and Live* which said that everyone had The Will to Fail and the way to overcome it was to say Yes to everything one was asked to do. It has taken me years to free myself from the chains I assumed during the brief period when I tried this. I was even made treasurer of some doomed organization; my successor never did get the books straight but simply burned them and began over again.

The Will to Fail is, I'm sure, a healthy instinct of Self-Preservation under a fancy name. People need time, they need long empty spaces in a day, they need to sit still and savor the moment. We had the Will to Fail practically all the time we were abroad and it simplified life wonderfully. For instance, we had hardly begun to go to the museums and read that fine print in the guide books when we felt a Will to Fail in these activities that was stronger than we were.

The fact is, trudging dutifully around museums, learning who was buried in which crypt, and trying to teach young children the principles of Gothic architecture are just other ways of interrupting the natural flow of life. I had escaped from Committees and Meetings (or, to be exact, the guilt resulting from avoiding them), Bob had escaped the Schedule Committee and the Every Member Canvass for the church, the children were free from the toils of school, cub scouts, and music lessons. Why should we take on the equivalents of these obligations and try to live up to other people's ideas of travel? Why should I feel guilty if I couldn't remember which French king had The DuBarry for his mistress? In other words, we abandoned all attempts to "do" Paris properly. Instead we sauntered without purpose in the beautiful light, under the chestnut trees and down the long green vistas of the Tuileries where birds sang and the children ran free, tumbling on the grass, walking on walls. In the spacious leisure of these hours, we simply did the equivalent of planting primroses. We lived in Paris as though we belonged there, and if we felt like sitting in the sun on some steps or talking to strangers, we did so. Having begun the simplifying process we went down hill like a runaway express train.

One of the first symptoms of our new way of life was that we stopped trying to force the children to wear "Sunday clothes" all the time. Then I gave up any idea of wearing The Little Black Suit purchased for Paris and went about in sweaters and skirts. When you consider that the denizens of the Left Bank, where we spent all our time, thought nothing of appearing in hip boots, riding breeches and sou'westers, it seemed silly not to be comfortable. Before long the children were wearing dungarees, flannel shirts, and cowboy holsters in the streets, and I remember wearing a plastic bag over my head one rainy day without the slightest embarrassment.

Then we began to eat picnics in our room because it saved money. We fixed up the bureau like a kind of bar-sideboard, and it was always loaded with wine bottles, cheese, oranges, and leftover bread in a plastic bag. We kept butter and milk in another plastic bag on the balcony. Every day we added to our supplies, and people would hack off a piece of bread or peel an orange any time they felt hungry.

Then one day I came in out of the rain and was suddenly struck by the similarity between our room and a George Price scene where a slatternly woman is stirring something on a pot-stove, a dipsomaniac husband is sprawled in a broken rocker, and cretinous children swarm all over the floor. I had spent the morning doing laundry in the washbasin and hanging it on our line. The size of the wash made it necessary to build a drip-gutter of wastebaskets and chamber pots from the bidet to the basin. The slumlike atmosphere was given the final touch of degradation by the picnic lunch eaten on the central table. Every inch of the rug was covered with crumbs; somebody had

39

spilled wine in the armchair and the whole place smelled of cheese and oranges.

It was hard to know whether these changes were freedom from responsibility or good old Will to Fail but whatever they were, we throve on them. We became part of the neighborhood because we did our daily shopping like everybody else. The French housewife buys food for one day only, partly because refrigeration is not a cult as it is with us but mostly because they prefer food that is really fresh. Bob and I covered the neighborhood in all weather carrying our string bags. First we went around the corner to the dairy where the window was full of cheeses, tubs of butter, and china swans with eggs in their backs. Then we crossed the Rue Marboeuf to the corner *pâtisserie* and entered an atmosphere sweet with smells of baking and hot from the ovens. The long brown loaves, graded as to size, were stacked upright in bins, *croissants* in dozens were hooked over wooden rods, and round loaves and *petits-pains* stood on racks. We always bought two loaves of the largest size and I carried them under my arm where they warmed my side nicely. Our last stop was Le Cercle Bleu, the little market, and there we filled the string bag with oranges and chose the day's wine. We always bought a *vin ordinaire rouge* and paid forty or fifty cents for it. The housewife in me longed to get busy among the pots and pans, chopping herbs, tossing mushrooms in butter, and feeling in my hands the nice wooden handles of French knives.

In a little while I began going to hardware stores, hardly the province of a real tourist, and came home with folding corkscrews, baskets, paring knives, butter curlers, and more string bags. We assembled all the necessities for a picnic including a bread board, wine glasses, and red napkins. I used to arrange our room like a little house.

"Your mother's *nesting,*" said Bob.

We did go to one museum, the Cluny, but this was by mistake and so turned out to be a delight. Also they had in there, if I remember correctly, a chastity belt and some instruments of torture which kept the children happy while we looked at the marvelous unicorn tapestries.

There were hours when we didn't do anything and the boys raced up and down the sidewalks in our block making gun noises. They made friends with all kinds of people, speaking in sign language or English, learned the names of dogs and watched the man at André's open oysters. I no longer expected rapists and kidnappers to be lurking everywhere, and pretty soon we let the children go alone to the movies.

There was an inexpensive restaurant nearby which had the kind of family atmosphere the French seem to create wherever people are eating and there we became so well known that the waitresses used to compete for our patronage. Bob, called *Le Papa,* had terrible difficulty with French, and every time he started to speak it he would raise his fists and shake them in the air. At the first sign of this, runners would be dispatched and Madame would come to his aid. Nothing could persuade her that we could read a French menu so she translated it every evening. Finally she practically lived at our table.

The sunny days came back and great smoky clouds chased the sun across the blue sky; the wet pavements shone with color; everywhere at the ends of streets between black chestnut trunks and over the rows of ivory shuttered buildings was the vaporous light of Paris, nostalgic and soft.

I felt so passionately about the city that I would go alone down the quays, watching the life on the river: the *bateaux mouches,* the fire boats practicing with hoses, the slow red-and-black barges, and the smoking tugs. Sometimes I went through the narrow streets on the Left Bank where the old houses leaned together, flaking and ragged with torn posters. Paris in winter is all pigeon colors, and this makes the print stalls and flower barrows look like something by Paul Klee. I used to go and bury my nose in the round bunches of violets, the narcissus, and the cottony candy-sweet clouds of mimosa. I visited the chestnut seller by Notre Dame, watched the old bookstall proprietor who fed pigeons, walked in the garden by the cathedral where lovers kissed and priests strolled, reading their breviaries. I listened to *The Magic Flute* in a music shop. I stood in the pale sunlight on the quays and looked at eighteenth-century prints of English flowers, prints of hummingbirds, of sea shells, of mushrooms, huntsmen, country houses, coaches, horses, and butterflies, and never bought one because I couldn't decide between them.

At the end of one of these solitary expeditions I would go to a patisserie back of the Louvre, a place as gay as a jeweler's, with glass shelves full of colored sugar candies and pastries. There I ate meringues and Napoleons and drank hot chocolate with whipped cream at one of the marble-topped tables.

Aha, I used to think, there will be a group meeting to discuss sewage at 7:30 on Thursday. Will you make cookies for the Brownie Valentine party on Friday afternoon? And then I would gloat again over my wonderful escape from responsibility (Will to Fail).

Now that we had stopped trying to see the correct things we discovered all kinds of ways to enjoy Paris. Bob took Pete to a soccer game because he coaches soccer every fall and never gets enough of it. He also treated the children to the Cirque d'Hiver which real French children love, and it was a great success. On sunny days I used to take the three youngest to the Rond Point in the Champs Élysées to ride donkeys. Here under the bare purple trees were the spidery iron chairs, the stiff horses of the little carousel, children dressed like dolls, and four gray donkeys with scarlet saddles.

Once I took Pete alone to an armor shop where he bought a very sharp sword of immense size with his own money. We were advised in this purchase by a man who looked exactly like Jesus in pink tweed and who acted as mediator between us and the rather sinister old gentlemen who ran the place. Pete spent every hour in the hotel polishing his sword and strutting in front of the mirror with it. I suspected that he had stolen a tassel off the draperies as a sword belt but pretended not to notice. War-like cries and sounds of combat used to come from the boys' room, and once Pete cut Billy in the back of the knee by mis-take, so we had to make a rule about dueling.

Still the car did not come, and then the rain began. We would open the shutters and see it driving like steel rods across the windows and balconies opposite. Down in the street where the paving stones shone wetly, people pattered by under dripping umbrellas, airing dogs or carrying their little milk cans and string bags of bread and oranges. The smoke from the chimney pots flattened out over the roofs and filtered down into the streets. Drenched cats scuttled across the open spaces and small glistening cars nuzzled each other and jammed up at the cor-ners, squeaking their brakes.

Four children cooped up in a hotel acquire after a few days a terrible power, like some great force of nature impossible to control or halt. When we were not hissing at them to stay out of the elevator and stop thundering through the halls, we were trying to settle disputes about who did what to whom first. In the intervals I ruffled feverishly through tourist pamphlets until I found one which said What to Do with Children in Paris. We had already anticipated most of the suggestions. The rest cost money.

Of course, there was their school work, and one whole suit-case weighing a ton was filled with school books. We had out-lines of the work they needed to cover before June. Somehow, though, nobody could face either studying or tutoring in Paris. We were too busy learning how to survive away from home and getting our heads far enough above water to savor our new life. Nothing seemed as important as for the children to see and understand the beauty, the sorrow, the strangeness and famil-iarity of old Europe. Americans are too innocent.

By this time we had been in Paris for two weeks and there

43

was no sign of the car. Paris is very expensive, and the situation began to be serious. Bob, horrified at the vast quantity of francs that we poured into the coffers of the Franklin Roosevelt, reviled the Volkswagen Company, the garage in Neuilly, our travel agent, the French, and the Germans, and grew more and more depressed and pessimistic. Once he took me out to the garage but we accomplished nothing and I caught a cold. To soothe him we used to go down to the Seine every day or so to hunt for books in the little stalls along the quays. In the striped shadows of the plane trees, their flower prints twirling in the light wind, these bookstalls were to us like honey to bees. All kinds of books were heaped up in fascinating disarray. You could find anything from *Winnie-the-Pooh* to rare first editions. One day, returning from a solitary orgy, I saw Kathy leaning out the window of our room.

"It's here!" she called. "They're driving around the block again trying to park. They've been doing it for ages."

Presently a silly-looking baby bus came bumbling around the corner with the grinning faces of the family framed in the windows and Bob enthroned at the wheel. They paused for a moment so that I could look inside. Bob was ecstatic, like a father at Christmas with an electric train. My affair with Paris was over.

The real difficulty about family travel is that each stage of the journey is like a sample life which you try for a while to see if you want to keep it. I did not want to keep or even remember the life tasted aboard ship, but Paris was different. Bob did not agree with me; he dislikes cities and thought that we would have more money somewhere else. The children were eager to be off and try the new car. Only I mourned our three rooms, and began packing again with the sinking feeling that we were leaving security behind.

Caesar and the Wine Road

We were up before sunrise on that last morning and in the sky above the chimney pots the wisps of smoke were like flames. We ate our breakfast in the dismantled bedroom and the new day, frosty and gay, hummed and clattered outside. I opened all the windows so that I could talk to the others who were packing the car in the street below. The regulars of the area, with their string bags, milk cans, and loaves of bread, interrupted their rigid routine to stare at this phenomenon, and soon quite a crowd assembled.

The sun had just risen when I went down myself. The street was still in shadow but the blue of the sky shone back from the wet paving stones. The warm air from the patisserie condensed in steam outside the door and I went up to the corner to smell the fresh bread. Bicycles spun past, one with a wicker hamper of new loaves on the handlebars. At one second-floor window a chambermaid in blue was shaking out a mop; at another a child in a smock stood with a bird cage. There was a tiger cat asleep on top of the oranges at Le Cercle Bleu.

After this valedictory look at our street, I turned back to the car. Bob was lying across the roof adjusting the intricate web of ropes which he considers essential to Outside Packing. I am an Inside Packer only, and my time had come.

Packing a car is a grim process, as everyone knows, but this one offered great advantages over packing an American car. The entire sidewalk in front of the hotel was waist-deep in luggage but there was so much room inside the Volkswagen as well as in the luggage rack on the roof that packing was relatively easy. Also nobody kept rushing out with boxes of sea shells, stones, African violets, or bowls of goldfish. A green fiber suitcase from the Paris five-and-ten did insinuate itself into the pile, but this was legal and held the new books. Pete's sword was a problem because he wanted it where nobody else could touch it.

Eventually, however, we achieved the ideal of getting everything in and still having seats *and* foot room for all. One child with its feet on a duffel bag can destroy the peace in no time. Also there was, or so we thought, nothing to fall on anybody's head. The children were separated from one another by small suitcases and duffel bags. Each had a window, so nobody, we were sure, would screech, "He's had thirty-two and a half minutes by the window and I only had twenty-nine." In our innocence we believed that we had solved everything, anticipated even the most unlikely contingency.

During those black drives to Canada in past summers we had discovered certain basic ploys or gambits for maintaining equilibrium. These were, feeding in a steady supply of crackers, cookies, Life Savers (but *not* gum), and fruit, or, in extreme cases which involved car-sickness, doping the children with Dramamine so that they slept much of the time. There were also the games: offering prizes to those who saw the most white horses, Fords, or whatever. The alphabet game (collecting letters from signs) used to silence them for long periods but it is risky, involving screams of, "You didn't really see a Z!" etc. Of course all these gambits take their toll and I still have to choke down the impulse to yell, "Forty-two—over there under the tree!" when I see horses.

Car-sickness, that nightmare of driving parents, is always a hazard, and some of my darker moments have been spent washing out car rugs at gas-station faucets while Bob led a green-faced child up and down nearby. The inventor of Dramamine stands with Pasteur and Dr. Salk, but even these sacred yellow pills are fallible and constant vigilance is still necessary, especially during the first hours of the trip.

The entire staff of the Franklin Roosevelt was outside to see us off. We climbed into the little bus and shut the toylike doors. Bob threw it into gear and the car jack rabbited forward.

"Hey!" we shouted.

"I keep forgetting about the shift," said Bob. "First is where reverse used to be in our car."

"Drive much, Fathah?" asked Pete.

Everybody on the sidewalk waved again and this time we rolled away and turned out onto the wide boulevard. Midget cars raced like water beetles on each side of us. The morning was wide open, merry and giddy with speed. The mist rising from the river spilled in a lake of gold over the city. Notre Dame was up to its waist; the Conciergerie's windows flashed crimson as the signal lights of a great ship. Everything was wet, varnished with sun, and I could feel on my cheek the first warmth striking through the river cold.

After the last ugly outposts of Paris, we ran through miles of nursery gardens. Plowed earth steamed, the eternal rows of poplars pierced the low mist, and horses pulling big blue two-wheeled wagons labored ahead of us. Occasional rows of pollarded trees raised clenched fists on each side of the road. Magpies flared up.

I sat beside Bob in a state of delight with the Michelin map spread out and watched the road, hitherto only a yellow squiggle on the map, become a real road and France turn into real fields and woods. In the forest of Fontainebleau the sun slanted down in long fans of light that opened and shut as we drove past. We stopped at the palace of Fontainebleau and fed the carp and were nearly attacked by a swan. At Sens we parked in the square and assembled our first real French picnic: a bottle of Château-neuf-du-Pape, a long warm loaf, cheese, butter, a string bag of oranges, and a bottle of lemonade so powerful that its stopper was clamped on with metal bands. We ate this meal on a hill overlooking a river which wound in broad silvery loops down the valley. Poplars with balls of mistletoe in their branches were reflected in exquisite detail on the surface and every little while a black-and-red barge would come nosing around the curve and break the mirror into a thousand pieces. Bob and I lay back in the dry, sweet-smelling grass and finished the wine while the children explored a cave below.

"You know where we are?" asked Bob, who had the map. "Champagne."

"Champagne," I said reverently. "Imagine all those poor people back home struggling around in blizzards."

"Everybody with colds," said Bob. "Faculty meetings."

"And we're drinking wine in Champagne," I said smugly.

It was not surprising, considering these complacent exchanges, that God saw fit to bring us back to earth. When we climbed back into the Kleinbus it seemed much smaller and all the children much bigger, as though they had been inflated by all the fresh air and space. There were words over who was to sit where. Somebody stepped on the doll, who uttered a squawk. Crumbs were everywhere and the smell of orange peel was incredibly powerful. Squeaks, thuds, and occasional whistling screams rose from the back seats; then the usual cut-it-outs, shut-ups, stop-its, and come-*ons*. But at this early stage I was determined to be a wise, serene parent never raising my voice.

"Look," I said, in a low cheerful voice, "there's Vezelay."

There it was indeed, its old roofs crowding upward to the

church at the top of the hill. Wood smoke lay in the air and when we stopped the car we caught the smell of it, spicy and nostalgic. On the edge of the road were some black and white chickens scratching around a straw stack and beyond them was space and a wide, dreaming landscape. It was the hour in the day when the low sun casts long shadows and intensifies all colors. Faced with that lonely lemon-yellow light, people go indoors for tea and children take comfort in television programs of reassuring violence. The place for families at the end of a winter afternoon is at home, *not* in a French medieval village (unless, of course, they live there). As we struggled wearily around the empty streets of Vezelay nobody was burning with the hard gemlike flame of appreciation. There was, we saw, no use attempting anything new after 2 P.M. because it would not register through the thickening atmosphere of wine-sleepiness, restlessness, irritation, and weariness that surrounded us.

Brooding darkly on this discovery, I was not surprised when it began to rain, and by the time we reached our hotel in Avallon it was pouring. We crawled out into the wet, all of us crumpled, tousled, and covered with crumbs, wine spots, and bits of orange peel. The concierge had, I think, expected a limousine full of rich Americans and seemed shaken by our bedraggled appearance. However, he soon recovered and saw that we were given hot tea and buttered toast in front of the fire in the lounge.

The following morning the *valet-de-chambre* opened the shutters on a medieval winter scene. Snow covered all the roofs and walls and lay between the neat rows of lettuces and leeks in the tiny gardens. After breakfast Bob explained, once again, that it was essential for him to see the place called Alesia where Vercingetorix had been defeated by Caesar. After the amount of time I had spent with atlases, magnifying glasses, and pre-Christian maps trying to find Alesia, I certainly agreed with him. (Why people insist on taking more and worse trouble to justify previous trouble is one of life's unsolved mysteries.)

49

It was raining and snowing simultaneously outside and I decided to buy berets for the boys. As for Bob, he had a hat when I married him, but lost it, and when I asked him to buy another he refused, saying that only Harvard men wore hats. Having once refused, he would rather kill himself than give in, so except for a ski cap he has remained hatless ever since. This morning I asked him nicely if he wouldn't please let me buy him a beret. He, of course, refused, and I went through the slush and rain and bought the boys berets, feeling that only one with British blood would prefer to die of pneumonia rather than change his mind. However, not long afterward, Bob said that he needed tobacco, and when he came back he, too, had a beret. I think he must have decided that a beret isn't technically a hat, so by getting one he hadn't given in to me.

The way to Alesia was through country much like Vermont in winter. The slushy snow ran down the windshield and sprayed out from our tires. After asking directions in a town of unmitigated hideousness we climbed upwards through small medieval farmyards sugared with snow to a dreadful and utterly medieval village. The rain poured down; dull-eyed, ragged women stared at us through open doors.

"Is this it?" I asked. "No wonder Vercingetorix gave up. He probably committed suicide."

Bob said this was the New Town, which is the way classicists talk about anything built after 400 B.C. He then left me and the car in an empty stable and departed with the children through the freezing wind and slush for the top of the hill. Kathy stayed with me and we read while the rain hissed on the cobblestones outside. Presently a ragged man came in and relieved himself against the wall. Pausing by my window to blow his nose on his fingers, he passed on.

"What a divine man!" said Kathy.

"Wasn't he?" I said. "And I do love this village! Maybe we could buy a house here."

Bob came back with the children, all soaked to the skin, and

I begged him to go and see if there wasn't a house for sale in Alesia. I told him about the man and suggested that we look him up and fraternize with him. Bob ignored these pleasantries and told us exactly how Caesar had outmaneuvered Vercingetorix, something that naturally we had never understood from the text. In fact, I don't remember in my youth ever realizing that Caesar was a Roman general. I simply thought the book was a lot of awful sentences made up by a Latin person to confuse and depress the young.

The next stage of the journey was one of my pet projects, planned inch by inch on the Michelin map with the aid of Samuel Chamberlain's *Bouquet de France,* a gourmet guide of the very first water.

We were to spend the night in the famous Hôtellerie de Pérouges which was a walled town of great antiquity. This Hôtellerie had four or five stars after it, meaning that the food was superb, and Mr. Chamberlain simply let himself go on the subject.

The Hôtellerie, besides being four-starred, was incredibly expensive, incredibly comfortable, and looked like a set for *The Three Musketeers.* It really was a set for *The Three Musketeers,* as a movie had been made here. The boys were overwhelmed. Out came the swords and off they went through the empty squares and tiny streets—D'Artagnan and Porthos. The girls took hot baths. Bob and I, who had cleverly fed the children earlier, spent three hours eating dinner in a private dining room. We spared no expense.

"Just once," Bob had said, and he is a man who keeps a promise. The bill for that one dinner was perfectly appalling, but he never said a word. He even bought the plates we used because I liked them.

The success of this venture was a fortunate interlude in an otherwise frightful journey. The next afternoon, following my plan, we picked up the highway below Dijon. This route, referred to by Mr. Chamberlain as the Wine Road, ran straight through the famous Côte d'Or, the great wine country where the vineyards of Nuits-Saint-Georges, Gevrey-Chambertin, Vougeot, etc., are situated. I had looked at the map so often that I almost expected to see a yellow thread strung with those beads marking towns and with red threads and blue squiggles flowing off it like pieces of seaweed. But the map is a hundred times prettier than what we really saw, which was an endless vista of sticks and gnarled vines rolling away into gray mist. The famous names were there all right, printed on the walls, but although the words "Clos de Vougeot" on a wall are preferable to "Coca-Cola" on a picture of a gigantic female in a bathing suit, there wasn't much to choose between the Côte d'Or and the New Jersey Turnpike. (The truth is that we never really saw it, because of the fog and rain, but I feel like reviling it anyway.)

Our first day in the car had been awful enough for Bob to offer a prize of Three Strokes of the Cat to the worst-behaved denizen of the back seats. In Avallon Pete had, by some miracle, found a real cat-o'-nine-tails in a store, and he presented this to his father as we drove off. So dreadful was the general tone of conversation along the Wine Road that Bob several times feinted towards the back seat with the cat and once I hit Margie's doll while trying to reach Pete. These outbreaks on our part caused the only laughter heard on that unholy ride and we arrived in Beaune in a fine state of exhaustion and mutual dislike.

The Hospice de Dieu was our destination, the ancient convent hospital which controls all the Beaune wine trade. I insisted on going in, more to get out of the car than from a desire to see the hospice. Margie went with me but all the rest said glumly that they would rather sit in the car.

I found myself viewing with complete apathy the magnificent medieval building and barely listening while an old man with a magnifying glass showed us the Roger van der Weyden hair-by-hair, pore-by-pore. A nun with a sail-like coif ushered us about, and we saw other nuns tacking and jibbing around the freezing courtyards. Actually we were too dulled by the rain and cold, too beaten down by the hours in the car to feel anything but a brutish desire for warmth and peace.

When we finally emerged, totally congealed, from the hospice, I nearly ran into a man who was standing transfixed on the sidewalk. Following his bulging glance I saw the Volkswagen. Inside was a kind of apocalyptic vision of Bob flourishing the cat while his children cringed in a heap in the back seat.

"For heaven's sake," I said, throwing open the door. "A nice bit of propaganda for Americans."

"Everybody thinks we're German because of the car," said Bob. "They expect Germans to flog their children. Anyway, I wasn't really hitting them."

"But you tried, Paw," said Pete kindly. "Jeeze, were you mad!"

"Yah!" said Billy, admiringly.

We had been determined to buy wine in Beaune and now did so, although Bob insisted upon taking a package deal of three unknown wines, rather than one good one, as I wished. This made me feel put upon. Back in the car, when I objected again to the purchase, my children sided with their father and said, "Oh, Mumm*ee!*" in world-weary voices. Self-pity overwhelmed me and I thought how ghastly a mother's lot is: nothing but drudgery, slavery, and discipline all day long while glamorous old Daddy comes home and gets all the attention. I huddled into my coat and stared at the rain dashing against the windshield.

Outside in the mist the ugly lines of vineyards whickered by like gigantic combs. I thought how fathers were always right, mother always wrong. Somebody in the back seat began throwing orange peel. Then darkness closed about us and the cold sank its fangs into my ankles.

During the day we had been lost every hour or so; after dark we were lost all the time. French road signs have a curious habit of mentioning a large city like Geneva once—say a hundred miles away—and then never referring to it again. Instead they have long lists of tiny villages with peculiar names like Cueilles or Pouilly-sur-Chaone, most of which are impossible to find on the map. At first Bob said to trust his sense of direction and I sat in martyred silence waiting, in fact hoping he would get lost. Of course he always did, and we would find ourselves jouncing down a rutted lane between trees like those spiked clubs giants carry in fairy tales. Every time we asked the way a small crowd would gather and begin to argue among themselves, smiting their brows and gesticulating wildly.

"*A gauche, monsieur—*"

"*Non, non, à droit—*"

"*Tonnerre!—*" etc., etc.

Excited streams of French would pour in both windows of the car and finally we would say, "*Merci beaucoup,*" and crawl off, leaving them all deep in angry debate.

"Just think," I said, "back home our friends are saying, 'They're going skiing in Austria,' and they envy us."

"The amazing thing is," said Bob, "that we came here of our own volition. Here we are spending a fortune to go crazy when for nothing we could have stayed home."

I groaned.

"What time is it?" asked Kathy.

"Never mind," I said morosely.

"I'm hungry," wailed Margie.

"Kin we stop and get a Coke?" asked Billy.

"*No!*" said Bob.

"But, jeeze, we're *starved*," said Pete.

"So are we starved," I said nobly, "but do you hear Daddy complaining? No," I answered quickly.

"When will we get there?" asked Pete.

"The next person who asks that will get—ah—something he won't like," said Bob darkly.

"What?" Pete said.

"Never *mind*," I said.

"That's because you don't know," said Pete in the voice of Donald Duck.

"One more peep in that voice—" began Bob, but suddenly a barrier loomed up ahead and a large sign saying "Genève."

The hotel was nice and clean but dull; the food also was very dull after France and the children were scornful at dinner and had to be curbed. Bob and I went up to the bar to cheer ourselves with some cognac, but it only made my head ache more. Bob read a French newspaper which contained a lot of snide cracks at the U.S.A., and I listened to some Chinese girls and a German woman talking German together. They glanced insolently at us and whispered to each other with frequent giggles. The German woman looked as though she had just whipped up some lampshades out of human skin, and I felt that I might somewhere have seen people I disliked more but couldn't recall the time.

At such moments it is hard to understand why anyone goes abroad, especially in winter, especially with four children. Nobody ever thinks of this when they picture their friends in Europe reeling from one glamorous spot to another in perpetual kodachrome sunlight. Sitting in that bar in Geneva I would have given almost anything to be back in our old winter rut—wet snow suits, dancing school, unhousebroken puppies, and all.

Over the Alps

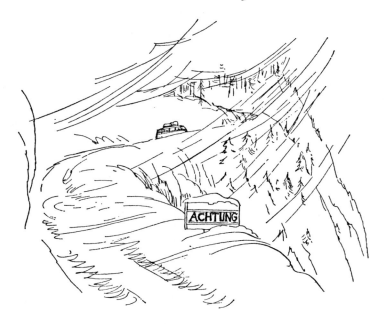

Bob and I had both had courses (at different times) in something called Group Dynamics, and as I lay in bed now, too tired to sleep, I reviewed this peculiar experience to see whether anything I had learned there could help in solving our car problem.

The main theme of those meetings (and one which I refused to accept) was that we had "punished" one member for leaving to have a baby. However, I hadn't had a baby for eight years now, and anyway most of the present group were ex-babies of mine, so I discarded this one. Another thing we learned was that people tend to sit in the same seats at meetings. Any good? No. Our members kept wanting to change seats and fought furiously about this.

Well, there was that business about the Leader being a Father

Image, how about that? As Bob was a real Father there seemed nothing very fascinating about his being regarded as one. Another thing. One person was often the focus of hostility. This united the group. Something might be done with this? I had been the focus of hostility during the afternoon because of the argument over wine purchasing. Had this united the group? No. They were also hostile to each other, although no one (except me?) was hostile towards that old Father Image at the wheel.

The Leader of the Group Dynamics Course had driven us all nearly crazy by saying, "Hmm?" and refusing to answer direct questions; however, we were not trying to find out how to drive this group crazy but the reverse. As far as I could see, Group Dynamics was absolutely worthless in our present situation and I decided that the only solution was for us to appeal to the Best in our children—in fact, cry for help—and also lay down rigid rules of behavior.

After breakfast in the morning we had a stern conference with our dependents and said that either they behaved with some semblance of human decency, or we would take steps. I said that I realized how dreadful I had been myself and that Daddy did too, but after all we weren't saints, nor were we made of iron. I would try to do better, I said. "All I want to say," Bob added, "is that whoever behaves like an animal will get a thick ear from me." I felt that this was not the right tone to adopt, at least at nine o'clock in the morning, so I made a short speech listing the activities which we considered beyond the pale. The children, intrigued, added a lot more. Here is the result.

RULES FOR CAR

1. Anybody who spits at anybody else (no matter what the provocation) will be severely punished.
2. Each person gets 26 inches to sit in and *no more* (doll gets 6 inches).
3. The Following Things are Forbidden:
   whispering to self
   sniffing

57

thumb-sucking
nose-picking
breathing loud on purpose
staring at each other
tapping
kicking *anything* or *anyone*
whistle-screaming
giggling in a silly way
pinching
singing any song people object to
burping on purpose
shoving
wrestling
pushing luggage on people
moving luggage to get more room than 26 inches
tattling
sucking Life Savers out loud
tickling, even for fun
sitting on each other

4. The following remarks are absolutely forbidden:
   stop it!
   come on!
   he (or she) started it!
   I got it first!
   that's not fair!
   shut up!
   bitch
   bastard
   cut it out!
   dirty stinker
5. No changing seats during the day (see 10).
6. No telling stories of movies unless asked.
7. No reading funny books (or anything else) in car (because it causes car-sickness).
8. Nobody can lie down behind anyone else or on their laps unless the person is willing.

9. *No imitating* each other.
10. Car-sick people have first choice of seats.
11. If anybody feels car-sick they must shout (also Bob *must* stop instantly no matter where we are).
12. Billy and Margie have just as much right to talk in Donald Duck speech as Pete.
13. Any timing of turns or measuring of seats to be done by Mum.
14. If a piece of food has to be divided, one person divides, the other gets first choice.
15. Margie's nest can't be bigger than other people's sections even if she has to hold her doll in her lap.

We asked the group members if they had everything straight. They said that they had. Of course, everybody knew that we had no idea what we would do to punish any infringement of the rules. After all, nobody could be left behind or deprived of television or movie privileges or sent to their rooms. Also, no matter how often we waved the cat, it was well known that neither Bob nor I could bear to hit any of them hard enough to hurt. Also, being seasoned parents, we expected to lose, and a defeatist attitude can always be sensed by children and animals.

However, it was a beautiful day, soft and springlike, and all of us felt happy and pleased with each other. Lake Geneva was a slippery, opalescent turquoise, magical in the rising mists, and all the leaves in the evergreen hedges sparkled like little mirrors. We soon began to climb and saw through clouds of moving vapor the steep hillsides covered with fruit trees where the neat Swiss farms hung like swallows' nests. The pink-cheeked, flaxen-haired children, the picturesque farmers and aproned women looked so exactly the way they were supposed to that it seemed like an affectation on their part.

We stopped in a cool scoured village and bought Swiss cheese and bread. The children were models of behavior but I felt cross with Bob because he hadn't spoken for miles. I think he felt cross with me because I had spoken too much and very boringly about people who wouldn't let other people get out of the car and savor the countryside. "Drive, drive, drive, that's all," I said. Bob is very good at these times and didn't even attempt to defend himself (didn't stop either).

Soon the snow peaks emerged into the sunlight and small villages with needle-sharp church steeples were reflected by polished lakes, in all their delicate dove-colors. We stopped on the edge of a valley and ate our lunch, and then continued our horrible progress. Hours later we skidded into Lucerne and I had to get out and chase two old ladies and ask them in German where the hotel was. Unfortunately, when I caught their attention I couldn't think of a single German word except bits of Wotan's farewell from *Die Walküre* and simply waved idiotically at them and fled.

"Nice work," said Bob.

"All right, you try it," I said. "Maybe they understand Latin."

Over a therapeutic drink of brandy in our room later on, I thought about our life in the car and began to laugh in a weak and hysterical manner.

"Hey, look at Maw," said Pete. "Drunk."

"I am not," I said. "I'm just losing my mind from living with all of you." I then thought about Group Dynamics and my own gadfly role during the day and mopped my eyes.

Everybody else began to laugh too and then Pete sang a few songs in Donald Duck, did a short but definitely off-color dance, and as a special treat said "Periwinkle" in duck talk seven times.

"Say," said Bob, "maybe we really are insane and don't realize it."

"I realize it," I said.

The next morning I went out and walked around Lucerne in the falling snow. The old part of the city looks like the illustrations in a book of fairy tales: onion domes, clocks with blue and gold faces, half-timbered baroque houses with carved shutters and beams and painted coats of arms, all in soft tapestry colors. I walked by the lake where hundreds of coots and swans were paddling near the shore, and then into a church where a service was going on. The freezing air and white and gold decorations made me feel as though I were in a book by Tolstoi. Outside again, I had to blink the snowflakes off; the whole sky seemed to be sinking silently earthward.

The car was being packed; the children stood with upturned faces catching snow on their tongues, and in the air was the atmosphere of excitement and mystery that comes with the first real snowfall. As we drove off, all the church bells were ringing, tumbling their iron dissonance into the white streets. Umbrellas jostled each other on the pavements as people flocked to church. The snow grew silently deeper and we stopped and bought strap chains in a garage. Then we left the city and drove into a whirling white void where small villages loomed up like islands.

My solitary walk in the snow had given me a chance to relax and also to enjoy in simple peace the flavor of the world outside the car. The brief period in the church showed me how much I had missed music in a quiet place. I could see that if I were to behave like a human being and not a wasp or adder I must have some time each day to be alone. Bob, being almost divinely patient and restrained, can sit through all kinds of bickering and think about Vergil, but I have to straighten things out. With some obscure idea of justice I cross-examine witnesses and weigh evidence until out of the chorus of "She hit me firsts" and "I did nots" I extract the pure truth that someone had put his or her foot in someone else's floor space.

This kind of thing wears down the nerves like a file and before I know it I'm telling Bob that he makes me do all the disciplinary work or that he ought to teach the boys carpentry. This gets nobody anywhere and as we drove through the snow I thought how dreadful I was, how good and patient Bob was, and how from then on I would be one of those wise, serene mothers like Mrs. O'Hara in *Gone with the Wind* or Marmee in *Little Women*. Even though I secretly have always thought Marmee a dismal and saccharine character and much preferred Jo as a female type, I spent a large part of that morning speaking in a low, gentle voice and telling Bob how noble he had been not to beat me the day before.

"Are you all right?" he asked.

"Of course I'm all right," I said.

"Well, stop being mushy," he said.

After a while we passed fields full of queer cement posts. They looked like huge cemeteries but they weren't cemeteries.

"What do you suppose those things are?" I asked.

"Can't think," said Bob.

All of a sudden the roadsides were hedged with fierce tangles of barbed wire.

"Look," I said. "It's like a battlefield. Barbed-wire entanglements."

"By golly," said Bob, "that's what it is! This is the Austrian border. Those fields of cement posts are tank traps." We all stared at this truly foreign sight. Tank traps. We could hardly believe it.

During lunch in a small village we studied the route to Saint Anton, where we had arranged to meet our friend Marquand from the ship. When we went out again the snow was so deep that we had to put on the chains. Every one of them clanked against the fenders with a noise like gunfire and at the same time the car jolted as though it were going over rows of large logs.

"Holy smoke," I said, "we can't go on this way. The whole car'll be destroyed."

"There's nothing else to do," said Bob.

Thumping and banging, we ground over the snowy landscape, and skiers three fields away started as though they had been shot. Farmers stood open-mouthed and watched us into the distance. Careful now, God, I said, this way madness lies. I take no responsibility for the future if you continue this horse play.

Presently we arrived at a place where there was a large sign right across the road displaying the words *"Achtung!"* and *"Schneeketten"* in scarlet letters a foot high. Beside the road was another sign, a regular metal highway sign, showing a man pushing a car up the side of a perpendicular cliff.

"What's *Schneeketten?*" I asked.

"Chains," said Bob. "Maybe this bird can fix ours."

The bird took one look at ours and shook his head violently. Somehow Bob and he agreed on an arrangement whereby he would purchase our chains and Bob would then buy new ones from him. By some miracle Bob sold the chains for more than he had paid for them, probably the only time in his life that he has or will make a profit on a deal. The bird put on our new *Schneeketten,* conversing all the time with Bob, who pretended to understand, and off we went again into the white void. We moved now with only a faint whirring noise that reminded us both of New England winters, unplowed roads, and our youth. Nostalgically we drove up the slight grade around the hillside.

"This is better," said Bob. "I'm glad we stopped there. Now we have nothing to worry about."

"Where are we?" I asked.

"Not very far from Saint Anton," he said. "Should be there shortly."

A few children on skis passed us and then a family on a sled. Nice reassuring sight. We wound upward into whiteness. The road was banked on each side with snow and it wasn't easy to see out. We didn't see anyone else and Bob changed into low gear.

"This is sort of steep," I said.

"It is, a bit," said Bob.

All of a sudden I looked down over my right shoulder and there was nothing at all but whirling vapor with the spear points of spruces piercing it in a very upsetting vertical way. I gave a squeak of horror and covered my eyes.

"We're going up a *mountain,*" I said.

"Do you know what I think?" said Bob as we crawled on and up. "I think this is a pass."

"You don't suppose this is *the Arlberg?*" I said.

"Yes, I do," said Bob.

Of course that's just what it was, and we were the last car over the pass before they closed it because of avalanches.

Once as we were skidding around a curve we came face to face with emptiness and a sign with a skull and crossbones on it.

"What's that?" asked Margie.

"Oh, just a sign," I said, biting my finger to the bone.

There were other signs shouting *Achtung!* and some forbidding the blowing of horns. Why? Because it might start avalanches.

The snow drove horizontally in a thick curtain that muffled everything in soft swirling folds. Spruces appeared momentarily like ghosts and vanished again. We passed more skulls and crossbones, but God, who really does seem to take care of children and fools, continued to do so and we arrived at snail's pace in Saint Anton just as darkness fell. Marquand happened to be in the crowd of homecoming skiers and stuck his head in the window of the car. He seemed startled by the hysterical warmth of our greeting and said he would meet us at the Schwartzer Adler down the street.

Presently we were drinking schnapps at a modern bar in a warm room surrounded by people talking English. There is no use pretending that we found this distasteful or decadent, although it certainly had no more resemblance to the real Austria than one of those fake chalets in the White Mountains at home. The truth is we were sick of being cosmopolitan and for a time needed the comfort of our own kind. Here were real Americans. We looked at them and listened to them with love.

Cowbells woke me the next morning and I crawled to the window to see a herdsman going by in the blue darkness with his two cows. Snow was falling thick and fast and the little Tyrolean village was buried up to its ears. Some houses had only a chimney visible. By breakfast time it was nearly as dark as it had been at dawn and the snow was driving swiftly across everything.

While I dressed I watched the school children flocking out, dear little things in tiny parkas, boots, and ski pants. Across the street they were diving off a wall into the drifts squealing merrily. Our smallest went out and did some jumping them-

64

selves. After breakfast Kathy and I struggled up to Hans Schneider's ski shop and bought blue parkas from his daughter. I told her how we used to see him every spring up in the White Mountains at Cranmore, all in gray with his gray hair and mahogany brown face. The whole atmosphere of the ski shop, the feel of ski clothes, and the universal snow, combined with these memories of home, had a bad effect on my state of mind.

"What are we doing here," I asked myself, "among all these Germans, when it's just as good where we live? Why did H. Schneider get out of Austria and go to New Hampshire? Because it's better, that's why." This atmosphere of Teutonic gloom was deepened by the news that six people had been killed in an avalanche while we were driving over the pass. The whole town was in mourning. The snow had a malevolence about it.

After lunch we set off reluctantly into the blizzard. The next hours were spent in driving blindly through a pure white world where everything except us was invisible. It was a queer sensation—rather like flying through a cloud. There was no earth, no sky, nothing but smoking white emptiness and in the center of it our wretched little box full of wrangling human beings, grinding on and on and on. Homeless waifs in a wasteland of snow. By late afternoon everybody was cold, hungry, and tired.

When we arrived in Innsbruck, and I saw the people floundering around in streets full of dirty snow or crawling along in the face of the snowstorm, I thought I simply couldn't stand one more second of anything. Still, short of throwing myself in front of a trolley car, there wasn't any way to avoid it. Also the children had to have ski clothes.

"I *know* it's horrible," I said to Bob, "but if we don't stop now and buy them we'll have to come back here later."

Bob said he felt it was always better to get bad things over with all at once, and as there would probably never be a worse combination of circumstances than the present, we might as well go shopping. Cars were skidding sideways through yellow slush —European drivers seem to have no idea of how to deal with snow—and people were parking anywhere. We shrank into our clothes and breasted the storm, dragging our young after us into a huge sport shop. There the ski pants and parkas were of inferior quality but out of sheer inertia and exhaustion we bought them anyway. Pete had a red parka, Margie, apple green, Billy, gray-blue. Bob refused to buy one.

After this we drove out of Innsbruck and up a long, well-plowed mountain highway between snow banks and towering spruces. We arrived at the Goldener Adler at 7:30 and staggered stiffly into a glacial hallway with skis stacked against one wall. We opened a door on the right and revealed a large room full of cigar smoke and people in ski clothes. Our entrance froze them all into silence and immobility, and the whole scene was like one of those photographs in the *Geographic* of polar explorers having a jolly evening in their shack at Little America. One man, who could have walked straight out of a ski-school poster, jumped up and came over to welcome us. The others turned back to their huddle around the radio.

The friendly stranger was a Dutchman called Adolf and he introduced us eventually to Herr Mann, the proprietor, who made us feel instantly at home. Herr Mann was a large, humorous person rather like one of our better American senators. He was so kind and fatherly that I wanted to throw myself into his arms and cry, "You take over from here. I've had it," but, needless to say, did not do so. He showed us our bedrooms where the temperature was, if anything, colder than outdoors and finally brought us an excellent hot dinner which we ate backed up against the white stove. Adolf joined us and told us the story of his life in the usual way, though his was rendered quite exciting by his very loose command of the English tongue.

We spent a short period breathing pure cigar smoke, our sensibilities dulled by the constant German shouting of the radio announcer reporting the Olympics. Then in a state of semiasphyxiation we tore ourselves away from the stove and sprinted upstairs. In our bedroom our breath smoked and as I flung off my clothes I said to Bob, "What was all that about the moun-

66

tains being warm because the Austrians understand cold?" He said that maybe it was the Swiss who were supposed to understand cold and we both dove under the feather beds. Outside our windows there was the absolute silence of deep snow and iron cold and above the mountains the stars burned like blue fires.

Cold

One of the special delights of travel is to look out one's window on the first morning after a night arrival. There framed before you is the unknown country revealed, as fresh as though it had risen from the sea.

I woke early on our first morning at the Goldener Adler because the traffic to the Olympics began at five o'clock. After a while I got out of bed and went over to the bay window where high above vertical blue snow-slopes a mountain peak glowed rose pink in the sunrise. On the ridge opposite the inn snow-covered spruces made gnomelike shapes against the radiant sky. All below was in shadow, as blue as ice, and when I peered down I saw an old lady hobble past carrying a milk can in bare red hands. With a sweet chinking of bells a yoke of oxen moved under the window driven by a farmer, and every hair on man and animals was white with frost. Across the street was the post office painted with holy pictures, and if I looked sideways I could see the church with its gilded dome and the few low-eaved chalets that made up the village. All roofs were several feet deep in fresh snow and the buildings looked top-heavy. The thick curves of the eaves, fat as down pillows, nearly met the swooping curves of the drifts on the ground. Windows were mere peepholes between waves of snow.

In my coat I darted down the arctic hallways and discovered that there was no bath, merely a pair of hostile-looking toilets operated by old-fashioned chains. Back in our bedroom where Bob was buried under his feather bed, I dressed like lightning in every piece of woolen clothing I could find. I am always the first member of my family to get up because I can't sleep after seven, so the beginning of each day is all mine. On this day I went down with the usual feeling of opening a new book and Herr Mann met me at the foot of the stairs.

"Guten Morgen, gnädige Frau!" he cried. "What for breakfast?"

"Guten Morgen," I said. *"Zwei Kaffee, vier Schokolade."*

In this way I began every day while we were there. However, on this first day I was so American as to add, "Oh, where is the bath? I couldn't find it this morning."

"Bath!" said Herr Mann scornfully. "And how would we have any hot water if you took a bath?"

"Not now," I said. "Any time that would be convenient."

"Nobody takes baths here in winter," he said firmly.

"Oh," I said.

After a while my family straggled down and we had breakfast. We then went out into the village to rent skis and boots. Children were trotting by on the way to school with little horsehide packs on their backs, and we kept meeting yokes of oxen pulling logs or loads of hay on light wooden sledges. Ruddy-faced girls in shawls with orange or blue head kerchiefs often strode at the head of these teams. I saw one tall pregnant Amazon helping unload logs as big as telephone poles. Some of the farmers carried

69

long black-snake whips which they cracked over the heads of their oxen with a sound like pistol shots. The Alpine cattle were very endearing—small and furry, mushroom-brown and cream color, with enormous velvet eyes, long-lashed like a movie star's. They moved with a dreamy slowness, the steam rising from their nostrils and warm bodies in a white cloud.

Bob bought a large roll of ski-school tickets for me and the children but not, I noticed, for himself, and after seeing us all equipped he took off by train for Italy. His departure on foot to the railroad station made me feel like Admiral Byrd watching the last plane disappear into the sky over little America.

My best friend for the first lone week was my bootmaker, a gigantic creature exactly like Hünding in *Die Walküre* but unlike Hünding, possessed of a most endearing personality. His shop, barely five feet square, was the warmest place in the village and smelled powerfully of glue, leather, oil, and Hünding. He and I, knee to knee, discussed by primitive sign language my feet and my prospective boots. We both laughed heartily most of the time, although I was never clear why, and Hünding kept hugging me, rather like a bear, to show good will and desire to please. The first pair of boots resulting from this fervent relationship was painful beyond my wildest dreams, and after the try-out on the ski slopes I was black and blue and blistered from boot-tops down. I consulted Herr Mann.

"These boots don't seem to fit," I said. "I can pick my whole foot up inside them."

"Of course they fit if Herr Hünding made them," he said. "You must put on more socks."

"But I have six pairs of socks *on*," I said.

"All new boots hurt," he said firmly.

I shuffled back to my room.

Two days later I was able to put Pete's galoshes on over my socks and limped over to Hünding's carrying the fatal boots. I pointed to them and shook my head, then put them on, bravely suppressing my screams of pain, and demonstrated to Hünding my ability to walk around inside the left boot. Hünding watched and then gave a great roar of laughter. Somehow he indicated to me that I was right, they did not fit. He then remeasured my feet and was once more overcome with bellowing mirth.

"*Bitte?*" I said timidly.

Hünding dealt me a comradely blow on the back that nearly disabled me and then crushed me to him with one arm. My feet, he finally made clear, were not the same size. He would make a new pair of boots.

I could not help but feel that in the movies the shoemaker would have been very handsome and a love affair would probably have followed. What happened to me? My feet were different sizes. Not romantic. Also, in spite of bear hugs, my relationship with Hünding was not the stuff of which movies are made.

It had taken me about half a second to realize that the ski resort depicted in the Vivien Leigh movie and our ski resort had only one thing in common—snow. Compared to Davos ours hardly deserved the name of resort because it was simply a tiny Austrian village with one galvanic rope tow and our inn. From the outside this was a typical Tyrolean inn, long and low with casement windows and walls painted with holy pictures. A sign, intricately concocted of metal flowers and gilded scrolls, swung over the door. It was supposed to be centrally heated, but this was more of a gesture than a fact. There were radiators but they were always quite cold to the touch. It is true we did not freeze to death in our beds, so perhaps there was some rudimentary heat in the pipes.

All the downstairs rooms except the kitchen and dining room were closed, and a large white stove heated these two, its firebox being in the kitchen right beside the table where the family ate. This kitchen soon acquired in my mind an impossible glory, like Valhalla—the home of the gods. It was enormous, with great iron stoves, scrubbed wooden tables of a marvelous whiteness, and a heartening array of copper and iron pots, all gigantic, where things bubbled and steamed all day long. In the mornings, in fact most of the time, it smelled powerfully of fresh coffee and new-baked bread. It glowed with light and it was as steamily hot as a greenhouse. When I ordered our breakfast I lingered as long as I dared, soaking up heat and envying Herr Mann who would be eating his breakfast about a foot from the infernal crimson of the open fire box. His wife, plump and quiet in a long apron, moved among her knives and cauldrons like a benevolent witch. The whole household spent every waking hour in the kitchen as far as I could see, and I longed to join them, since the dining room with its fake Tyrolean furniture and German magazines was to me a sort of hell.

There are three things which can render a room uninhabitable —noise, dim lights, and cigars. The dining room combined all three with the physical torment of straight wooden chairs and insufficient heat, thereby reaching a new high in what is now called the "discomfort index." From dawn until far into the night the radio bellowed out news of the Olympics and by ten o'clock the air became totally impregnated with cigar smoke. Far from complaining of the cold or the crowded evenings in the cigar-filled dining room, our children absolutely reveled in everything. Children are like litters of puppies—they flourish in the teeming noisy warmth of the pack.

Watching their happiness I wondered whether we might not have stumbled on some formula for raising young, hitherto unsuspected by Gesells and Spocks. I'm sorry to quote Thoreau again, but he is really one of my mentors, despite the fact that I can never forgive him for being unmarried and childless. He says, "Why should we live with such hurry and waste of life? We are determined to be starved before we are hungry," and "Simplicity, simplicity, simplicity! I say, let your affairs be as two or three and not a hundred or a thousand." We had certainly reduced our affairs to two or three, namely: eating, sleeping, and skiing. It was a life completely on the physical level and although I told myself that it was genuinely Austrian and therefore more "real" than Davos or Saint Anton, I often longed passionately for the pleasures of unreality and decadence such as light and heat.

I know we are all taught to despise Americans who complain about the cold in Europe, but this is because we can't comprehend the effects of cold in countries that are poor or without natural resources like ours. Nobody who lives in New Hampshire minds cold in itself. In Austria the cold outdoors was crystalline, dry, and invigorating. But inside!

First of all there was no welcoming blaze of open fires because they use stoves. Also wood was scarce.

Then there was no real light. This was because the cold was so intense that Herr Mann's electric power plant froze. First, he explained, the stream froze, then the turbine filled with ice. This was why the lights went down until they were mere filaments and the men had to stagger out with kettles of boiling water to thaw out "the screen," whatever that was. Sometimes the lights went out altogether and one man wrote letters by the flame of a votive candle.

Since there was inadequate light it was often impossible to read in the evenings and because of the cold everybody was shut up in one room which was never subjected to one scrap of fresh air.

I think that even Thoreau might have grown a bit restless under such conditions, but after about a week I was hardly able to imagine life on another level. At times I missed light and privacy to the point of desperation, but I soon accepted cold and cigar smoke as normal. As we came to know the Mann family and Adolf, we spent hours sitting around the stove talking, and we grew so fond of these good kind people that we dreaded leaving them for Italy. The rapidity and ease with which families send down roots wherever they come to rest is one of the nicest things you learn abroad.

This world in which we were now rooted was a snow-world where one could not imagine the presence of grass or earth. The brittle blue and white of the days often faded at dusk into the gray feather-softness of snow which fell swiftly and silently covering the marks of oxen, sledges, and skis so that each morning was immaculate, like freshly laundered damask. It was the kind of dry, crystalline snow that sends off jeweled flashes in the sun and lies lightly, flake upon flake, improbably fragile.

Our days fell into a pattern. We rose with or just before the sun. The valley would still be in blue shadow, the spruces on the upper slopes so encrusted with hoar-frost that they looked like rock candy. Above in the sunrise the snow-peaks burned from shell-pink to rose, to gold. I went from room to room waking the children who were totally invisible under feather beds, washed my face in ice water, and put on woolen underwear, two pullovers, a Bavarian cardigan covered with woolen flowers left over from my youth, three pairs of socks, and ski pants. Over the socks I wore ski slippers to put off as long as possible the anguish of the new boots.

These splendid articles were rather like the hoofs of Clydesdale horses with soles an inch thick. When I wore them I could barely lift my feet off the ground and was forced to assume a gait more like that of a mechanical robot than a human being. When I went down to breakfast I carried the things to warm them by the stove, shouted, *"Ein kaffee, vier Schokolade!"* through the kitchen door and went to watch the sun creep down the slope opposite the inn. The street outside rang with cowbells.

Pretty soon the children, all heavily sweatered and booted, would come clumping in, and we waited for our breakfast. Herr Mann brought it with a loud, *"Guten Morgen, mein Herr!"* to Pete and we began hacking away at the rolls.

After this we sorted out mittens from the drying rail, put on our parkas and caps, shouldered our skis, and marched out into the brittle nose-prickling cold. The snow squeaked under our boots, tears filled our eyes in spite of snow goggles, as we climbed out of the blue shadow onto the blinding white slope behind the church. My feet began to hurt about there.

On the next slope was the short and primitive ski tow and

beyond that a degrading hillock where the ski school suffered from ten until twelve and two until four daily. The school faculty consisted of Sepp, an old man the color of a cigar with a frozen moustache, and a tall dark god in a kind of Mercury helmet whose every glance filled me with despair and hopelessness. He was kind but sorrowful as he watched my turns. It was easy to see that he, too, was hopeless about my ability to acquire correct form, but he continued to repeat gloomily and reproachfully, "Ach, *no*—ski to de mountain fore–ward."

At home I am able somehow to ski down a mountain trail without being instantly killed. This seemed incredible now. However, on second thought I think I can do it because on our New England trails I am not observed by gods in Mercury helmets— at least none who are paid to teach me. Also, at home I am happy and at peace among the pine trees and birches whereas at this school I had not only my own children and the instructors watching me, but three strange Germans as well. The Germans couldn't ski at all but Pete passed from Beginners into my class in one morning and was soon alone in Advanced.

"You have champion there in ten years," Sepp assured me as Pete in a scarlet parka, illegally plastered with resort insignia, swooped past in a lovely turn.

Billy, on the other hand, seemed incapable of keeping his skis from crossing and gyrated slowly around until he was facing uphill. Nobody, not even the god, could figure out why this was. Margie wilted like a cut flower in Sepp's arms and merely rolled her china-blue eyes at him in a feckless and female way. Kathy after one day of struggle decided to stick to ski bobs (a kind of ski bicycle), the stove, and cups of tea.

We went back at noon for lunch—myself in a pitiable state of pain and exhaustion—and then limped back at two for more of the same. I would have given anything to leave the ski school and the god forever. One day I suddenly realized that he couldn't force me to attend my lessons; I also convinced myself that if I did leave him he wouldn't come ravening after me.

In fact, I decided the hell with ski school and the next morning climbed a mountain trail behind the church. After considerable scrambling I arrived at a point high above the village where the sun shone with a fierce brilliance. I could see up and down the whole length of the valley, and framed in snow-buried spruces were vignettes of distant peaks folded and creased with shadow. The intervening slopes were so dazzling that even with sunglasses I was nearly blinded. Shadows as blue as sapphires flowed over these pure hillsides and in the bright air flakes of hoar-frost glittered like prisms. It was so still, so clear that it was like being inside a diamond.

On the way down I collected wisps of hay that had been brushed off the sledges on the sides of the trail. The Alpine grasses were still green, mixed with dried field flowers, and gave off a summery sweetness.

Having made the break, I never went back to the god in the mornings. Instead Kathy and I would climb the mountain trail or explore the village. Every afternoon when the lessons were over, we all had hot tea and big wedges of chocolate cake. I used to have rum in my tea and drink it out of a glass, which made me feel rather Russian.

The three younger children were in seventh heaven and spent all day out on the slopes either on skis or ski bobs. Sometimes the boys would not be in at sunset and I would go out into the pale-blue twilight and hunt for them. The snow, hardening in the frigid night air, creaked under my boots; the first stars shone above the mountain peaks, and my voice calling my sons echoed hopelessly from one blue slope to another. I always panicked and expected to find them with broken legs frozen stiff and always felt the same blissful relief when I heard them in one of the empty little valleys.

In the evenings Herr Mann told us stories of the war: how the Germans marched past the inn for a month on their way to invade Italy; how after their defeat by the Allies they were ordered to line up in the roads by the Brenner Pass and await orders; how the French came in through the front windows and burned all the furniture, and how the Americans bombed Innsbruck when his little son was there in school.

"*We* bombed you?" asked Billy, horrified.

"Of course," said Herr Mann. "It was war. We would have done the same."

"What happened to your little boy?" asked Margie, whose tender heart is particularly vulnerable to babies and small children.

"He was to leave his school for the day to buy flowers for his mother's birthday," said Herr Mann, drawing on his cigar and leaning back against the stove. "He was to take the one o'clock train home." He paused dramatically, being a born storyteller. "The Americans bombed the railroad station at one sharp," he said.

The children stared at him as though he were the Lone Ranger on television.

"Naturally the train did not arrive here. I met all trucks from Innsbruck bringing refugees, then I got a ride with a man and we went to all the stations. I remember how it was snowing hard and at each station they said he was not there. So then I came back here and we went to bed. Of course, we did not sleep."

"Did he come?" exploded Billy.

"Was he bombed?" asked Margie.

Herr Mann held up his hand and slowly blew out a cloud of cigar smoke.

"Let me tell it in my way," he said sternly. "We will come to that. My wife and I, we lay there and waited. At two o'clock I hear a knock at the door. I think maybe it is the Americans coming or maybe it is news of my boy. I go downstairs. I open the door. There," he held up the cigar, "there on the step is my son with his bunch of flowers. 'I am sorry I am late,' he says."

I was naturally unable to speak and Herr Mann seemed to be having difficulty himself. He chewed his dead cigar.

"Well, there is your war," he said to the children. "How do you like that little boy? He was same size as you," he went on, pointing the cigar at Billy. "What do you think of that, *Mein Herr?*" He chuckled and went off to get someone a beer.

Except for the inmates of the Goldener Adler, we saw no one. There were, it is true, transient guests who stopped for a beer or a meal, but these were all Germans, heavy, blond and stolid, who stared at us but never spoke.

Finally, however, a new interest appeared in the shape of a curious trio—a pink, wholesome female and two men who dressed alike. One man was small and pallid and was known to us as the Little One, the other was big and lard-colored and was known as the Eskimo. Of the two the Eskimo was on the whole the more repellent, but it was nip and tuck. The female was in love with the Little One and between the Little One and the Eskimo there was a bond of some sort, better left in obscurity. They were all German and we were only able to deduce the plot from our interpreter, a local girl who spoke English. The Eskimo, she said, paid for all three.

Kathy and I used to watch this trio for hours, exactly like people watching a movie in a foreign language without explanatory captions. Then we would rush to Elsa for clues. The combinations, recombinations, fights, and crises were constant. The female spent days in her room weeping while the Two went off together, then she and the Little One would go off, etc. etc. There was, however, no question but what this was Love. The Little One might be revolting to everyone else but she loved him with as pure a flame as Juliet loved Romeo.

"And so," I said to Kathy, "she deserves respect and sympathy." At the same moment I wondered if the emotion between the Eskimo and the Little One deserved respect and sympathy, but instantly rejected the thought. Sometimes we all played games with the Trio and Adolf. The Eskimo once challenged me to a bout of Indian wrestling. This honor I declined with (I hope) well-concealed revulsion. Kathy played Ping-pong with the girl and one night I unwisely embarked on a game called "Damen," a bastard form of checkers. The boys played chess with Adolf or entertained the company with Donald Duck talk, a feat which never ceased to amaze the most hardened characters.

"Valt Deezney!" they would cry, and Adolf would proudly ask Pete to give them an encore.

There were times when I could hardly credit the kind of evenings I now enjoyed, and occasionally Kathy and I would sit on the window sill and talk Brooklynese to each other. Kathy's favorite expression was, "How about dat, spawts fans?"

One never knows how one will react to certain atmospheres. Some people, trapped in an Austrian ski hostel, teach themselves German or read philosophy; others talk Brooklynese. The time arrived after a while when I could barely imagine any other kind of existence, and at this point Bob came back from Italy saying that he had found a wonderful place for us to live in Florence. It was a convent run by an American Mother Superior. It was warm. It was in its own gardens. Here, if anything, was the exact opposite of our present sample of life. However, like all real men, Bob is a rotten reporter and when I pressed him for details he grew vague.

"What does the Mother Superior look like?" I asked.

"Look like?" he said. "Oh, like anybody."

"What about our rooms? Are they nice? Are they well furnished or are they cells? Think!" I said.

"Oh, they're fine," he said. "Like any rooms."

"Is it cold in Florence?" I asked, abandoning all hope of detail.

"Coldest in the memory of man," said Bob, "but the Mother Superior is an American so they have oil heat at the convent. Also hot water."

"We can have hot baths?" I asked, amazed. Bob said that we could but I didn't really believe him.

Just then I received a card from a young German I had met on a train in 1938. We had both been very young; he had been slender and good looking and we had talked about music and books instead of Hitler, which in 1938 was refreshing. We had exchanged addresses and after the war I had received my ad-

79

dress back, written in my own handwriting on a leaf of notebook paper. With it was a letter asking for food and clothing for his children. I sent some, then Care packages. And after the war was over, he sent Pete a toy steamer. Now he was at Cortina and wanted to stop in and see us. Well, this was more like it. I showed the card to my children, thinking that they should be impressed at the long-term effect of my fatal attractions.

"Twenty years, almost," I said.

"Gee, he must be *old* now," said Pete.

"Old!" I cried. "He's just my age."

They looked at me sideways.

"Well, I suppose I'm old to you," I said stiffly, "but I don't feel old."

"You *aren't*," said Billy indignantly. "She isn't *old!*" he said accusingly.

"Who said she was? Jeeze," said Pete.

I went up the street in a blizzard and had my hair done in a microscopic hairdresser's where an oil stove filled most of the room. The problem of explaining my Parisian coiffure was almost insuperable and I was forced to do my whole head in pantomime, curl by curl, which took hours and hours. However, the result was satisfactory and I felt prepared for any contingency.

The next day Rupert telephoned from the station and Bob and I drove up to the next town to get him and his wife. As I climbed out of the car, a short, thick-set stranger advanced upon me with glad cries. He wore a chesterfield and a homburg and looked rather like Cary Grant, which was all for the best, but how could he be Rupert, who had been tall, slender, and poetic? He was, however, and I was considerably gratified that he had recognized *me*. After the ravages of twenty years I was identifiable and I fully intended somehow to get this across to my young.

During lunch Rupert reminisced about our romance, as he called it. This seemed to me an extreme way of describing two hours in a train compartment, but after lunch Rupert began to set up glasses of cognac all around and he and I toasted one another with sentimental references to Our Past. On the third cognac Rupert said that we were a Symbol of International Good Will. We were a link between America and Germany. "That's right," I said, and downed a toast to us as the Link.

After a while we went out into the sunlight—now absolutely dazzling—and drove off to the station. Rupert kissed me several times while his wife and Bob looked at their fingernails. Finally we parted, promising to meet again very soon. On the way back from the station, Bob said, "I wish you wouldn't kiss people all the time because then I have to kiss their wives. It's very embarrassing."

"Did you kiss her?" I asked, fascinated.

"Certainly not," he said stiffly. "We hardly exchanged a word."

"Well, I don't kiss people all the time," I said. "Rupert and I were old friends."

"Oh, I don't really mind," said Bob. "It's just that I don't want to kiss everybody's wives."

"You don't mind *all* of them," I said.

"That's true," he said.

"Oh, it is, is it," I said, sitting up. "Exactly which ones don't you mind?"

"Now don't start attacking me," said Bob grinning, "I think you're pickled."

I said I thought so too and climbed out at the inn feeling much younger and better looking.

Get Thee to a Nunnery

We left the Goldener Adler in a snowstorm and Herr Mann threw a snowball after us as we headed for the Brenner Pass. At the border the officials spoke Italian and had black mustaches. I like people to look the way you expect them to, and they certainly did.

As we came out on the Italian side of the pass the snow stopped, the clouds vanished, and beyond the peaks ahead was the most miraculous light, soft and nostalgic as though the air were full of gold dust. The snow disappeared from the ground and soon we were driving down a long valley of orchards and vineyards, between steep cliffs.

Going away into the distance were layers and layers of mountains, each layer paler than the one before, until the far ones dissolved in light. On the slopes of the hills the vineyards made black scribblings; cypresses clustered around red-roofed villas and there were ruined castles high up against the sky.

At Lake Garda we drove down into summer where fruit trees bloomed on the edge of the water and the air smelled of strange pungent herbs. We saw our first olives flickering silver and gray, the close-packed spears of cypresses rose from hidden gardens. Fish nets were drying on walls in the sun and their colors were pale green, rose, and silver; in the little inlets brightly painted boats floated above their reflections. Once we saw through a stone archway a boy driving a flock of sheep up from the water. He carried a new lamb in his arms and with his ragged garments and black curls seemed a being from another age.

After the snow and cold of Austria it was a miracle to be warm, as though you had shed a skin. Ordinarily summer comes slowly; you are prepared by spring for its luxuries, its illusion of eternal happiness and youth, but here we came down into it as a swallow might, flying over the Alps on its southward journey. The whole experience seemed even more illusory and dreamlike when we drove up and out of the lakes and re-entered the prison of winter. We spent the night in Verona where winds like knives sliced through the streets.

Everything after Verona was a white nightmare of snow. It blew across the Po Valley like smoke, and of all the dismal stretches of country the Po Valley in winter takes the prize. The misguided inhabitants train the grapes on elm trees whose branches are all cut off. These rows of gnarled claws stretched to the horizon on all sides. A few scrofulous towns dotted the plain and along the highway at regular intervals were signs advertising *"Supercorte Maggiore—Agipgas."*

"What a foul place," I said to Bob. "Why do they do that to those trees?"

"Well, it's very interesting," said Bob. "Vergil mentions in the *Georgics* that they trained grapes on trees and cut off all the branches every year for firewood. Exactly like this."

We passed a few solitary figures fighting their way through

83

the blizzard. All wore long black cloaks which they wrapped around themselves like villains in melodramas.

"Hey, is Italy all like this?" said Pete from the back. "This stinks."

"In a poor country," continued Bob, "every stick of wood counts."

"I hope Florence isn't like this. Jeeze," said Pete, "what a dump."

"That's why the trees on all the highways are pollarded like that," Bob went on.

"Hey, there's a man going to the bathroom!" yelled Billy.

"Where? Where?" cried Margie and Kathy. Shrieks of laughter followed.

"Listen to what Daddy is saying," I bellowed. "It's *interesting*."

The two days trapped in the car had had their usual brutalizing effect. We had been tossed from winter into summer and back again into winter so quickly that all of us were a little shaken. Also Italy was so strange, so unlike anything we had ever seen. The cities were incredibly old and crumbly looking; people seemed to make no attempt to fix anything and there were houses with no windows in the battered openings, houses half tumbled down with old blankets for doors. The walls were all scaling and patched with tattered posters but the over-all effect was warm and rich.

The colors were fruit colors: apricot, peach, tangerine, and exactly the bruised, speckled yellow of overripe bananas. Even the earth was unfamiliar and looked like powdered brick. The trees were all peculiar and unreal—and the cypresses and umbrella pines were like artificial trees, dense and motionless as shapes carved from ebony.

The smell of the country was strange and not too pleasant, being powerfully flavored with the excrement fertilizing the fields. The cold narrow city streets also held the strong odor of excrement mixed with other smells—smoke, coffee, rotted orange peel, and carbon monoxide from the hundreds of motor scooters and little cars that screeched and hooted past us at top speed.

We drove over the Apennines in a blizzard and, as nobody seemed to plow the roads in Italy, got stuck on top of the highest pass. After a while some truck drivers pushed us out and we continued creeping and skidding for hours and hours into a cone of whirling gray snow. The sight of it coming toward us in that funnel shape hypnotized me into a sort of trance.

"Watch the edge of the road," Bob said in a dead voice every few minutes.

In the rear seats cold and exhaustion plus Dramamine had reduced all four children to inanimate lumps. Two were actually asleep.

I kept my eyes on the edge of the road where a few weeds, bowed down with beads of ice, were visible above the drifts.

"It seems to me," I said angrily, "that you can't go anywhere in Europe without going over an Alp."

"This isn't an Alp; it's an Apennine," said Bob. "Godalmighty, why don't they plow the roads?"

The fact is, we think of Europe as entirely civilized and rather compact—neat and sophisticated because it's so very old. Winter driving in Europe, however, is more rugged than anything I've seen in our country—more like what I imagine Alaska to be or wildest Tibet.

Our first view of Florence was a dim scattering of lights floating in the bottom of a valley. To one used to the brilliant jewelry of American cities, Florence seems at first like a tomb. When we drove into it, all the steel shutters were down and the high narrow streets were as dark and cold as mine shafts. Newspapers blew about in the gutters and starved-looking cats dashed out of sinister alleys.

There was a light in a little bar and we went in to buy a bottle of cognac. The place was jammed with chattering black-eyed men in berets who rolled their eyes at me in a startlingly obvious way. I felt a hand slide over my thigh and held tightly to Bob. In spite of this, I was sorry to leave, it was so warm and steamy, and gay with bottles and cheeses. Outside, a piercing wind searched our vitals and the air felt damp and raw. Bob was, I think, lost, because we kept driving around and around the same circle and finally were held up for ages at a level crossing waiting for a train.

At last we stopped before an iron gate in a long garden wall. Bob rang a bell and the gate opened. We drove into a courtyard in front of a long peach-colored villa. There were rows of French windows, bay trees in tubs, and a single dim light burning in a window out at the back. Bob rang another bell and after a considerable time the door was unlocked and we saw a tiny nun, young and rosy and smiling, who spoke to us in English. We all staggered in—children looking incredibly rumpled and owl-eyed, and me clutching the cognac bottle under my coat. We were in a pale blue-and-white vaulted salon with murals after Boucher of pretty bare-bosomed ladies and their lovers. Venetian glass chandeliers, curly gold furniture, parquet floors. Much pink marble and very slippery white stairs like blocks of Ivory soap.

The sister took us up to see the rooms: there was a choice between large ice-cold marble bedrooms and small less cold tiled bedrooms. We chose the latter. The children instantly began to fight about which would have which room and I was obliged to squelch them in whispers. All this time I had a curious feeling of being back in school under the eyes of Miss Fine, the headmistress, although nothing could have been less like the regal Miss Fine than this diminutive nun.

We were told to come down and eat in ten minutes, and Bob and I shut ourselves into our bedroom and drank two very swift cognacs. Bob sat on the bed and I on a small straight chair. There was a black crucifix over his head, a picture of the Virgin Mary over mine, and I felt guiltier and more worldly every minute.

Dinner followed, in an immense dining room with a coffered ceiling and a cavernous hooded fireplace. A pretty, dark-haired waitress named Corinna served us with spaghetti, an unknown meat dish, greens (unidentified), and fruit. We drank a whole decanter of Chianti. The lighting of the room—a few naked bulbs high up—together with some fairly dreary oil paintings of lobsters and fruit, caused a sinking sensation in my soul. What if this were to be a Bad Thing, in fact a mistake? Shivering, we crawled into the inner salon, another vaulted blue-and-white room with more Boucher murals and several unprepossessing armchairs. A single floor lamp, heavily befringed, made a dim pool of light around the small radio. We crouched before this and I twiddled the dials until from somewhere in space came the music of an orchestra playing Mozart. Far and faint, it whispered the familiar themes and was soon drowned by the heavy thrumming of a jazz orchestra. Kathy and Margie backed up to the lukewarm radiator hugging themselves, the boys looked at photograph albums of nuns in a kind of incredulous daze. Bob sat speechless with weariness in a Victorian arm chair. All around us were empty rooms, darkness, silence, and cold.

After a bit, a young black-eyed sister tiptoed noiselessly into the room and whispered something in Italian which Bob said meant turn out the lights when we went to bed. I then was inspired to produce my hot-water bottle, which luckily called for no explanation. She vanished and reappeared with the hot-water bottle in a state of white heat.

"*Buona notte!*" she breathed.

"*Buona notte,*" we whispered, and she seemed to be absorbed by the darkness like a creature of smoke.

"Jeepers," said Kathy, "this is cheery."

"Let's go to bed," I said, still in a whisper.

It was glacial in the bathroom and I felt that never again would I be warm and free inside my clothes, but it was nice in bed with a hot-water bottle. My hands congealed when I tried to read, however. Bob plugged in our own portable bed light, which gave out an unhealthy acetylene glare, and promised to blow all the fuses before long.

I put on my mittens and began to read a copy of *The Experiences of an Irish R.M.,* picked up from a bookstall in Paris.

Irish fox hunting was so remote from Italy that it seemed almost insane—a lot of people sitting on large animals chasing a smaller animal with the help of a pack of other animals. I put the book down.

"All these crucifixes and things make me feel guilty," I said. "We shouldn't be here in bed in the same room with a crucifix and that picture of the Virgin."

"Don't be an ass," said Bob.

"No, really," I said, "don't you feel wicked?"

"Certainly not," said Bob.

Lying in bed listening to the rustle of leaves I felt completely uprooted, utterly at sea.

The apprehensive mood in which I had gone to bed was, however, instantly dispelled when morning came and I looked out of the casement windows into the gardens. The formal garden, covering about an acre, lay below me with its box-edged beds, fountains, and statuary. Enormous unknown trees in full dark-green leaf rustled high overhead and there were cypresses, sharp and ink-black in a long alley at the end of which was a white crucifix. Just under the window stood an eighteenth-century aviary, shaped like a bird cage, where doves cooed sentimentally and parakeets and canaries flew about.

Beyond the bay hedge which bounded the garden, I could see far hills with more cypresses upon them and olive trees in silvery clouds. There were a few red-tiled roofs just visible among the cypresses, but otherwise there was no sign at all of the city. The whole scene was exactly like the background of an Italian painting—a Gozzoli fresco of gilded nobles on horseback with hawks on their wrists and ladies on palfries. Secular.

I took a cold bath (no hot water) and later put on three sweaters, a wool skirt, fur-lined boots, and my coat to go down to breakfast. The children's clothes were hopelessly wrinkled from weeks in duffel bags, but at least they were clean. We went down to the dining room where the table was set for twenty people although we never found out why. There was no sign of a nun, and we were greeted by Corinna, who brought us rolls with crusts as hard as wood and coffee of a fearsome blackness. The rolls, once we had hacked them open, were fresh and hot and the Italian coffee, although new to us as a beverage, was good as well as boiling. We even had orange juice and shirred eggs. The sun poured through the French windows and, outside, two ducks waddled quacking to the fountain.

"This is so good there must be a catch somewhere," I said.

"It's the bathroom," said Bob. "When I shaved the water wouldn't drain out."

"That's nothing," I said. "The only thing I really mind is being cold all the time, but maybe I'll get used to it."

The children, still mourning the ski slopes of Austria, showed their customary indifference to exploration when questioned.

"Don't you want to go out with us and *see Florence?*" I asked.

"No," they said. They went on to say that they would stay there and read funny books.

"Oh, no!" I moaned, but then realized that this meant I was free to explore Florence myself while Bob went to the consulate. Sister Celia, the pretty nun of the night before, appeared and said that, of course, the children would be all right. She then produced from behind her a curly-haired bambino about five whose name was Sandro. He and Billy stared at each other like owls.

"Say, 'How do you do?' " said Sister Celia.

"Howdoyoudo," said Sandro in one word.

"Say *buon giorno,*" I said to Billy.

"Bun jorno," said Billy.

"Cowboy-Indiano?" said Sister Celia and Sandro dashed away. "He's gone to get his pistols," she explained calmly.

"Are you sure this is a real convent?" I asked Bob as we drove out the gate. "I thought they were always ringing bells and praying and that everybody lived in stone cells. This place is a perfect palace."

"It's a guest house. A fourteenth-century villa," said Bob. "I think the nuns live somewhere out back."

"Did you see that good-looking man in the hall?" I said. "Who's he?"

"How should I know who he is?" said Bob. "All I know is that I did see the Mother Superior and she's an American so she must know what she's doing."

This seemed to me specious reasoning but I let it go and looked at the city. We drove along the Arno in a stream of speeding scooters and midget cars. Trolleys and buses were circling about by one of the bridges, and donkey carts of great charm trotted in and out of the traffic bringing from the country loads of vegetables and huge wicker-covered bottles of wine. The Arno looked strange after the Seine, shallow and muddy, with water the color of *café au lait*.

Bob left me at the Ponte Vecchio where I stood wrapped in delight for about one second before I was hit amidships by a man on a bicycle. Several Italians darted out to support me and the man on the bicycle collapsed in the street with Italian imprecations.

Following this incident I spent a short time window-shopping and nearly froze solid. The Italians seemed to have anticipated this because at the moment when I could no longer feel my lower limbs I found a window full of very unseductive woolen underwear. Inside I was welcomed by three men in overcoats smoking cigars who courteously ushered me into a small storeroom piled with cartons. Here I put on thick pink panties and wool stockings of an unattractive shade of brown. The latter were apparently planned with a giraffe in mind and would have reached to my armpits if not impeded by anatomical barriers. These garments made me feel like a stuffed Teddy bear but were very successful in other ways.

I walked happily out and down the tall narrow street with no idea of direction. It began to snow and the unfamiliar stone façades were delicately veiled. Suddenly I came around a corner and saw Giotto's campanile and the Duomo looking fragile and unsubstantial in the falling snow. I stood there staring and 1 think smiling like an idiot. The cold air smelled of freshly ground coffee, snow, and a spicy kind of smoke.

Several people bumped into me and one young man in a very tight-waisted coat and pointed shoes lingered nearby in a hopeful and slightly lecherous way. This pleased me because it was exactly the thing people said would happen, but I also felt a bit apprehensive, after all I had heard about Latin men and blondes. Giving my admirer a cold glance, I went over to the Duomo and warmed my hands furtively at a votive candle.

When Bob and I returned to the convent we found the girls sitting in a welter of comic books, eyes faintly glazed.

"Where did you get all those?" I asked.

"A nun gave them to us," said Margie. "Hey, guess what? There's a comic book all about *nuns*. Look."

I looked and there was. On the cover as usual were a lot of horses but on the horses were not cowboys but nuns.

"It's no good," said Margie, dispassionately.

Through the window we saw the boys in their Austrian parkas, dungarees, and French berets, trying to fish a ball out of the fountain. Sandro was with them.

I tapped on the window and they all came in. Sandro was dressed as a cowboy.

"Gee, Sandro's got about a million guns," said Billy enviously. "Gee, look at that cowboy suit. I wish I had one."

"Have you had fun?" I asked.

"Yah—hey, do you think I could get a cowboy suit like his?"

"What does everybody want to do this afternoon?" asked Bob, who was looking at the nun comic book.

"Go to a movie," they all said.

"Certainly not!" said Bob.

"Over my dead body!" I said.

This condition was nearly fulfilled two hours later when I leaped from the car and darted through heavy traffic to the lobby of the movie theater. We had been driving round and round the square trying to find a place to park but this was impossible.

It had taken us far too long to find the movie chosen by the young but finally the snarling scarlet face of a vampire two stories high showed that we had reached our goal. The character in the box office—curious family resemblance to the vampire—instantly rejected my money and me too.

"But *pourquoi?*" I asked piteously.

A small wasp-waisted man who had been watching now came to my aid. "Room gone," he said. "Full. No sit down. O.K.?"

"Oh," I said. "Thanks."

This information was not well received by the inmates of the Volkswagen and we were obliged to take them to a very expensive patisserie for hot chocolate and pastry. Then we somehow were talked into buying fur-lined boots with very pointed toes for both Pete and Margie. After this we drove back to the convent with the children in heavy dispute over who should ring the bell at the gate.

Upstairs, Bob and I locked our door and took the cognac bottle out of the wardrobe.

"I wish you weren't going away so soon," I said in a quavering voice, "Greece and Turkey are so far off."

"I wish you were all going with me," said Bob nobly.

"In a pig's eye, you do," I said.

The World Within the Walls

Until we moved into one I believed that only nuns were allowed inside convents. My sole preparation for convent life was a garbled, inaccurate, and sentimental collection of facts about nuns acquired inadvertently over the years.

I had read in school a bad novel called *The Unwilling Vestal* and in college I read for history something called *Ancren Rule* or *Rvle,* which I think was a list of rules for those in a twelfth-century priory. I also had seen a movie with Lillian Gish called *The White Sister* and read romantic novels in which girls were saved from convents at the last minute by their lovers thundering up on foaming horses.

Then, too, the pretty French sister on the boat had told me there were strict rules against idle or purposeless conversation. A nun showed no curiosity about the lives of others. She had no personal possessions. The Mother Superior reads all mail. Did any of these rules apply to me? Would the Mother Superior read my letters, for instance? After Bob left I felt that the maid Corinna was my only support because she was married, had a child, and wore lipstick. I was talking in pantomime with her at breakfast one day when the Mother Superior, who had been ill, swept down upon us, her robes and veils streaming behind her and all her cohorts flocking around to witness our meeting. The Cloister and the Hearth—there we were.

The Mother Superior was about my own age, but far more impressive, and reminded me of a President of the Student Council before whom I had been summoned for bumming rides. When she spoke with a New York accent, I felt a bit less awed but not much. There were so many nuns around that I couldn't push my chair back and remained in a far from dignified semi-crouching position.

Her attendants beamed upon us as we exchanged the initial courtesies, and I tried, unobtrusively, to get rid of my egg spoon.

"Your little boys are so full of life," she said after a while, "running about everywhere. I'm sure that they aren't destructive?"

"Oh, no," I said nervously. "They haven't broken anything, have they?"

"Someone has put Scotch tape on one of the beds," she replied, "and would you see that they don't play football in front of Our Blessed Mother?"

"In front of—?" I said blankly; then I remembered the statue of the Virgin out in the garden. "Oh, no, of course they won't again."

After very kindly inquiring into our comforts, La Superiore retired, leaving me in the company of her cohorts. They crowded around smiling, asking questions, and apparently commenting upon the whole episode and its implications, but naturally I could not understand one word. The whole business, even in Italian, seemed to me to have a strong flavor of curiosity and even idle and purposeless conversation, but I couldn't be sure.

Presently Sister Celia, who spoke excellent English, came to my rescue, and I was charmed to find that it was quite permissible to converse in any way, curious, idle, or otherwise. Through Sister Celia I dealt as well as I could with the barrage of eager questions. Did I come from New York City like La Superiore? Where did I come from then? New Hampshire. Noo Hahmpsheer! Ah, that was a funny word. Gay laughter while various members of the group relayed this information to less articulate ones on the fringes. How old was I? Ah, see I am the twin to Sister Elisa (*"Simile, simile. Simile Suore Elisa"*). And so it went on, while they regarded me during my rather self-conscious speeches as though I were a kind of miraculous toy that worked just like a real person.

A Catholic friend of mine tells me rather impatiently that I obviously was most astonished when the sisters showed themselves most human.

"But I thought they weren't allowed to act human," I say.

"But they *are* human!" he replies.

I had certainly read all the wrong books.

The day that I was to take the children to school I woke to find that it was snowing hard. Down in the garden the ground was already white and the familiar hissing whisper of flakes came to me as I shut our windows. There was no other sound; it was as though the works of the city had stopped like a clock.

The Mother Superior met me in the hall and said that, of course, I wouldn't be taking the children to school in this terrible storm.

"Storm?" I said. "Why it's only about half an inch deep."

The Italian nuns looked at the Mother Superior, who interpreted my remark. They then looked back at me with horrified admiration.

"We're closing our school," said the Mother Superior. "All the stores will be shut."

"I'm sure Miss Barry won't close the American School," I said, remembering that vigorous little New Englander.

The Mother Superior interpreted this too and I left a black-and-white bouquet of nuns jabbering excitedly by the radiator.

95

Outside the windows of the dining room, the falling snow swayed like a veil between us and the fountains. The statues of the four seasons on the edge of the garden had snow on their heads, and in the baskets of fruit and flowers that they offered to the sky. Overhead the ilex oaks were incongruously green and lustrous. The nuns stood by the windows exclaiming in rapture. One of the younger ones went out to sweep and presently I saw her having a snowball fight with Sister Celia. They laughed, and scampered through the snow making a picture so delightful that I longed for the camera. Sister Celia came in on a wave of cold air with snow on her veils and her cheeks pink as roses.

"This is like Morristown!" she said gaily. "I once got stuck in a drift there in the station wagon."

"Did you say Morristown?" I asked stupidly. "You mean in New Jersey?"

"Of course," she said. "I was in the guest house there for ten years. How do you suppose I learned English?"

"You drove a station wagon?" I said blankly. "How did you get out of the drift?"

"Shoveled myself out, naturally," she said.

I couldn't picture this.

All the nuns were watching us from the front windows as we started out for school. The phalanx of faces made me nervous and I couldn't get the gear into reverse.

"Drive much?" asked Pete, who was waiting to shut the gates.

The gears screamed and so did I, but eventually we bumped out into the street. The city was in a very relaxed state and an almost carnival atmosphere prevailed. There were hardly any cars about, and everywhere people were taking pictures and merry groups were engaged in snowball fights. No attempt had been made to clear the streets, although I did see a very old lady scooping a path with a large spoon.

The American School was in the Via dei Bardi in a *palazzo* that used to belong to Petrarch's mother. The street was about one car wide with a high wall on the left and the rough stone

96

palazzos on the other unchanged from the days of the Medici. Great iron rings to hold torches stuck out of the walls and there were stone benches where servants used to wait in ancient times. We went in through a medieval-looking courtyard and opened the inner door.

The headmistress wearing a fur jacket welcomed us with great briskness, rather like a small general reviewing new recruits. She dispatched the children to separate rooms with no ceremony and a refreshing matter-of-fact assumption that they needed no help. All of us liked this. Then I waited for the Reassuring Little Talk that headmistresses give to parents. It didn't come.

"Well," she said, "goodbye."

"Oh, goodbye," I said. That was that.

I went back through the courtyard, climbed into the car and in five minutes was hopelessly lost.

Words cannot express how involved and confusing I found it to drive that Volkswagen around a city whose street plan was worked out several centuries before by people riding horseback or herding goats. The concentration necessary for manipulating the five gears and translating street signs was constantly shattered by shouts of enraged policemen, warnings screeched by nearby pedestrians, and the incredible bedlam of traffic. Everybody blew horns, screamed, and sang, but the scooters and motorcycles drowned even these sounds in their endless steam-drill roar.

I couldn't stop to look at the map; every other street had the Don't Enter sign on it; some of them were torn up altogether and reduced to mere chasms full of pipes and some ended in wooden barricades. I drove around for hours and hours, emerging into strange piazzas, squeezing again into tubelike alleys, until I found myself driving the wrong way on a street called (in Italian) The Street of the Pig. "————!" I yelled. "————! ————!"

A policeman ran out ahead of me and opened his arms. He then came over to my window and screamed at me in Italian.

"Je suis perdue!" I shouted.

He paused.

"Madame," he said in French, "are you then an American?"

This seemed to me an insult to my French but I accepted it as preferable to arrest. The policeman kindly directed me back to the school, it being then lunch time, and added apologetically that he had thought I was German because of the car.

My children came straggling out full of comments on their classes, classmates, and teachers.

"Our Italian teacher just gives us candy," said Billy. "We don't do anything. But it's a neat school."

"Jeepers, some woman's trying to teach me about Edward the Confessor," said Margie. "Who's he?"

"Jeeze, there's a kid from New York in my room and is he a *creep!*" said Pete.

"Have a nice morning, Mum?" asked Kathy kindly.

"No," I said.

During lunch, while the children described in detail the behavior of the other Americans and listed all the supplies that we had to purchase *that afternoon,* I brooded darkly on the prospect of two weeks shut up with children and nuns. At that early stage I was acutely aware of my worldly status and didn't know whether nuns were supposed to laugh or how hideously I might offend them by lighting a cigarette.

I had no clue as to what was going on in the private world of the convent, no idea what I should or should not do or say. I was in a fine state of apprehension most of the time and hardly dared speak. I was, however, intensely curious about everything.

The two things that impressed me at once about the convent were the appearance and general behavior of the sisters and the very secular elegance of the villa and its gardens. At home I had acquired a kind of composite picture of the typical nun made up from cursory glimpses of sisters of charity on the streets or in trains and on steamers. This symbolic figure had a face of waxen pallor, colorless lips pressed in a tight line, and steel-rimmed spectacles half concealing the pale, cool eyes. In the Italian order there was no one remotely resembling this. The young sisters were dimpled, black-eyed, and pretty, almost always smiling, almost always running with veils and robes flying behind them.

They chattered and laughed together going about their mysterious errands like birds nest-building in spring. The bubble of their laughter and the gay swirl of their hurrying wings were infinitely charming. One of the older nuns was so exquisite to look at that it was breathtaking to watch her float down the marble stairs. The habit of the order with its white coif and wimple tightly framing the face was very becoming. The nuns who worked in the kitchen or in the garden wore white robes and veils; those who taught in the school or supervised the workings of the villa wore black.

The cook and the garden sister were much older than the rest—real country women, ruddy and heavy-set. These two could have existed nowhere but in Europe because they were the true peasants, simple, good, and dedicated to hard work. They were not modern people at all, any more than the convent itself was modern in most respects. There were times when I felt that I could easily be looking at part of the fourteenth century, because within the high walls of the convent's domain the middle ages still seemed to live.

The uniform dress of the nuns and the fact that I could not understand their speech gave me perhaps a curious advantage. For instance, in our own country we are instinctively aware of an individual's background and upbringing by his choice of clothes, his regional pronunciation, his vocabulary, his manners —all those superficial and often deceptive details that camouflage the inner being. I saw the Italian nuns absolutely uncolored by anything except their own essential personalities, and these —merry or grave, kindly, gentle, or boisterous—shone out clearly.

Only the two Americans seemed to be comprehensible, identifiable, and familiar—which was, of course, quite unfair. Still it was interesting to observe that these two Americans, highly intelligent, nervous, and energetic as they were, had none of the quality of merry serenity or serene merriment which characterized the Italians. They were the only ones who ever lost their tempers or showed worry, anxiety, and distress of any kind. This was completely understandable in the case of the Mother Superior—she carried a load of responsibility comparable to nothing I could even imagine. The other American was younger and I felt, perhaps wrongly, that she was having a rough time adjusting herself to the ancient and prescribed routine of the order. She acted as I might have done, only I would probably have been much worse. The other sisters were like happy children, completely cared for and directed.

The elegant and romantic character of the villa seemed to me equally surprising and unlike anything one has any right to expect in a convent. It had been furnished in the style of Louis Phillipe, probably the most frivolous and worldly style in existence, and La Superiore received visitors in a small salon, all pale blue, white and gold which was pure Watteau. Then there were the Boucher and Lancret murals which were not only secular but obviously portrayals of illicit rendezvous, amorous intrigues, and carnal preoccupations. Mirrors framed in gold arabesques reflected the bewitching lovers as well as the flying figures of the nuns moving across the parquet and between the delicate columns. There was a sunporch decorated in Chinese red lacquer and beyond its French doors lay the garden where there were some half-naked stone figures, a delightful head of Pan playing his pipes, a large white crucifix, and a lot of white marble gods and goddesses, frankly pagan in nature.

The villa combined beauty, comfort, and extreme discomfort in a way peculiarly Italian. Living there was almost as luxurious and as painful as it must have been when the villa was first built centuries before. Even with my severe training at the ski

100

hostel, I was still annoyed by the immense amount of effort it took to achieve even minimal bodily comfort. American standards are taken so for granted that it is nearly impossible for one of us to understand why Europeans can't learn about things like heat and light.

"I thought you had a furnace," I said to Sister Celia once when we were leaning up against a blood-warm radiator.

"Oh, we do," she said, "but we turn it off during the day when the sun's out."

"What for?" I stupidly asked. "It's still freezing in here."

"Because there isn't enough oil in Italy," she said.

"Why not use the fireplace during the day to save oil?" I said, still thinking like an American.

"Because there's no wood in Italy," she said.

To me this seemed perfectly incredible. Still it was true. Wood was as precious as gold. You bought it stick by stick in little baskets or collected twigs and grape prunings.

These aspects of my ignorance involved me in so many difficulties that at first I thought I would never have time to do anything except adjust. The children, on the other hand, fitted in at once, never mentioned the cold or the peculiarities of life among nuns, and acted as though they had lived there since birth.

In the process of adjusting I was constantly coming up against unexpected barriers and felt rather like a person trying to run through a forest with cobwebs in the face and briars grabbing the ankles.

There were, to begin with, crises over the domestic trivia of living. There was a very confusing business with the key to the hot-water boiler which was kept by Sister Celia. She would turn the thing on before dinner and turn it off after breakfast, she said, thus allowing us to have hot water for baths at both times.

"You know," she said, with her sweet smile, "you can't have hot water here the way you do in America."

This was no surprise to me, but either we didn't take enough baths or the boiler was turned too high, because every night it nearly exploded. It would roar and I would go into the bathroom in the middle of the night and turn on all the faucets to let the steam escape. I complained about this to Sister Celia, who laughed heartily and finally left the key on the window sill, as it was against the rules to let me have it.

Then our portable bedside light blew all the fuses. The Mother S. told us that the Man said we were using a powerful bulb (no doubt American) which had overloaded the circuit.

"But it's a European bulb," I insisted, "and only about forty watts."

"Ah," said the Mother Superior. "Probably it's French."

"It's *Italian,*" I said. "I bought it here."

She smiled sadly and said that a bulb of 15 watts or even less was quite sufficient. The one I finally got was 7 watts but by a certain amount of bulb snatching from other rooms I managed to secure a 20.

One activity in which I wasted untold hours was getting comfortable enough to read. Although it was spring outdoors most of the time, it was winter inside, and the cold striking upwards from those stone floors made it necessary to prepare for sitting in a chair as though one were going on a dog sled through the Arctic. After putting on my alpaca-lined coat, gloves, and scarf (I *always* wore fur-lined boots indoors), I spread a sleeping bag out on a chair in front of the heater, arranged cigarettes, books, glasses, and a pile of pillows neatly on the bed, built a structure of books to bring the lamp practically onto my shoulder, and then crawled carefully into the bag, zipping it up to my chest.

Usually I knocked over the lamp or swept my glasses off the bed in the process and had to crawl out to get them, or I might forget the matches or an ash tray or a handkerchief. However, once in the bag, I built another structure of pillows on my lap to hold the book right under the light bulb. The trouble was that all that wriggling around, the building of structures and adjusting of equipment, would leave me angry and exasperated, with all my clothes twisted the wrong way. In such a state of mind I found it impossible to concentrate on reading Italian history or studying the language. Also the meter for the electric heater was right in front of me rolling up the score for which I would be charged.

Another constant problem was that of maintaining some kind of order in our three rooms. We had no place to store anything except in three small bureaus, under beds, in or on top of three wardrobes, or in corners. As a result we were all buried in possessions. Across the hall was a double room where the girls lived waist deep in dolls, comic books, recorders, music, duffel bags, and cartons of books, as well as hundreds of bits of paper advertising Argo, a protective agency which sowed the landscape with tiny handbills every night. The boys lived in another double room and threw all their clothes on the floor with soccer balls, swords, and more Argos, Bill and Margie being rival collectors of these useless articles.

Every day I ordered them to clean up, forgot to check before school, and was obliged to do it myself, so that Sister Celia wouldn't find out how lax my discipline was. This method didn't fool her, though, and she gave me a lecture one day on Neatness. My children, she said, were not Neat (no news to me). I replied that no children were neat. Sister Celia said that they must be trained. I agreed and said that I was working on this, but did not say how. (Didn't know.)

After she left I built up a magnificent theory that the reason why I didn't enforce neatness was that I didn't want my relationship with the children to consist entirely of disciplinary encounters and constant needling. If, I told myself, I were to succeed in making them neat, I would have to speak of nothing else from morning till night. Also, I told myself, Sister Celia had no children and very few, if any, possessions, so she could hardly understand my position.

This argument made me feel pleased with myself but I still

had to get the boys' room picked up myself as usual and the old familiar guilt once more assailed me; I was a bad mother.

Besides the innumerable hazards of life inside the walls, there were the infinite and varied hazards of the unfamiliar Italian city outside the gate. Every day I had to drive the children to school, collect my mail, and do certain basic shopping. I also had to baby-sit with Billy in the afternoons, an activity which I thought I had outlived. Looking back on those first weeks, I can't imagine how I found it so difficult or why I took so long to get free of all my foolish preconceptions and expectations. By the time we left the convent, I felt as though we had spent all our lives among nuns in Italy, but at first I was still too conditioned by American standards of all kinds. It is quite impossible to appreciate the comfort and freedom that we enjoy in our country until you are deprived of them.

As for trying to understand the point of view of Catholic nuns, I gave up. I think that with all the best will in the world it is impossible for anyone brought up as a Protestant, with sixteen years of marriage and motherhood behind her, to put herself in the place of a person trained from birth in the Catholic tradition and dedicated to poverty, obedience, and chastity. The reverse is also true, or so I believe. Peaceful coexistence on the subject of religion was the final solution of both the sisters and myself. I think the matter was settled when we tried to discuss the Pope. This incident occurred on the Pope's birthday and I was met in the hall by several nuns, one of whom asked me in Italian if it was true that I didn't believe in a person called Eel Papa.

"Eel Papa?" I repeated vaguely.

"It's his birthday today," said Sister Celia, regarding me mischievously. There was a brief pause while I wondered whether they were talking about somebody's father and then it came to me. *Il Papa.* The Pope.

"Oh yes, of course," I said, "I believe in him. I think he's a wonderful man."

"But you don't believe him to be infallible, do you?" asked the Mother Superior who had joined the group.

I saw that this was somehow a test. I felt very inadequate, and into my head came unbidden the words, "Diet of Worms." I had in school been so charmed by this production of Martin Luther's that I had never forgotten the name. All I said now, though, was, "No, I guess not," in a feeble voice.

"Why not?" came the ominous question.

"Well—" I said, nervously, "he's only a man and no man is infallible."

There was a dead silence.

"He is not only a man," said the Mother Superior.

I could see no way out of this but for us to go on saying, "Yes he is," and "No, he isn't," until eternity, so I smiled at her and said that I didn't know enough to discuss the matter. I then departed to take the children to school.

The period of initiation into convent life is intimately associated in my mind with cold. It's true that outdoors the temperature was mild to a New Englander and the few inches of snow which fell seemed a mere sugaring to one used to wallowing around in real blizzards.

The snow lasted only a day and then disappeared, but the cold stayed, and all the sisters went around with hot-water bottles clasped to their stomachs. I bought four new ones, and every night these were filled by one of the sisters from the kettle in the kitchen. In the afternoons the children and I went out into the vineyards and collected grape prunings for the evening's fire.

We used to have the fire in the black marble fireplace in the Mother Superior's office and she would sit with us and talk about the cold. Nobody ever spoke of much else during this period. The olives were frozen. Hundreds were starving in the south. Food was being flown in. I found it hard to believe these dark reports when the ground wasn't even frozen and I could pick violets out under the hedges.

One day we had a fearful crisis precipitated by the cold and my American officiousness. There was an orangery out back—a glasshouse where the ancient orange and lemon trees spent the winter. The temperature now fell so low that the poor gardening sister stopped watering these precious trees; she was afraid to "freeze the roots." Of course, this was a fatal move and presently I noticed that the oranges were dying. If I had been an Italian I would simply have shrugged my shoulders and said, "So they are dying. That is the will of God," and forgotten the whole thing. Not being Italian, I reported it to the Mother Superior.

The result was rather like General Quarters on a navy ship. Alarm bells shrieked, nearly lifting me out of my chair on the porch; nuns flew past me with scared eyes and the garden was full of streaming veils. I went outside and heard the Mother Superior's voice raised in anger. A stream of Italian poured over the hedge and then she herself, hot-water bottle clasped tight, sailed through the opening and back to the chapel. I, overcome with guilt, went by devious routes to the greenhouse where I expected to find the sisters flagellating themselves with knotted thongs. On the contrary, the younger nuns were squirting frozen lemons at each other in gales of laughter, Corinna's husband was fixing the broken windows, and the old garden nun was watering the trees. I sought out Sister Celia and abased myself before her.

"I'm awfully sorry," I said. "It's all my fault."

She laughed merrily and offered me a piece of lemon which I sucked, although it nearly ate the skin off my lips.

"That's all right," she said. "You didn't know."

"What happened?" I asked when I had recovered from the lemon.

"The Superior thought we had forgotten to water the lemons. It was a mistake. We had been advised not to. We were very sorry for her. Now she will be sad because she lost her temper."

That afternoon the Mother Superior referred quite humorously to the whole affair and her own part in it and went on to discuss the difficulties of working with people as relaxed as the Italians. If it snows, she said, they wait until all the roads are blocked and then say, "Alas, we can go nowhere." If something needs fixing they wait until it breaks and then say, "Alas, nothing can be done." If they lose something they don't look for it but simply wait until it turns up.

This system is so exactly like the one under which we operate as a family that I had difficulty in showing sufficient disapproval.

"Honestly," said the Mother Superior, "sometimes I think I'll go nuts!"

I stared at her and then we both burst out laughing. Suddenly we were just two Americans. Later on I met some of the younger sisters and Sister Celia returning from the orangery and all of us giggled in a conspiratorial way, remembering the lemon squirting. Sister Celia put her arm around me and gave me a hug, her pretty face full of mischief. We went through the French windows into the dining room and out through the passage toward the kitchen. At the kitchen door they all paused. Beyond them I looked into the huge tiled room where the cook was stirring something over the stove. The blue gas flames were reflected on shining steel surfaces, copper pots winked brightly, and there was a wonderful smell of onions and olive oil.

"Now I will iron my veils," said Sister Celia.

"I'll come and watch you," I said, feeling at last part of the group.

There was a cool pause.

"I'm afraid you can't," said Sister Celia, smiling sweetly. "Everything beyond this door is cloistered."

Someone to Talk To

The exclusive company of children and nuns had one great drawback: all conversation had to be heavily censored. After a certain period the law of diminishing returns set in, and I used to go out in the vineyards and talk to myself in a very uninhibited manner. I even became interested in the opinions put forward by my worst self and would often howl with laughter at something the coarse creature said. This way madness lies, I have always been told, so I decided that unless I got outside the walls and saw people the world of fantasy would claim me. I had, it is true, spent every morning exploring the city, memorizing the routes to various places and wandering about the streets and through museums and occasionally getting winked at by a policeman or patted by a guide, but this was not really satisfactory, nor was it conversation.

Then it happened that I was asked to a cocktail party by the wife of an American friend of a friend of ours. Much excited I made an appointment with a hairdresser called Signor Florio and thought, ah, launched into society at last! Somebody to talk to without censorship. Interesting conversation with erudite and cultivated members of the International Set. Meeting Italians who were not vowed to poverty, obedience, and chastity. In this happy state of mind I set out for Florio's and on the way was accosted by a tall, rangy Englishwoman in tweeds who asked if she could help me. I explained my mission and she instantly told me to go to her own hairdresser, much better, cheaper, etc. As her hair at the time was rather like an old bird's nest with a few hairpins poked into a doughnut at the back, I felt that she was hardly a recommendation for Hairdresser B. Thanking her, I went off in the right direction but the minute she passed from view reversed my steps and followed back alleys to Signor Florio's. I had spoken to somebody, yes, but on the whole I preferred my own conversation to hers.

I had my hair cut and curled high in the "Italian boy" fashion and later put on my black sheath, pearl earrings, and spike heels—all very painful after such a long time in comfortable clothes. When I arrived at the old palazzo, the scene of the party, I was ushered into an enormous stone-floored room where a fire was burning and introduced to a group of American ladies, every last one dressed in a black sheath, pearl earrings, and spike heels, with their hair done in the Italian boy fashion. Here our resemblance ended—well, we were all women—but aside from that we had nothing in common. They were all in their fifties, all rich and all divorced, and had daughters who later arrived with names different from theirs. One woman took me aside and said that a person present had flown back to New York for a night to pick up her dog.

"Her what?" I asked, thinking I had misunderstood.

"Her dog," she said. "She missed him so."

"Oh," I said.

The conversation closed and I moved into a corner by a comfortable old lady in a pink cardigan.

"Have a drink," she said.

"I'd love it," I replied. "Will you have one?"

"You're damn right I will," she said.

Subsequent to this meeting of souls, I talked to a girl with pancake make-up and dark circles under her eyes.

"You know," she said, "there's someone here who flew back to New York to get her dog."

"Oh, really?" I said falsely. "What for?"

"What for?" she said. "She missed him, of course."

"Oh," I said.

Soon afterward I went home and took off sheath, earrings, and spike heels. My left ear lobe was completely numb for the rest of the evening. The erudite and cultivated conversation I had enjoyed with the International Set made me so angry that I drank half the decanter of chianti at dinner.

"Guess what?" I asked my children. "There was a woman there this afternoon who flew back to New York for one night to get her dog."

"*What!*" they all exclaimed.

"Ask me what for," I said.

"What for?"

"Because she missed him," I said bitterly.

The next day I went to the American Library thinking that there must be someone in there to talk to but found only a very young man with a light green shirt and greasy hair. I looked through the magazines and nobody else came in so I went over to the American Express. There must be somebody, I thought dismally, somebody in this whole city who wants to talk to somebody else the way I do.

I was absolutely right. There was. The first thing I saw was a superb coat of blue mutation mink standing at the mail counter. Above it was what looked like a wig made of unraveled manila rope. The coat moved aside as I went up for my mail and, glancing sideways, I nearly screamed at the sight of a face exactly like that of a Siamese cat. The eyes were pulled wide and painted bright blue, the mouth stretched upward in

110

a catlike shape. Obviously a face-lifting job gone wrong. Suddenly it spoke.

"Pahdon me, dear," it said in exactly the low gin-cured Brooklyn voice now a specialty of Kathy and myself. I almost said, "Hiya, kid," but instead said, "Yes?" in my own voice.

"I'm ssawry," said the cat, "but I gotta prawblem here." Her *s*'s hissed like snakes.

"Oh, can I help?" I asked.

"You sure can, dear," it said. "You know anything about this nice?"

"Nice?" I asked. "Nice what?"

"Nice," she said. "N-I-C-E, get it?"

"Well, not exactly," I said.

"It's a place, dear," she said. "Some goddam place in Yourrup. My husband says in this telgraham he's at this Nice and wants me to come. What I wanta know is where is it, see?"

"Oh," I said. "Nice. Oh, it's pronounced Niece—as in niece," I added weakly.

"Neece, eh?" she said. "Where is it?"

"On the French Riviera," I said. "It's a resort. Place to swim. Beaches and things."

"Oh, swell," she said. "You're a real doll. I knew you'd know about it minute I saw you. You and me click. I sez to myself when I saw you c'min, that kid's my type."

This, I must admit, shook me terribly.

"Y'know," she said, "ya like people like I do. Gawd, c'mon out and let's getta cuppa coffee. Got anything on for lunch? C'mon and have lunch. Gawd, I haven't talked to anybody in this dump for a week that knew anything. Most of 'em can't even talk Inglish."

"I would simply love to," I said, "but I must collect my children and go home with them to lunch."

"You got kids? Gee, y'lucky," she said. "Well, y'never know. Maybe this Neece'll do it. I'm ssawry you can't come to lunch." She looked wistfully at me, pathetic under her heavy make-up.

111

"I'm sorry, too," I said, and somehow I was. "Well, goodbye and have fun in Nice."

"Sure, dear," she said. "Goodbye now."

That afternoon the children informed me that there were two new people at the convent, guests like ourselves. When I went down to tea I met them in the salon—a German doctor and his wife, kindly looking, gray haired. They could not speak English so we spoke French and after a bit I turned on the radio and found a station playing classical music. Bob and I have a game in which we see who can guess the composer and the composition, or, if not, the century of the work. I suggested to the doctor that we guess the composer of the work now in progress.

"Baroque, peut-être?" I said, as a starter.

"Vivaldi," said the Herr Doktor.

"Corelli," I said.

"Bach," said the Herr Doktor's wife.

We listened for a moment.

"Vous avez raison," said the Herr Doktor finally. "Corelli."

It was Corelli; we were pleased with ourselves and talked about music. Kathy joined us and then brought her recorder and played a little piece of Handel's. The doctor and his wife applauded. We then began to tell about ourselves and I explained that my husband was in Greece.

"Il est professeur," I said.

"Oh," said the doctor in French. "Then how do you have the Kleinbus I saw outside?"

"We need it to drive around in," I said.

"Ah," said the doctor. "Americans. Your husband is showing off, I see. Rich. In Germany such a car is the bus for the whole town."

I felt as though the doctor had stuck a knife in me. The amount of the hurt surprised me.

"Oh, no," I said. "We aren't rich at all. We have to have a car because we can't afford trains, you see. Also we carry all our baggage this way. It's cheaper."

The doctor laughed. "I know the Americans," he said. "After the war they came to our house. It was a big house full of old things, paintings, furniture, all that we possessed. Some of the paintings were very valuable. The Americans came in and stole everything. They burned what they didn't take."

There was silence. His wife looked anxiously at me and said in a soft voice, "It was really very bad, but that's war. War is always very bad."

"I'm sorry," I said. "The whole thing was bad. Hitler was bad. Nobody behaved very well."

"Let me tell you an amusing story," said the doctor, now smiling in a frightening way. "I had a friend, my dear friend. He was taken by the Nazis because of something he said against Hitler. He was shot. It was I who said the thing, not he. It was a mistake. *C'est amusant, n'est-ce pas?*"

Change the subject, I thought.

"Tell me," I said, "that scar you have. Is that a dueling scar? We have always heard of the student duels in Heidelberg."

The doctor's eyes glittered. He rose and bent his head so that I could see the top of his bald head where there were more scars.

"I fought many duels," he said. "The scars are, you see, all on the head."

"C'est pour le sport?" I asked.

"No, it is not for sport," he said. "It is to kill."

"Is it like fencing?" I asked, now quite terrified of the doctor's eyes, which were ice-blue. "Go get your sword," I said to Pete. "Show him your sword."

Pete returned with his sword and Billy followed with a cheap tin one from the Florence five-and-ten.

"Aha," cried the doctor, "now I will show you how to duel. Take the other sword."

I took Billy's short toy sword and the Herr Doktor swept Pete's out of its sheath with a shriek of metal.

"En guard!" he cried.

I put up my sword.

Suddenly I was in the center of a flickering haze of blades. Every now and then his sword clashed against mine but most of the time the point of it was at my throat, my eye, my cheek, or my mouth.

"Touché," he would yell, and he shouted other things, too, dueling terms I did not understand in French.

"Mum," said Kathy from behind me. "Don't. Stop. It's awful."

I put down my sword. The doctor's eyes, now absolutely diabolical, laughed at me.

"You're dead," he said, mopping his face with his handkerchief.

I went upstairs and sank down on my bed. Kathy collapsed in the chair and covered her face with her hands.

"I thought he was going to kill you!" she said.

"So did I," I said faintly.

"His eyes!"

"Yes, I know."

"He hated you!" she said.

"No he didn't really," I said. "Oh, dear, I wish Daddy was here. Don't think about it. Remember the music." *You* remember the music, I told myself angrily.

"Look," I said, taking a firm line, "it was only because we reminded him of the war. He had more than he could take back there when he was in the underground."

"But Herr Mann didn't talk that way," said Kathy, "even when he told about the night we bombed Innsbruck."

"Well, no," I said. "It's the difference between people."

After Kathy went off, apparently calmed, I began to feel most peculiar, with a strong desire to lie down flat somewhere and weep. A familiar horror seemed to be approaching through the darkness outside, a featureless face, and around it fear out of all proportion to the incident of the doctor. Well, I recognized it all right. The Germans are coming, my life-long nightmare. I remembered a poster with a spiked helmet and a dripping scarlet hand. *The Kaiser's Hand is Bloody,* it said. Where's Pop? we asked, sitting in the sand dunes eating sandwiches. He's in France. He's at the Front now. Then he came back, bringing me a French doll, and he also had helmets, bayonets, a hand grenade, and a piece of shrapnel, all picked up on the battle field. This was interesting at the time, but I used to dream about faces in spiked helmets coming over the edge of a trench.

The worst part, much the worst part, was the next step in this sequence—our own personal war, and Bob going off in his naval officer's uniform, me driving home with the babies—Pete's fist clutching my hair, Kathy interested in the fact that I was crying. Where's Daddy? she said later. He's on the ocean in a big boat. (No news for a month).

At this point I went and got the cognac out of the bottom of the wardrobe because I knew what was coming next. I poured myself a stiff hooker and then sat there thinking, all right, go ahead. You have four children. If they drop an atom bomb when they're in school shall I go out and look for them or not? It's against civilian defense regulations, but do I care? I do not. If they come and I'm at home with the children—say they're asleep upstairs—what's the best thing? Shall I get a gun and keep it upstairs? Supposing they say, "Tell us where your husband is or we'll shoot your children?" In five years Pete will be nineteen.

There was a tap on the door and Sister Celia's pretty face peered around it.

"Hello," she said.

"Hello," I said. "Come on in."

"Having a little drink?" she asked, sitting as straight as a saint in a niche.

"Yes," I said. "Are you allowed to have some?"

"Oh, no!" she said, laughing.

Presently she smiled at me in a compassionate way and said, "You miss your husband, don't you?"

"Yes," I said curtly.

Oddly enough, the business of the doctor and my recent hideous revery had abolished the barriers between me and a nun. At least they seemed of no importance at all compared to "Tell us where your husband is or—" etc.

"Why on earth did you become a nun?" I asked, looking at the bewitching little face in its white frame.

"I wished to," she said.

"But why?"

"Well," she said, "I was so—in our house in Naples there was no peace. There were too many children. Too many people. Too little money. When I was eleven years old I made my parents take me to the mother superior in a convent in Naples."

"Eleven!" I said. "Margie's eleven!"

"Yes, my parents felt that way. They were against it, against me all the time. The mother superior said I might stay with them at the convent but I could not be a postulant for ten years. I had to wait."

"Did you ever have doubts?" I asked.

"Yes—yes, I did. When my sisters married I said to myself, 'You can have that, too.' It was very hard. There was a time when I had to fight my parents and myself, too. You see it is against nature in some ways."

"But why did you stay?"

She looked dreamily at me, as though she were remembering something sweet and as though she were trying to think how she could make me see it, too.

"Think how you feel about your husband," she said. "That is how we feel about Jesus Christ, as nearly as I can explain. We are brides of Christ, you see. Oh, the time comes when we put on white dresses, bride's dresses—so lovely! I wish you could see. Veil, long white dress, crown!"

"Don't you ever wish you had a real husband that you could see, and children?" I asked bravely.

"But I have them," she cried. "All my children at the school."

"Well, I couldn't do it," I said. "I couldn't bear to miss anything."

"Listen," she said, "you are braver than I am, to live in the world. All you have—husband, children—will leave you. They will die and you will have nothing left. What I have I will never lose."

No, I thought. You'll never have to picture your sons in uniform. Not for you the panic when they are late, the sudden fever that could be polio, the terror of speeding cars, breaking ice, fire in the night.

The door thudded open and Billy entered.

"Hi," he said to Sister Celia, then came and leaned against my chair.

"Hey," he said, "are we getting our allowance over here?"

"I suppose so," I said. "What did Daddy say?"

"Oh, he always forgets. So do you, too."

"I know," I said. "I'm sorry."

"That's O.K.," said Billy comfortingly. "I just thought if I saved up my allowance, *if* you gave it to me sometime, I might get a holster like Sandro's. Do you think I might?"

"Yes," I said. "Probably."

"Say!" he said, suddenly. "You were good fighting that man. Was it fun?"

"Oh, yes," I said. "Lots of fun."

"Well, he hacked some places in my sword," said Billy, "but that's O.K. Gee, you were pretty good!" He moved on thinking about holsters.

I looked at Sister Celia.

"What about that?" I said, and all the atom bombs, the spiked helmets, the Gestapo agents, and Kaiser's hands dwindled down into nothing. "Don't you envy me *that?*"

"No," she said, "I have never regretted anything. I have only known the most perfect happiness."

In her radiant upward look I recognized my own emotion. Only I was remembering the doctor bringing me Billy and saying, "It's another boy!"

Primavera

Comparatively few Protestant wives and mothers, to say nothing of American Protestant wives and mothers, find themselves living in convents. I do believe, though, that those who do may be excused if they undergo a brief attack of cabin fever. My attack ceased with the beginning of my real friendship with Sister Celia, and presently I didn't want to go outside except to explore the city like a wandering gypsy, unencumbered by social obligations.

The Herr Doktor, having purged himself in the duel, now proved an interesting and cultivated conversationalist. By watching his eyes I could tell whether the topic under discussion was going to remind him of either Americans or Hitler. Then I would instantly change to another. The safest topics were archaic Greek sculpture and archaeology, but even here I was nervous, as the word "underground" was implied in excavations. On the whole, though, this skating on thin ice was a stimulating exercise, and I became quite fond of the doctor and his wife. The effect of the Hitler regime on people of that age was like a mortal wound, and one evening he said as much. It was a remark we had heard many times before in Europe.

"You cannot understand. It is an illness. Europe is ill. We are all ill. You in your country are young and happy and you do not know what war does."

No, we don't, but I was able to see something of what it does by knowing the Herr Doktor. I would have liked to discuss war with him but this was impossible.

Another doctor, a Basil Rathbone type who came to the convent to give vitamin shots to the sisters, used to talk to me for hours about kodachrome slides and once cornered me in the sun porch and showed me his collection.

Aside from these medicine men I saw no one but the nuns and stayed in the convent like a mother fox in its den, brooding over my little ones. When I sat outside in the sun guarding my litter I really felt like a mother fox—placid, content, but watchful. If anyone had attempted to harm my cubs—and there were troops of urchins in the Bobboli Gardens—I would have sprung at them, snarling and snapping. I hadn't been so purely maternal, in this basic animal way, since my babies were born, and it felt rather nice.

Still, there were moments when I had seen enough nuns, doctors, and children, and once I took my young to an American movie, thus reminding myself that home still existed and currying favor with the children at the same time. When we emerged from the theater the car had its first attack of what we later called the Sickness Mongo, and we didn't get home until dark. Following this disaster I never went anywhere in the car after I had collected the three older children at four o'clock.

The only one of us who achieved social success in the outside world was Billy. He used to play with the son of the American consul and drive away from school in the back of the consular

Cadillac. Once I went to pick him up at the consulate and saw him and Jimmy crawling through the railings of a deserted villa nearby. A short distance away from them two uniformed guards were baby-sitting.

Billy climbed reluctantly into the front seat, his eyes snapping with excitement.

"Boy, do we have *fun,*" he said. "Boy, I wish I lived there!"

"What do you do?" I asked.

"We chase cats," he said. "There's this empty old house and a yard all full of bushes and they're just *millions* of cats in there. One almost clawed me today," he added with relish. "Jimmy has this enormous dog and we hunt with him. Boy, you should see him go after those cats!"

The pattern of our life now became as follows. We rose at seven. At breakfast, just as we were eating our eggs, two ducks waddled quacking past the French windows and splashed about in the fountain. The children then collected the dozens of thin black notebooks required by the school and clumped in their fur-lined boots through the marble halls to the front door. One or two of the sisters were usually leaning up against the radiator and we all said, *"Buon giorno!"* The three younger members of the family then fought about who was to open the gate and who-ever won did so.

We then rolled out into the street in our Volkswagen, bumped over the trolley tracks, and began the usual race with scooters, donkey carts, men on bicycles, men pushing carts full of wood or carrying piles of chairs. There was always the same very small donkey with red harness and gay little cart decorated in blue and scarlet. It was always driven by an old man who seemed to be going to the wine shop on the corner. Big green No. 6 buses just missed colliding with us at all the intersections. Five trolley cars were always circling at the entrance to the Ponte San Nic-colo, and a good-looking conductor was just walking across the corner. In a kind of cave in the street wall, two men would be piling wood and coal into baskets.

In the cold, sunny air the Arno steamed like a boiling kettle; the melting frost on the pavements and wet, glittering bay hedges sent upward a silvery vapor. All the exhausts of cars smoked gaily and this added to the general feeling of excitement and motion.

I dropped the children at school, went to the American Express for mail, visited the secondhand book carts to see what was new, bargained with certain raffish characters in the straw market where I was working down the price of a tablecloth, and then did some exploring. Every day the warmth of the sun grew more intense. I used to wander down unknown streets where the squared paving stones were smooth as water-worn pebbles, and find shops selling baskets, or antiques, or copper or religious candlesticks. Once I discovered a courtyard full of fat cupids holding dolphins, scallop shells, and mermaids, all the furniture for Italian gardens collecting moss and lichens among the dank weeds.

There was a high arched window in one of the *palazzos,* and every afternoon on the way back to the school I saw in the cavernous room beyond a great chandelier of Venetian glass, iridescent, unsubstantial, suspended in the darkness. It was like an inverted crystal tree, every branch blooming with tulip-shaped sconces. On some evenings it was lighted, the brightness bringing out a thousand rainbow sparks from the glass. This chandelier seemed to stand for all that I couldn't see in Florence, all the real living of people in their homes, as secret as the inner chambers of a hive. All we saw were the workers flying back and forth, the honey gatherers on the flowers and the guardians of the swarm.

Before tea the children and I walked again in the gardens and vineyards collecting twigs for our evening's fire. We found hickory nuts and cracked them on stones; we picked wild daffodils and grape hyacinths. Then I had tea and the boys played soccer or pushed things around in the fountain while the girls occupied themselves with a surprise for Bob's birthday involving hundreds of scraps of cut-up comic books and all my Scotch tape.

121

They did this in a small garden room containing an unused wall fountain and a set of children's furniture.

Dinner was announced by a gong. We filed in under the eyes of the boiled lobsters and a painted tile saying, "All that glistens is not gold." The meal began with some kind of *pasta* and had main courses composed of interesting cuts of meat and vegetables cooked in olive oil and garlic. It was always very good and ended with a bowl of apples and oranges.

"*Molto buono,*" I would say to Corinna.

"Mummy—don't say that *every day!*" Kathy said.

"*Grazia,*" I said to Corinna, rising.

"*Grazi-*e," moaned Pete.

"Mummy, aren't you *ever* going to learn Italian?" Margie usually asked and I usually replied, "I can't seem to speak anything but French."

Then the long, dark cold evening began.

Once in a while the Mother Superior provided a terrific treat for everybody and showed movies in the dining room. The machine even had a sound track which gave us the noises of gunfire and horses' hooves, but, of course, provided only Italian words. These movie parties were fraught with hazards because at any moment the Mother Superior might exert her powers of censorship and switch off the story in mid-passage. She did this whenever the action was "too exciting" or "too stimulating." My children, who go to the movies only for the purpose of being overexcited and overstimulated, were indignant beyond words when the film stopped just as the Good Guys and the Bad Guys were shooting it out.

One evening while crouched in my sleeping bag reading a detective story, I heard an operatic tenor voice echoing through the villa in the most romantic way. The children and I met on the stairs and hurried down to the marble entrance hall. There we came upon an enchanting scene. A young man with two baskets of groceries at his feet was sitting on one of the gold-legged sofas beside the Mother Superior, singing his heart out.

122

The nuns were grouped around him, some standing with rapt faces, others—the younger ones—leaning on the backs of chairs tapping their feet and humming.

When we appeared the Mother Superior introduced the young man as Tullio, and in my honor he sang *Arrivederci Roma,* which mentions an English girl. Afterwards he sang all kinds of songs, mostly about love, mothers, babies, and home. The love songs went perfectly with the Boucher murals over our heads.

When we went upstairs I was melted down to a mere puddle of sentiment and in this mood leaned out my casement to look at the moonlit garden. The cypresses speared the luminous air; one pierced the full moon. The garden was alive with the rustling of leaves and the sound of fountains. A dove murmured sleepily from the aviary and the whole thing was so incredibly romantic that I couldn't help but feel the waste of it with no man around.

On other evenings the Mother Superior would play the organ with Kathy, and I would sit and listen nearby in a little blue-and-white salon of extreme frivolity. Sometimes the Mother Superior played Bach and sometimes she played a virtuoso number about a squirrel, full of difficult runs and trills that squealed and echoed through the marble rooms. Most evenings, though, the children worked and I read.

I read about the Medici and the beautiful Simonetta Vespucci, the model for Botticelli's Venus. Kathy read about early Italian painting, entranced with her first taste of art. Pete was sculpting a head in clay. The small ones seemed a little unclear as to what they were studying, but their Italian improved daily.

Following the progress of the Medici family I went each day to a place associated with them and became more and more submerged in the past. Then overnight the spring came and the past faded, receded, and dissolved in the brilliant light of the present.

The Italian spring, the *primavera,* is an experience comparable to first love. Its arrival after the weeks of cold was almost more than I could cope with in a balanced way. One morning, waking to the sound of singing birds and fountains, I leaned out my window into a soft stirring warmth—air from which all edge of cold had melted. It was as though a great oven door had swung open somewhere and through it poured the heat and sweetness of the coming summer that was baking there like a cake. Wood smoke lay in the valley, making all the distances pale blue and silver. The sky ballooned up high and empty and under its enormous bubble of blue all sounds echoed in a muted, nostalgic way.

Drunk with this taste of the day, I decided to abandon the city and its dark streets, forget museums and Medici, and spend every minute outdoors. After driving the children to school I collected the mail and bought a bunch of violets from a ragged man on the street. Down on the Via Tornabuoni against the rough brown stones of a wall, the flower seller had placed a whole almond tree. And below in the cans and jugs were armfuls of narcissus and lily of the valley, striped red-and-white tulips, anemones of scarlet and grape-blue, and, as a kind of *pièce de résistance,* a large curved basket packed with tight bunches of Parma violets and blue hyacinths.

There was a dress exactly the color of violets and almond blossom spread out in a very expensive dress shop next door and beside it a pair of earrings made of opalescent sea shells. I went right in, smelling my violets.

"I want that dress," I said.

"Certainly, madam, we will make one to madam's exact specifications," they said.

"How much is it?" I asked weakly.

It was quite a lot but not too much on such a day. I made an appointment for a fitting and drove back to the villa where I took off my stockings and put on my old sneakers. Now! I said to myself and going into the boys' room selected a bamboo stick to carry. The first walk in spring requires sneakers and a stick to swing. Everybody knows this who knows how to go on a spring walk. When I went down the marble stairs I passed two of the nuns, who stared at my bare legs, at the stick, and then at each other.

"*Primavera*," I said.

"*Si! Si!*" they agreed, smiling vaguely.

Out in the garden the garden sister in her white robes was raking the earth under a baby almond tree. I greeted her and went on between the stone lions, past the boxwood maze, the head of Pan on his column, the second fountain, and on through the bay hedge into the valley. From somewhere came a flowery perfume mixed with smoke and the smell of manure. At the end of the valley the monastery bell was ringing. This valley stretched for about half a mile to where the monastery's tower showed above some bunched olive trees. On the right it was bounded by a high stone wall and up against this were some small farms set in olive groves. Beyond them the hillside rose up gray with more olives and punctuated with cypresses of all heights and degrees of blackness. The floor of the valley was criss-crossed with long paths of grass that divided the gardens into squares. On each side were rows of clawlike elms with grape vines festooned from one to another. Under the trees and between the vines were rows of leeks, lettuce, turnips, and artichokes or the combed emerald lines of wheat and rye. Men were always gathering up the prunings and one used to drive a donkey with a cart containing a load of evil-smelling manure.

As I went out into the valley I saw this man. The donkey was about the size of a large dog and violet-gray in color and the load of manure towered over him like a haystack. His master kept up a steady scream of curses, belaboring the tiny creature with a whip the while. This, combined with the terrible and malevolent odor of the manure, made me feel a little sick. I turned the other way and went down to the dike where I explored the bank for new flowers. I found some tiny cyclamen with leaves no bigger than a penny. While I was picking one I heard a sound behind me and, turning, saw two men—heavy, brown, and ox-eyed—staring at me. There was a peculiar expression in those eyes, a kind of bovine leer.

"Buon giorno," I said, nervously.

They exchanged glances and the larger one said something to the other with a lecherous grin. Neither spoke to me, but their eyes went up and down, resting finally on my bare legs. I got out of there fast and crossed the valley on one of the grass paths. Several women in long earth-colored dresses were grubbing in the dirt and raised their eyes to watch me. I smiled. They did not smile but simply stared in stolid, hostile disapproval. They were as remote from me as though this were a spring day in the fourteenth century into which I had strayed by mistake.

Nothing in my life had prepared me for this, and I realized with surprise that these farmers and their wives disliked me. Why? Because I was an American? My tweed suit made that fairly clear. Because I had bare legs? Sneakers? Because I carried a stick?

Then I remembered a friend of mine whose sister had married an Italian. She had given me a short lecture on being a woman in Italy. She had said that in Italy a woman's place is *really* in the home, either in bed or in the kitchen; that it is not only improper but actually dangerous for a woman to walk alone in the country; that a woman never converses with a man in Italy unless she is willing to be seduced by him. At the time I thought this a lot of balderdash, like the business about taking along twenty tubes of toothpaste and never drinking water or milk. Also I remembered the friend saying that she had been pinched in the bottom by a soldier during an audience with the Pope. Yet I still couldn't believe that anything could happen to me on a spring morning, so I decided to leave the valley for once and see what was outside the wall.

I crossed through an orchard of exquisitely pruned peach trees all colored turquoise with spray. A man at work with a curved pruning knife raised his head and gave me an impudent glance. I hurried past him and almost ran to the gate. It was luckily ajar and I slipped out, closing it behind me.

I was in a narrow road with the high brown walls on each side, making it impossible to see out. No one was in sight and I began walking up the hill feeling like a runaway child. Nonsense, I kept saying to myself. This is silly. What on earth could happen to you? I concentrated on the beauty of the cypresses that rose above the walls, their stone-gray trunks and dense green-black foliage crisply outlined upon the brilliant sky. These trees emphasized the strangeness of Italy, where nothing seemed to strike a familiar echo. They were recognizable only from backgrounds to Italian paintings, those dreamlike formalized landscapes behind groups of improbable angels.

Presently I came to a drive which branched off the main road and led to a large villa that was apparently an institution of some sort. The wall beside this drive was a low one, and tiptoeing over to it I looked down into a miraculous garden, a garden full of strange scents and unknown bird song. Tall oaklike trees with shining dark foliage towered above me and in their depths invisible birds kept up a liquid warbling and chirruping. Their full-throated notes were like fat, silvery bubbles crowding to the top of a glass and running over the brim. Hundreds of smaller birds darted back and forth in the bushes below. A walk ran underneath my wall through a delicately arched arbor upon which jasmine was trained. Beyond this the thick green grass fell away under olive trees. There was a tree among the cypresses that seemed made of silver tinsel. Eucalyptus?

A noise made me look around. A young man in some sort of uniform was getting off his bicycle just beside me. He gave me the unmistakable glad eye.

"Oh, for God's sake," I said under my breath and made off as fast as I could without actually running. Once more in the road, I angrily turned upward, determined to get to the top and enjoy the spring even if I had to hit some man with my stick.

127

"Just animals, that's what," I said angrily.

A man in a small car slowed down and smiled at me. I gave him a black glare.

"Go away," I said. *"Basta!"*

Around the curve the walls sank down until they were like our stone walls in New England. Beyond them the olive groves with their silvery twisted trunks were amazingly like apple orchards. Under them, among the green lines of wheat, were clumps of wild daffodils, exploding in gold as far as I could see. When I reached the top of the hill I saw between the olives all of Florence spread out below, dreaming in a violet haze. The Campanile and the Duomo rose above the surface of the haze, and up from the valley came a sudden tumbling din of bells. All the bells of the city were ringing in some sort of celebration. Entranced, I perched on the wall and listened.

Presently I was aware of footsteps coming up the road. Two men this time, both in wasp-waisted sharp-shouldered dark suits with hair like patent leather.

Well, here it is, I thought, feeling curiously breathless.

I stood up and walked away down the hill, shaken from head to foot by the pounding of my heart. One of the men called out in honeyed tones, *"Signorina!"* The other called out something else. I began to run. I heard them laughing behind me. After a while I stopped running and looked around. One man was standing in the road, the other was still coming toward me. As I turned he made one of those famous gestures that people are always making in books by Steinbeck. He also beckoned to me. I had always wanted to find out what these "age-old gestures" were, but the knowledge gave me no particular satisfaction now. I went down that road like a bolting horse, only stopping when I saw ahead of me a nun hand in hand with a small child. It suddenly occurred to me that she of all women in Italy was free to go where she pleased unmolested. No wonder Italian women entered convents.

Indirectly chaperoned by the nun, I reached the gate in the

wall and, averting my eyes from the laboring peasantry, went primly back to the convent hedge and into the garden. Italians! I thought furiously. Really, what a bunch!

I passed Corinna's husband pruning the bay hedge.

You! I thought. Satyrs, all.

When I reached the door to my room I was shocked but hardly surprised to see the silhouette of a man against my window. Even as I said to myself, "Wouldn't you know!" I recognized Bob. An ecstatic reunion followed, and eventually he produced a bottle of *ouzo* (a Greek drink), a box of Turkish delight, and a pack of Turkish cigarettes, suggesting that we have a private orgy in celebration of his return. Anyone can reproduce my sensations while enjoying these delicacies by drinking paregoric and smoking a cigar in a bathroom full of cheap talcum powder. I would not advise the experiment.

That night we celebrated Bob's birthday and the children produced the objects they had been making in the garden room. These were a series of paper hats which Bob was to wear during dinner. They grew more complicated with each course and by dessert he was wearing a creation like a small sailboat with a jib and mainsail as well as two braids which hung down on each side of his face. The sight of him in this hat, eating imperturbably, nearly incapacitated us all.

"It's not that funny," he said. "Hurry up and eat so we can get out of here."

Several nuns peeked in the door at him, their eyes a bit glazed. Corinna watched us all, obviously waiting for an explanation.

"What's the word for birthday?" said Bob to Kathy.

"*Natività?*" asked Kathy.

"Could be," said Bob. "*Natività mia,*" he said to Corinna, and pointed to his hat.

"*Ah, si?*" said Corinna in some confusion.

"*Now* what have I said?" asked Bob.

After dinner we had games in the salon. One involved racing the length of the room with suitcases, opening these and putting

129

on our nightclothes, getting into sleeping bags, and finally galloping back to the starting point. Bob, who was sure that he would be discovered by the nuns in his pajamas, was in a pitiable state of apprehension. The children had to lie down on the floor from laughing.

"That will give them a nice idea of American family life," Bob said as were going to bed.

"Where's the color camera?" I asked him. "Did you leave it on the train?"

"Yes," said Bob. "Now go to sleep."

Venice

I have a theory that all children are born Italian and only become Anglo-Saxon as they are forced and pounded into the polite mold demanded by our northern society.

If you think about it, you see that almost all manners are artificial. It is unlikely that emotional restraint is a natural attribute of man, and it is something the Italians don't bother about. We noticed that as we moved farther south in Europe the contrast between our behavior and that of the local population became less and less apparent. The seething atmosphere of Italian streets, where people sang loudly, yelled, and argued, was just the atmosphere in the Volkswagen.

Italy is part of a lustier world than ours, an older world, happier, sadder, dirtier, noisier, and much more beautiful, and the world of children is like this. It is a world where somehow the meticulous details of scientific baby care, the pronouncements of child psychologists, and the self-conscious report cards of progressive schools take on a quality of fantasy. The truth is, there are certain places where the idea of, say, judging a child's character by his reaction to a lot of ink blots seems perfectly sensible —Cambridge, Massachusetts, to name but one. There are other places, Venice for instance, where such a process seems not only bizarre but insane. I don't say the Rorschach tests *are* insane; I just say that these and practically all the lingo of the psychologist *seemed* insane in Italy and in the company of children.

If you hunted for years you couldn't find a place less like Cambridge, Massachusetts, than Venice, and yet to our little band, products of New England though we all were, Venice was more spiritually compatible at this stage than Cambridge. It exactly suited the rakish, raffish, merry, and abandoned state to which we had been reduced.

By this time the position of Bob and myself as parents had been deeply undermined, and as far as I was concerned my secret suspicion that I was an imposter and not a real mother was almost confirmed. Steady and relentless observation on the part of our children over a period of months had uncovered all our weaknesses, our pitiful pretences of authority. The advice, "If you can't beat them, join them" seemed the only solution to our situation and although we never applied reason to the problem, we gradually became as Italian and relaxed as our young.

We came to Venice at sunset. Over the city all the bells were ringing and canaries were singing from cages on balconies overhead. We swept down the Grand Canal in the soft opalescent glow of the spring evening, past the lacy pink *palazzos* and under the arched bridges. The air was shot through with rose-colored light and seemed to quiver constantly as the sunset glanced upwards from the oily waves. In the canals the noise was incessant. The buzz of outboards, the sputter of motor launches, cries, laughter, music. These sounds were inseparable from the smells of orange peel and exhausts, coffee, and the cool, rotten salty odor of the sea among slimy pilings. Above our heads rose the fantastic palaces and beside us under their stone sills the garbage surged back and forth. Dead cats and empty

Chianti bottles, a thousand orange peels floated in water iridescent with oil. Rainbow gleams of turquoise, bronze, and violet ran out from our thrusting prow.

Our gondolier shouted to other gondoliers and occasionally burst into scraps of songs. With his single oar he sent the gondola through the pink evening like a bird through the air and this swift silent flight put us all under a spell. We simply smiled at each other, incredulous and enraptured. Billy, who sat in the bow with the curved beak of the gondola rising behind his head, was too overcome even to smile. Solemn as a little owl, he stared at the people who waved at us from bridges. Everyone seemed to share our delight.

Our *pensione* was facing the lagoon and we came to it along a side canal that was a kind of ghastly punch bowl of garbage. Steamers were bellowing like melancholy cows from the lagoon and the running lights of smaller boats slid through the blue twilight in pairs and clusters. The Pensione Seguso was a tall, narrow house rather like part of a set for *The Merchant of Venice*. Inside, it was divinely warm and the standard of comfort was so high that we were not surprised to find that everybody there was either British or American. The furniture was antique and charming, the bathrooms excellent, the food superb.

The first person we met in Venice, not counting the gondolier and a man in a dirty T shirt who got a tip for steadying the gondola, was a charming American lady who knew all about the Rorschach or ink-blot tests. The second person we met—well, not exactly met but became involved with—was a small drunken Italian in an outsized beret. The lady psychologist accompanied us everywhere we went, and most of the time the drunk did too. In fact he eventually became a kind of guardian spirit, if you can imagine a guardian spirit like an intoxicated Mickey Mouse.

The contrast between our American friend and Mickey Mouse was so dramatic that it added a certain piquancy to all our encounters. We would be listening to one of her descriptions of ink-blot tests and suddenly our drunk would lurch out of a bar and make for the table, an expression of lecherous joy on his

133

pointed face. Frankly, I found him a perfectly bewitching character and toyed with the thought of showing him an ink blot.

The children were, naturally, completely at home in Venice after the first hour. They freely admitted that it was a "neat place," and although hardly five minutes passed without somebody asking when we could go in a gondola, they found plenty to do.

On the wide promenade along the edge of the lagoon they played cowboys or hopscotch or simply ran. There were always steamers unloading somewhere and the boys were usually present. They chased each other between the iron tables of the outdoor cafe and over the little humped bridge across the side canal. Once I saw Pete and Billy rocking violently in a large rowboat that was tied to a ring in the wall. Sometimes, sitting out at one of the tables, I would have the curious experience of watching two little boys in berets strolling along in the crowd and only later recognizing them as my own. There was nothing they enjoyed more than going off without us and exploring. They usually went in pairs but sometimes one of them would say that he wanted to go alone.

"Take Billy along," I said once to Pete.

"No," he said, "I want to go by myself."

"What are you going to do?" I asked.

"Oh, have fun," he said. The classic answer.

Sometime later I saw him coming along the quay, hands in his pockets and his beret on one side. He seemed to be doing absolutely nothing but he did occasionally spit in a bored way. On his face was an expression of haughty detachment; the look of one sated with experience.

Under ordinary circumstances our children kept us under strict supervision when in public places, checking instantly any display of enthusiasm. I was a great trial to them, crying "Oh, look!" all the time and often going so far as to break into song. Bob, being male, was no trouble.

In Venice they relaxed vigilance and, inspired by our Mickey

Mouse drunk, used to stagger ahead of us, waving our empty wine bottles or hanging onto each other and speaking thickly. Pete here developed an artificial limp which convulsed the other three. In this merry and irresponsible mood we went to Saint Mark's to feed the pigeons; we stood on the curved bridges and watched the traffic on the canals; we walked through the twisting alleys where the markets were, and here the smells were garlic, fish, spilled wine, cheese, crushed lemons, perspiration, olive oil, fresh bread, salt water, and *pissoirs*. The great greasy cheeses were right out there in the open, being hacked apart by long dirty knives. Raw meat lay exposed on ancient, hollowed-out chopping blocks buzzing with flies, and there were cats curled up on top of the vegetables.

When you buy food in Italy, you know it, and our air-conditioned, odorless supermarkets, full of packaged products and polite clerks, are bloodless in comparison. In Italy the customer is always wrong, and the stores resound with arguments and accusations.

After a while we gave in and hired another gondola from the steps by Saint Mark's Square. It was midday and the traffic on the Grand Canal was turbulent. We slid between whale boats full of piled oranges and elegant white launches driven by beautifully dressed ladies. We saw all the vegetables for the city streaming past us in open boats: artichokes and eggplant, red peppers and potatoes heaped like treasure around the feet of the oarsmen. There were flat barges carrying wood and coal. There were enormous punts loaded with Chianti bottles, with brown, dirty men standing at the oars. There were glittering heaps of silver fish and coral fish and fish the color of lapis lazuli. In between these slower craft darted outboards and launches of every kind. Our gondola shot through the traffic, stopped with it at, of all things, traffic lights, and floated between the candy-striped posts that marked what seemed like parking places for private boats.

The noise, the color, the rank smells were all part of that highly flavored unrestrained world of the south, where the life-

135

force is not hidden. The men in the boats had fiercely brilliant black eyes, and their hair curled violently under torn hats. They screamed out songs or shouted curses or roared with laughter. This same bursting vitality shakes the house containing a lot of children; it causes older people to leave movie theaters on Saturday afternoons.

The gondolier left us on some steps near the museum and we told the children that we would treat them to ice cream if they would go inside with us (bribery).

"For how long?" asked Pete, suspiciously.

"Oh, not long," we said.

"If we come in, kin we ride in a gondola again?" asked Billy.

"No," said Bob, who had been royally cheated by our last gondolier and forced to tip three unidentified characters in uniform.

"Maybe," I said, always the coward.

The gigantic canvases of Venetians eating and drinking left the younger members very cold, but fortunately we found paintings of the Martyrdom of Saint Ursula which had great appeal. Martyrs often have interesting if revolting things done to them, such as having their insides wound out on a species of clothes wringer or spool. Saint Ursula, a terrible shade of green throughout, was obviously in rough shape, and the children gave each panel the most minute and scholarly scrutiny.

On the last morning I went out alone to do the marketing for the noon picnic. The air was clear and crisp. As I walked through the dark cool passages and the yellow sunshine of the little squares, I felt gay and light-hearted. People seem to know it when you feel this way and everybody smiled at me. A gondolier threw me a kiss as I leaned on the stone of a bridge watching him swoop underneath. I impulsively threw the kiss back, and several men in rowboats cheered. Men in Italy would throw kisses to anything female that looks directly at them. It is an automatic reaction, not flattery, but it is nevertheless pleasing. Of course, a real Italian lady would never catch the eye of a gondolier but I was still acting American.

In an alley with shops it was so dark that the lights were on and the small, brilliant interiors were like a row of paintings. I bought our wine in a room where straw-covered flasks hung from the ceiling in clusters; our cheese and butter next door; our blood oranges in a narrow cell where red peppers and braided garlic bulbs brushed against my hair. On the way back through one of the squares I stopped and watched a fish peddler cleaning some bright pink fish. There were squids and sea urchins in wet piles on his table, and his arms were covered with mother-of-pearl scales to the elbow.

We left Venice unromantically on a motor launch, but the bells were still ringing and in their wooden cages against the house walls the canaries sang their hearts out.

The enormous garage where we joined the car was like one of those decompression chambers where divers are readjusted to normal conditions. The marshes on the other side of the garage were as flat and colorless after Venice as the earth must look to wanderers from undersea gardens.

The Kingdom of Summer

In the late spring we took the two older children on a trip to the south, leaving the small ones with the nuns. We left Florence on a gray morning with rain imminent and drove all day through country as strange to our eyes as the illustrations in illuminated manuscripts. The colors were those of stones dried in the sun, bleached bones, silvery weathered wood, and brick dust. Sharp hills rose up in the midst of the plains, crowned with ivory-colored towns. Olive groves clothed the hillsides with shimmering silver; the wild lavender grew in gray tufts from the gray rock.

The farmers were out under the olives, cultivating the earth with yokes of cream-colored bullocks. These creatures were astonishingly beautiful, with great dark eyes and polished horns and hoofs. They were decorated with harnesses of scarlet leather and moved under the trees with slow majesty. Crumbling farmhouses clung to the hillsides like old wasps' nests to the side of a barn, and each had its cluster of tall yellow strawstacks, its blossoming almond, its flock of harlequin chickens.

Driving with the two older children was so simple that it was almost unnerving, and I was rather pleased when we had a violent argument about where to picnic. I wanted an olive grove with anemones in the grass; somebody else wanted a hillside with a view; another a place near water. It is not surprising that we finally found ourselves sitting beside a sign advertising Agipgas, with a fine prospect of a dump.

We came to Rome at dusk in the rain and we might just as well have been entering Pittsburgh. Our *pensione* was on the top floor of a building near the Spanish steps and our first impression of it (and our last) was depressing. Three elongated English spinsters in tweed were talking about Brussels sprouts in the sitting room and never even glanced at us as we shuffled in. I looked at an old copy of *Punch* and the children kept coming in to describe the horrors of the plumbing.

"Nothing but old telephone books for paper," said Kathy.

"O.K., O.K.," I said in a whisper.

"Boy, does it *stink!*" said Pete with relish.

Nine o'clock found Bob and myself seated on either side of a small table in our bedroom with a half gallon of Chianti and two tin mugs. The Eternal City lay below us in the driving rain and from the window we looked out on a vista of dirty apartment houses, a leprous wall covered with arsenic green posters, an enormous lighted sign advertising Chianti Ruffino, a taxi-stand, and, above it all, acres of chimney pots silhouetted upon a sky of pink and blue neon. The night was torn with the grind of gears, the roar of Vespas, and the growl of heavy trucks. The smell of Italy—olive oil, coffee, *scaldini,* and auto fumes—rose up to us, rich and strong in the wet air.

"*Roma bella!*" I said, toasting it.

"What did you expect—all white classical buildings full of men in togas?" asked Bob.

139

As a matter of fact that is exactly what I had expected. My Rome was a reconstruction of the Forum which hung in the Latin room at school.

The next morning it was still raining hard, and without the neon signs and electric lights the scene from our window looked even worse than it had the night before. Across from us was a balcony railing where a row of frozen aspidistras hung like rags over the sides of their pots. A scrawny cat was slinking along below them. It was Palm Sunday and we decided to attend mass at Saint Peter's. Here again our reactions were all wrong. Instead of feeling overpowered by the great church, we were distracted by unimportant details. I thought the nineteenth-century sculpture looked like chewing gum and Bob was outraged by a cardinal who kept scratching himself. Finally we had to leave.

We subsequently learned that the Pope had given audience to ten thousand people in Saint Peter's Square a few minutes before we arrived there. This did not surprise us because we were constantly reading in the paper about things that had happened immediately before or after we had been to a place. Sometimes, in fact, the thing was actually going on when we were there and we never knew it. We had, it is true, noticed a great many people streaming away from Saint Peter's, and the whole pavement was covered with fragments of palm and olive branches. Still, in a foreign country one never knows what to expect and we read about the audience in an American paper the next day as usual.

After Saint Peter's we went to the Forum, which looked in the rain rather like a group of bombed banks and factories. We went down into it, huddled into our coats, and wandered about while Bob explained to us which buildings were which. The use of brick by the Romans never ceased to disturb me. Somehow a ruined brick building centuries old looks just like a ruined public library or railroad station.

Pete was able to secrete about his person several pounds of the Forum and after getting back in the car took some pieces of green paving out of his beret and a slab of marble out of the seat of his pants. I protested but Bob said he was sure the tourist agencies dumped loads of rubble into the Forum every month for people to steal.

It was still raining when, after lunch, we went to the Colosseum, and this was so magnificent that we were properly awed and I was impressively terrified coming down from the top. The Appian Way, however, did not fare as well; we stopped on it to let someone go to the bathroom behind a bush. This was hardly correct procedure for the Appian Way so we stopped again and plodded through the rain to look at a tomb. This was the low point of our Roman holiday, and although we tried even then to see the Sistine Chapel a man in a red bathrobe leaned out of a window opposite the entrance and said that it was closed. This was perhaps for the best considering our general condition.

Brilliant sunshine and a seductive warmth lay over the city on the second morning. Bob had to go to a bank after breakfast so I took the children around the Borghese Gardens in a red-wheeled Victoria. The cherry blossoms were out, an artificial chalky pink, the green of the grass was incandescent, birds warbled in a full-throated and voluptuous way. We drove to the terrace at the top of the gardens and saw all Rome dreaming below in the hot spring sunlight, her towers and domes dimmed by a blue haze of smoke. The divine and irresponsible air blew sweet and warm upon us as we drove down again, and a soldier on horseback waved gaily to us.

Bob said what about taking a picnic and going out to Tivoli to see the cascades that Horace described.

"He had a villa nearby," Bob said, "but I think there's no record of its location."

"Any ruins out there?" I asked.

"Not that I know of," Bob said, and I agreed that it sounded ideal. We then bought an enormous bag of fresh, hot bread, a hunk of cheese, butter, a string bag of blood oranges, and another half gallon of Chianti.

Out in Tivoli the olives grew on terraces that went around the hillside in a series of long steps. These groves are so old that the trunks are often mere gray shells, gnarled and twisted into fantastic shapes. We chose one of the high terraces looking out over the valley; far below, sheep grazed in green and gold pastures and there were clusters of tiny buildings, sharp and clear like things seen through the wrong end of a telescope. Rome was a violet haze in the distance.

We spread the picnic on a limestone outcropping above a stream and near a large patch of anemones. These ranged in color from deep purple-blue to white, but they all had the fringed black eye in the center that gives them such an exotic look. Among the anemones were scattered clumps of star-shaped blossoms, orange and lemon-yellow, and thyme and lavender made thick aromatic cushions. We lay back against the slope of the hill and looked up at the olives that flickered from green to silver in the hot blue sky. The sun poured down upon us, the air smelled of crushed thyme, and there was no sound but sheep bells and the infrequent patter of donkeys' hoofs on the road below.

We wedged the Chianti bottle in a crevice and began our ritual of cutting bread and cheese. The butter softened in the summery heat and the hearts of the fresh loaves were still warm. We had chosen a perfect cheese, not too sharp but sharp enough, and the combination of all these flavors and the good raw taste of the wine seemed the taste of the day itself. After we had eaten all the bread and cheese we passed around the blood oranges and sat there happily dripping juice on the anemones.

Such a day, such a moment comes seldom in a lifetime and all the museums in Rome were not worth those full Italian hours under that flawless sky. We had captured, as it were, the essence of the day, the gypsy freedom of the springtime, the simple delight of being alive that was more ancient than ancient Rome itself. This is the Italian way to see the world, a far cry from the German and American way of seeing it through cameras and guidebooks.

The children finally went off into the olives to look for Roman coins and bits of pottery. Bob lay on his back with the Chianti bottle on his chest and I moved up into the anemone patch so I could look at them sideways, against the sky. Bees nuzzled in their fringed black hearts with the drowsy sound of all summer days. The light shone through the petals, illuminating them, and at that level each blossom looked enormous like a great tinted parasol of silk.

"What about the Sistine Chapel?" I asked after a while.

"The hell with it," said Bob. "There's just enough wine for each of us to have one more."

We had one more. Then we lay there half asleep. I could hear the little brook percolating down between the rocks with small silvery noises, like coins chinking together. Wine and sunlight combined seem to melt all the northern, Anglo-Saxon energy and anxiety out of one's character. Lying there, I could see why the Italians are such rotten politicians but such marvelous musicians. I could not escape the dangerous thought that everybody up north was crazy. Even the Bible says, "Eat thy bread and drink thy wine with a merry heart," and there in Italy this seemed the highest wisdom.

We drove back to Rome and after parking the car went and sat on the Spanish steps and watched the people going up and down. After a while Bob and Pete played soccer on the terrace with a ball of rags. Various other people were sprawled comfortably in the sun, smoking, dozing, or chatting together. We were as much a part of the stream of life as the pigeons or the flower seller or the old lady knitting.

We rose early the next morning and all the chimneys of Rome were smoking in the sun. From the cool streets the smells of freshly ground coffee and new bread rose strong and exciting, and we ate our breakfast with the windows wide open to the spring day. To be up so high and at the same time in Rome made even the sordid balconies and Chianti signs seem romantic, and I told Bob that it was a great pity we were not living in sin.

"Well, it's too late now," he said.

Our first view of the Mediterranean, the ancient sea, came suddenly. We had been driving between the walls of a valley when, around a turn, the whole world opened wide like a great blue morning glory. We climbed wonderingly out of our little car and crunched down over the pebbles to the edge of the water. The air had a living freshness moving with the rise and fall of the swells. Just offshore on the slippery turquoise slopes, two fishing boats were riding at anchor. They were scarlet and blue like the ones in the Van Gogh painting. Everything else was poignantly familiar, for the sea is always the same. The light sweetness of salt in the breeze brought back all our summers in New England. Blue-and-white days of clouds and sky and sails and sea blotted out the toasted gold rocks of Italy.

In one instant we were all sick for home, for our own stretch of seashore and our own boats.

"I wish we could go for a swim," said Kathy, longingly.

"I wish we could go for a *sail*," said Pete in a depressed voice. "Jeeze, is it *hot* here!"

This was an unfortunate shift of mood, since we had a long drive ahead as well as the city of Naples. To all of us one thing was anathema in summer, and that was the city. People sometimes had to go up to The City to the dentist or to fix the car and we considered it a hideous ordeal. Cities in summer were a hell symbol the exact opposite of the cool blue-and-white heaven of water and sails.

We drove on along the edge of the Bay of Naples through the citrus groves where donkeys carried *paniers* of oranges up between aisles of burnished trees. The gutters smelled of crushed fruit and we stopped and bought a long string of blood oranges. Presently the car reeked of orange peel.

The heat stood up like a glass wall and through it all objects were edged with light. The orange groves gave way to orchards of almond blossom, the color of cotton candy, and above their frivolous clouds of petals Vesuvius floated, detached from the earth.

We crushed the bursting orange sections into our mouths; the juice was all over the car and all the door handles were sticky. Our fingers were sticky and our clothes clung to us. The only

144

thing anyone wanted to do was swim, and it was at this point that we arrived in Naples.

We drove by mistake into the waterfront section of the city where the bombs had reduced acres to rubble. Here in hideous squalor, in ugliness and filth, people were living.

In caves of masonry and ruined cellars we saw men and women so miserable and hopeless that they had no reserve, no decency. They screamed at us, hatred in their eyes. Some merely stared, apathetic, uncaring. Beside our car ran the packs of wild children famous for their viciousness, yelling like hyenas at our two through the windows.

"My God," said Bob.

Our children stared.

"Look at that old lady," said Kathy. "She's eating something out of the street."

There was a baby lying on the sidewalk, its eyes full of flies and a tiny girl naked from the waist crawled in the gutter picking over refuse like a little animal.

"What happened to all the buildings?" said Pete. "They're all wrecked."

"We bombed them," Bob said.

"Your own uncle was here on a destroyer," I said. "Look at these people and never forget them."

After this the art museum was an anticlimax, even though it contained the treasures unearthed at Pompeii. It was very hot, the streets of Naples were still in the process of reconstruction, and we eventually drove down a flight of steps and escaped into the country.

We stayed in a bright pink hotel on a cliff in Sorrento. Below our window was a shelf with a garden on it, and here were camellia trees like artificial bouquets of wax. Strange birds sang in a grove of lemons and beyond the garden wall was space and the stretched silk of the sea.

After dinner we sat on the terrace drinking Falernian wine and every time one of the children went near the railing I screamed.

145

"Let's not get neurotic about this," said Bob.

"*Get* neurotic," I said, "I am neurotic about it. Why not bite the bullet? You have a wife with agoraphobia."

"Agoraphobia is fear of the marketplace," said Bob, "and you certainly don't have that. It's acro-phobia—fear of heights."

"Well, whatever it is, I've got it," I said, "and anybody who looks over that railing goes straight to bed."

"Jeeze, Ma, how silly can you get?" said Pete wearily.

Anybody with any sense knows that the Amalfi Drive is the very quintessence of acro—or height—but we didn't, and the next day set off blithely to drive down it to Salerno. It was a Mediterranean morning of marvelous clarity, everything was bathed in the upward flood of light from the water, and on the horizon Capri had the transparent blue of a gas flame.

We drove along the cliffs and saw the sea glittering between umbrella pines. Then the road plunged over the brim of the land and leveled out on a narrow shelf halfway between the surface of the water and the sky. Above and below us, in the porous honeycomb of limestone, bunches of aromatic herbs exploded in green-gold and silver. We were so close to the cliffs that I could see the gray undersides of the rosemary bushes and the bees burrowing in the hooded blue flowers. Over the edge of my window there was nothingness like a punch in the stomach and, at the bottom, surf, noiseless with distance, feathering the base of the cliffs.

"Hey!" I cried, "turn around. I really do have that thing. Go back!"

"I can't," said Bob, simply. "There's no room to turn around."

Surely no place on earth is more beautiful than the Amalfi Drive. Purged by terror, ravished by blue, I was like a super-sensitized plate recording every detail and at this moment I can see the lizards pinned to the golden rock by the heat, the olive roots clutching the crumbling terraces, the very texture of flower petals and the orange glow in their cups. Every few minutes I moaned and put my head in my lap and then I steadied myself by looking off over the serene reaches of the sea where strange islands rose up, flat as glass and as translucent.

"Boy, oh, boy," the children said. "Look at her."

"Whatsa matta, kid?" asked Kathy in our Brooklyn voice. "Goin' crazy or sumpin?"

Once, approaching a blind corner, we heard the familiar yodeling of one of the tourist buses. The road here was about the width of the car, and the cliff on the inside bulged over our heads. The outside edge, marked by a few tottering stones, projected over the abyss like a pulpit. We met the bus halfway around the curve and, as we were on the outside, we were able to look directly down to the surf below.

We drove into Positano right after this and Bob stopped the car in the town where there were walls on both sides as well as houses. Both of us were shaking, and he was a curious shade of green.

"Maybe we can get off the drive here," he said and unfolded the map. I climbed out of the car, tottered over to the wall, and took hold of it. The stone was hot in the sun and all over the place in every crack and corner grew clumps of wild sweet alyssum, that edging of every New England cottage garden. Its honey scent mingled with the odor of orange blossoms, mimosa, and the sea.

"Let's stay here," I said.

"We either have to spend the rest of our lives here or go down to Salerno on the drive," said Bob. "There's no other way out."

We did stay there for a while, reassured by the solidity of our surrounding and enchanted by their beauty. Positano spilled down the cliffs like a box of sugar lumps. On the terraces below the road were narrow groves of lemon trees where ripe fruit glowed through the enameled leaves. Tiny gardens had been made on every level bit of ground and in them the neat rows of vegetables looked incongruous, high in the blue air.

After half an hour we took a deep breath and continued what I now considered our last ride together.

147

We came down to Amalfi into mid-summer. Chalk-white and coral, the town climbed vertically to the sky, now a deep gentian-blue with noon. The tiers of houses were like boxes at the opera; the whole of Amalfi faced the immense and empty stage of the sea, whose level floor seemed cut from a single sapphire. It stretched to the horizon, waiting. Not a ripple stirred, not a whisper of air moved. We were transfixed in a white glare of light that bounced back from the dazzling Saracen buildings and threw watery reflections along the walls.

We walked up narrow streets zebra-striped with sun and shadow. The feel of the sea was everywhere. Even in the darkest alleys its dazzling presence was apparent, and the air was rich with odors of kelp, iodine, and salt, tar and fish. In the blocks of shade the fishermen's barrows were heaped with treasure: sea urchins, squid, fish like silver dollars cascading from baskets, rose-red fish beautiful as jewelry, snarls of eels, torpedo shapes of blue and cold green. The paving stones glittered with scales and everything shone and slithered with salt water.

Bob, who was for some reason collecting sponges, bought two from the long strings of them hung by the shop doors. I was buying the lacy raffia baskets made in the area, Kathy was obsessed with string bags, and Pete, who collected everything movable, wanted a carved bottle stopper with a sailor's head on it. This was on his mind to the exclusion of all else.

"Do you think I can get it?" he kept asking. "How much do you think it costs?"

"How should I know?" I said. "Probably it was made in the United States, anyway."

"Well, gee," said Pete, "I just asked. There's Daddy buying another sponge."

After a decent interval we let him buy the bottle stopper and went and sat in an outdoor café on the waterfront.

The extreme beauty of the place and day, the voluptuous heat, and above all the infinity of blue at our feet gave to the present moment a supreme importance. Amalfi seemed the very source of life, the kingdom of summer.

For our noon picnic the family selected a narrow terrace halfway up the cliffs beyond Amalfi. Here some peasant had carried a few feet of earth and planted grass and one olive tree. I was persuaded to climb up the cliff's face by a goat track, but I could have told them how it would be. When I turned around and sat down, I saw beyond the toes of my sneakers nothing but space and the remote surface of the sea, dusted with silver. The earth reeled under me and I said in a weak voice that I thought I might faint.

Bob instantly took command and dragged me down the cliff by the wrist. I slid most of the way on my bottom, to the great joy of some passing sportsmen, who cheered and tooted their horns.

When the others came down to my level, Bob stated that he would rather sell the car and walk home than return by the Amalfi Drive, so near Salerno we took the inland road and went to Pompeii.

Somehow, volcanic eruptions are just the sort of thing you would expect to happen in a place like Southern Italy, where violence of one sort or another is the order of the day. I myself, shaken to the marrow by all that beauty and terror, brilliant life and brutal death, could hardly take in anything more, and I fought against the thought that Pompeii looked just like parts of Trenton, New Jersey, with the roofs ripped off. We had a guide who never missed a chance to stroke my arm when Bob wasn't looking and who picked me a bunch of violets in some nobleman's bedroom.

The only person thoroughly enjoying Pompeii was Pete, to whom it offered undreamed of opportunities for collecting rubble. He immediately vanished through a doorway and we could trace his progress by the sounds of minor avalanches.

Bob, Kathy, and I were overcome by the sad spirit of those

149

empty streets. The blue day had clouded over, matching our mood, and we walked drearily up and down the narrow terracotta vistas. We saw the casts of the dying, contorted in agony, and the tragic room where a whole family lay, the babies beside the mother.

If Amalfi had been the source of life, Pompeii was the home of death.

"Let's get out of here," we said almost simultaneously.

Pete crawled out of an alleyway, his pants nearly dragged off with the weight of his souvenirs. Sidling up to me, he loaded the pockets of my coat with shards.

"Stick around," he said. "Boy, there's more stuff here!"

But by then life had become so terribly short that there seemed hardly time to get to the gates.

We ran out into the parking place, swept aside the screeching hoard of souvenir vendors, and rocketed away to Sorrento. It was a near thing. I felt as though we had just made it.

The Life of a Journey

We left the convent for good on the last day of March and spent the next two weeks in the car. This vehicle, which for reasons clear only to ourselves we had named Tom Thumb, now became our home as a ship does on a long voyage. Theoretically it is romantic to roam at will through Europe stopping at picturesque inns and eating one's bread and cheese in a new field every noonday. It is romantic in fact, too, but extreme fortitude and self-discipline are necessary to keep this truth in mind all the time when trapped in a car with five other human beings.

It was always difficult for us to leave a place where we had stayed for any length of time, and on each trip we went through the same phases. The life of these shorter trips reflected the life of the journey as a whole; their development was almost like that of a living organism.

The wrench of leaving the place where we had been settled was like the shock of birth; next came infancy, a stage when primitive emotions were loose and we were all victims of our immediate surroundings. Adolescence followed, a hideous period of adjustment and reorganization in which the organism—in this case the family—achieved some sort of equilibrium, and finally the triumph of maturity when adjustments had been made, resilience acquired, and it was possible at last to enjoy life to the full. Then came the inevitable decline into senility, usually extremely rapid, and followed by collapse when travel was anathema to us and all we wanted was home.

We had lived in the convent for two months and the wrench of leaving was fearful. We loved the gentle sisters; the villa and its gardens were our own private preserve.

On that final day Tom Thumb stood in the courtyard with all his doors open and Bob and I tried to fit together the gigantic jigsaw puzzle of possessions there assembled. Bob, lying on his stomach on the roof, built a huge structure almost as large as Tom Thumb himself, while I, bent double, tried different ways of combining a crated Della Robbia reproduction (about two feet square), two copper water jugs, my baskets, two cardboard tubes containing rolled-up pictures, Pete's sword, some full wine bottles, and a *scaldino* (charcoal handwarmer) which I had bought when nobody was looking.

The new soccer ball was one of the worst items, as it kept rolling off and out of the car, but the most exasperating objects of all were the dozen rolls of toilet paper which we had been advised to bring and which were fitted into crevices in the car. These were continually bouncing out and unwinding across the courtyard.

Every time we went off to get another piece of luggage, one or all of the children would get into the car and start building a nest like a dog afraid to be left behind.

"For the love of heaven," I cried after this had happened three times, "you'll be in the thing all day. Why start now?" and they crawled out, protesting and knocking over some of my precious construction.

Whenever the nuns appeared I spoke to the young in soft

honeyed tones for their benefit. Thus a false appearance of calm was maintained. At last we were ready. Each child in his corner had at hand whatever he or she needed to survive the journey. They were very efficient now, and packed their own overnight bags, assembled whatever equipment they needed for playing games, eating, etc., took their Dramamine and adjusted various blankets and duffel bags to achieve perfect comfort.

Bob, having paid the bill, climbed in behind the wheel. I checked the Dramamine bottle, the crackers, the oranges, my handbag, and my reading glasses. The nuns flocked around us saying goodbye, then stood back with the Mother Superior while we drove off. We waved and the gate closed. The moment was too poignant to dwell on, so we turned to practical matters.

"Did you case all the rooms?" I asked Kathy, automatically. The "casing" was her job.

"Yes," she said. "I found one of Daddy's pipes and Billy's other slipper."

"Did you check both cameras?" asked Bob.

"Kin we buy some Life Savers?" asked Billy.

"It's my turn to give them out," said Margie.

"No, it isn't, it's mine," said Pete.

"That isn't fair, you've just been *on* a trip and it's *my* turn." etc., etc., etc.

"*Quiet!*" bellowed Bob, "I want everyone to understand that if there's any quarreling *nobody* gets any Life Savers or Cokes or oranges. Is that clear?"

During the first day or two of any trip, everyone's tempers were so short as to be almost nonexistent, and the slightest incident was apt to set off a series of explosions like a string of firecrackers. However, as likely as not the whole group would be hysterical with laughter five minutes later. There was nothing hypocritical about us, if that is a virtue. The minute anyone felt or thought something, he or she expressed it either in words or violent action. Our resemblance to Italians grew more and more marked, and although Bob and I made sporadic attempts to be dignified and mature, we were never allowed to stay that way.

153

The children spent half their time analyzing us and saying in amused voices things like "Mummy always laughs like this," or "Daddy always goes this way when he's mad" etc.—a process which made it all but impossible to remain calm. Before we knew it we'd be saying, "Well, at least I don't act like a wild beast at meals the way you do," or "People who laugh like hyenas shouldn't talk."

The truth is that in a car each person's idiosyncrasies take on a fantastic importance. It was hardly possible to move one's fingers without being convicted of "twiddling"; any sound repeated more than once caused screams of outrage; meals were made unbearable by accusations of chumping, smacking, sucking, and drooling barked out from all sides. "Feckling"—a word we invented to describe feckless behavior—was applied to almost everything anyone did.

As we had started after lunch, we only had half a day's driving that first day, but this half was so dreadful, what with crawling up the mountain roads behind trucks and the fresh shock of being cooped up together, that we were all worthless when we arrived in Rapallo. The hotel had curiously high unsympathetic rooms painted red and yellow, and the effect of this atmosphere was to plunge us into the depths of depressions and homesickness. All these reactions are typical of the first part of a long journey after a period of being settled. No weight should be attached to decisions made or emotions undergone during these times.

Bob and I drank a very nice white wine at dinner that night to console ourselves, and this is a good policy. There is no use trying to economize on food and drink when grappling with one of these melancholy moods. This is the moment to spend money. The other time to spend money is when everybody is on top of the world. In between you can save.

One of the good things about these low points is that the next morning is always better because it couldn't possibly be worse or even as bad. Characteristically the second day was beautiful —clear and brilliant—and we drove along the coast of the

Italian Riviera beside a sea like the eye of a peacock's feather. Little towns with coral, cream, and pink houses crowded the steep hillsides above blue-green harbors full of fishing boats.

Between towns were limestone cliffs where the bunches of herbs sent out a pungent odor. Among the silvery and gray-green kitchen herbs were all kinds of fascinating small plants: heaths covered with red-violet bells sweet as honey, yellow clover, rock roses, calendulas, and anemones. I identified them all in an Italian flower book stored in the glove compartment and every now and then we stopped and picked bouquets to decorate the car. The ash tray always contained a bunch of flowers but unfortunately these wilted quickly because we couldn't keep water in the ash tray.

I felt deeply sentimental about our re-entry into France and told everyone that I could tell the difference the minute we crossed the line.

"We're actually on the Riviera," I said. "Remember that movie *Catch a Thief* with Grace Kelly? Well, it's going to be exactly like that."

"You mean where she drove with Cary Grant?" asked Billy.

"That's right," I said. "We'll be on the same road and we'll go right past Monte Carlo."

"You mean where she married the Prince?" asked Margie.

"Yes," I said, "only that's really true."

"But I thought she was going to marry Cary Grant?" said Billy.

This kind of talk went on for some time until the older children attacked the smaller ones, screaming in exasperation.

There seemed to be no difference between the Côte d'Azur we were in and Atlantic City, but I told everyone that pretty soon it would look like the movie. However, we continued to drive along a dirty cement highway with peeling villas on one side and a railroad track on the other. There were a great many rusty, frazzled palm trees and stretches of cindery earth where unknown weeds flourished.

155

All through these revolting areas I kept saying that soon we would get out of this and reach our hotel. It was right on the beach, I said, but it was not in a resort town so it would not be crowded. It was certainly not crowded. In the late afternoon we came to the place where it was supposed to be and we were still on a large highway driving between the beach and vast wastes of gravel and sand. Ahead was a single structure like a large Frigidaire built apparently out of solid cement. It had a porch in front—a kind of cement tank—in which a shabby man was blowing his nose on his fingers as we drove up.

"Holy smoke," I said. "Don't *stop*. We can't stay here for one second."

"But we have reservations," said Bob, who is a moral man. "It wouldn't be fair to the manager." He stopped the car.

"It won't be fair to us," I hissed. "I think it's some sort of den of vice."

It was too late. He weakly allowed the manager, who looked like a cross between a sex fiend and a murderer, to lead us into a glacial foyer painted poison green. Behind the desk was the manageress who could have doubled for Lady Macbeth. She stared at us with evident hostility, and I kicked Bob in the ankle to indicate that he must get us out of there. However, he ignored this and we all followed the sex fiend up two flights of wide, dark stairs.

This place was without question the most revolting hotel I have ever seen or imagined. Our room was a cell of matchboarding the color of fish glue, with long coffin-shaped windows, dark green shades, and bedspreads of a fungoid design. The hallways had olive-green walls and bare board floors that stretched away in a nightmarish perspective. At the end of each Dali-esque vista was a malevolent and filthy toilet with an odor that dealt one a stinging blow across the face. On the inside of the door was a sign saying in two languages, "Please leave this bathroom as you would wish to find it." In order to do this, Bob said, we would have to take up residence there for a month and work day and night.

As soon as we were alone I said that I would rather starve than risk eating there, and ruffled frantically through Michelin while the children appeared at intervals to describe one more hideous attribute of their bedrooms. There was a four-star restaurant at Old Cagnes and we decided to go there. It required all my courage to tell the manager this. He didn't take the news well, and said that they expected the residents to eat in the hotel. I said that we preferred to eat out and rushed outdoors to the car where we outdid one another in reviling the manager.

The influence of atmosphere on wanderers is almost frighteningly powerful. In the same way the effect of people's personalities is more immediate and deeper than in the cushioned safety of your own environment. The spirit of the manager, made visible in his repellent hotel, seemed to show the world as a hostile, vicious place full of ugliness and cruelty. Conversely, the old restaurant and its proprietors gave forth a glow of reassurance, of happy benevolence.

It was in a starlit square on top of the hill and its small paned windows, curtained in red, shone cheerfully in the darkness. When we opened the door music came out and we saw a leaping fire, a long low-ceilinged room, and a bar where a fat old man and a young couple were drinking. An enormous bearlike dog advanced across the floor to greet us, and the three at the bar smiled welcome. The young couple promptly whisked two tables together in front of the fire, spread red-checked cloths over them and set out baskets of crusty bread *"pour les enfants."*

Soothed and content, we drank our wine while a row of chickens turned on the rotisserie before the fire. After a while the girl brought in some *piperade*—a Basque dish of scrambled eggs, tomatoes, green peppers, thin ham, and olives—and then a salad, well tossed in a wooden bowl. The chickens came crisply browned and tender and we ordered another bottle of wine.

157

It was a greenish-gold wine in a square bottle covered with silver wire and had a light, delicate bouquet. Bob and I drank a bottle apiece, and what with the heat of the fire and exhaustion were in a very relaxed condition by the end of the evening. The children had two rounds of "Coca-Colà" and played with the dog under the beaming supervision of the fat man. The spell of the hotel manager was exorcised; we felt that the world was full of joy and good will, that people were kind and to be trusted.

At the end, Bob showed me the enormous bill in reverent silence. We took another bottle of wine home and I nearly lost my shoe down a drain outside.

Although our reservations in the manager's hostelry were for a week we left the next morning, after a slight delay when Pete tried to play an electric football game. Having fed 100 francs into this machine, Bob was unwilling to leave it without a struggle and spent half an hour banging and rattling the football game and arguing with the manager in broken French. We left with black looks on both sides and headed for Saint Tropez, the one place where we knew of a specific hotel. This was the Ferme d'Augustin which I had written on the back of an envelope and kept in my file marked "Route." Incidentally, this was the only time the file proved to be of any value.

The efficient notebook in which I had recorded the contents of our luggage had disappeared and would not, in any case, have been any help. This was partly because Bob had caused every extra article of clothing to be lashed to the roof of the car in inaccessible bags. He said that he would rather buy new things than undo his sacred web of ropes and straps. I couldn't help but feel this a short-sighted attitude. Being always on the move made adequate laundry impossible, and picnics left stains of wine and butter all over our clothing. Bob burned a hole in his overcoat by putting a lighted pipe in his pocket, and the buttons came off everybody and couldn't be found. In fact practically nothing could be found at this period, as we had not then perfected the art of car packing.

Another difficulty of this time was that of the noon picnic. On the Riviera, or more specifically on the Moyen Corniche, one of the famous roads along the coast, there was simply no place to have a picnic. Every available level space near the highway was either private property or an open-air privy. We tried several romantic glades under umbrella pines and some olive groves, but in every case they were unbearable for the second reason. This seemed an unnecessary addition to our sufferings but was somehow consistent with the way things go in the early stages of a trip.

Even Tom Thumb was suffering—from a mysterious disease called by Bob the Sickness Mongo. For no apparent reason T.T. would begin coughing and wheezing stertorously and then pass out. We would drift to a stop and there we would be. No garage could help us although a man once fixed it by stirring up some wires around the engine. Another time we drained out all the gas and administered a transfusion of Agipgas. This was when people believed the difficulty was caused by water in the gas. Nothing ever worked twice and the only cure seemed to be to allow Tom Thumb a short rest. Bob held that his trouble was Air, mysteriously introduced into the system on steep hills. In any case, we never did solve this problem, and the imminence of the Sickness Mongo lent one more element of insecurity to our existence.

You can either spend all your time abroad worrying about reservations, luggage, cleanliness, thieves, and car engines, or you can trust simply in the general goodness of life. For some obscure reason the more you plan ahead the more likely it is that you will get fouled up, the more you worry about hygiene the more certain it is that you will succumb to the European complaint, and so forth. The secret of successful travel, I think, is to throw yourself on the mercy of the world, trust everyone, eat everything and fear nothing. It takes a while to be able to do this, and we didn't take the plunge until after the episode of the manager. The turning point was Easter Sunday.

The Life of a Journey, Continued

The psychologists who invented group dynamics are too apt to attribute changes in what they could call the Group Behavior Pattern to causes deeply connected with one's self-image, id, ego or whatever it is. Actually, the most trivial and irrelevant incident or thing determined the mood of our group in the course of a few minutes. It was often, most regrettably, something indecent but humorous which made everybody laugh but it could just as easily be something beautiful which illuminated all of us with delight.

Such was the harbor at Cannes on Easter Sunday and here we stopped, still in the jagged, angry mood resulting from our last encounter with the manager. It was a morning of purest radiance and to the horizon the sea lay smooth as glass and as polished, reflecting the light upward in a blue-white glare. The wide brimming harbor was filled with fishing boats in brightly colored rows, and beyond the long wharves yachts lay at anchor drying their sails. The water was a mirror of sliding reflections, the air tremulous with the clouds of canvas, and we walked down the wharves in a flood of light. The whole morning smelled of salt and seaweed, fish and tar. Fishermen in clean clothes sat in their boats mending nets, tinkering with their engines, or simply smoking in the sun. The place had the happy feeling that somehow lingers around boats in a sunny harbor.

As soon as I saw the boats and smelled the special harbor smell, I knew everything was going to be all right. These things are deeper than reason and it was perfectly true. We found the hotel at Saint Tropez in time to picnic on the beach nearby; a pink villa among the vines was given over to our use and the dinner served up by Augustin himself was perfectly superb. We had a gigantic tureen of *potage aux légumes,* young chickens fried with thick bacon, a tossed salad, and the incomparable French bread, crusty outside and tender and warm within. We drank a good red wine and walked back to our pink villa under a sky of stars.

This period of two days gave us a chance to get properly organized and also to rest. On the first morning Kathy and I heated water in our minute saucepan over our even more minute pocket stove and by repeating this again and again managed to wash out all our dirty clothes in the wash basin. We then hung them to dry all over the plane tree by the terrace. After this we went to the beach where we swam, and sat in the hot sun watching the antics of the French getting undressed and into Bikini bathing suits right there in front of us.

The next day we went into the town of Saint Tropez to buy our picnic, driving slowly through the narrow streets where pale pink houses with shutters of faded blue leaned toward each other to frame a strip of sea. At the end of one street we saw the clustered masts of many boats and came out on the stone quay of that most exquisite of harbors. In the opalescent water, yachts were moored in elegant rows, their bows to the quay. Painted fishing boats lay on their sides on the cobbled beach, and in the background curved a long row of pastel-tinted houses. The air was sweet with salt; sea gulls wheeled over us with mewing cries. We saw fishermen in forget-me-not blue spreading nets to dry and yachtsmen in striped jerseys drinking *apéritifs* on cabin tops with ladies in tapered slacks.

Kathy and I made an attempt to buy some of these so-called "Italian" slacks at a fashionable sport shop but were prevented by Bob, who made us watch the rear action of women wearing them. This was quite enough to discourage us and we bought striped jerseys instead.

This was one of those days when much is accomplished in the way of family solidarity. It is such days that justify trips like ours, that are the best of all arguments for having large families, and are money in the bank, figuratively speaking, to draw upon in more dismal times.

In this case it was not hard to see why everything went well. We were in a beautiful place near the sea, it was a summer day, we were dressed in our summer clothes, and we were going on a picnic. As everybody was on top of the world we naturally began to spend money lavishly in order that our picnic should measure up to the general level of perfection. We bought sausages and then had to buy a grill to cook them on and a fork to poke them with. We bought some bread, cheese, butter, and a bottle of Château Minuit in a waterfront store where the yachtsmen were also outfitting themselves.

For once we looked and behaved like everybody around us, or so we thought. Everyone was in dungarees and jerseys like us and the feel of boats, cruising and the sea was in the air. We all felt very light-hearted and decided to cook our sausages on the terrace of our own villa. This we did, over a fire of grape prunings. Bob and I drank all the wine and he became very raffish and gay and joined the boys in a degraded form of soccer on the terrace with his beret on sideways.

Later, using the Tom Sawyer fence-painting gambit, we organized our dependents into housecleaning the car. We washed

162

it all, even to the hubcaps, swept it out with a broom made of grass (that I'd bought in Tuscany), and even threw away some rubble from the Forum.

Fired with inspiration, Pete built a wall of luggage down the center of the car, dividing the two back seats into four compartments, one for each child. He pointed out that it was impossible even to see over the barrier and that this would prevent a great deal of warfare. We all recognized the brilliance of this idea and even felt that it should be publicized for the benefit of traveling families.

I cleaned out the glove compartment, which contained obsolete maps, bits of the Colosseum, a Roman brick, envelopes full of bay leaves, and a paper container for airplane passengers to be sick into. This had been used only as a kind of address book and was invaluable. Billy polished the headlights and Margie finished the job with a bunch of violets in the ash tray.

The next day we were ready to go on, and set forth with clean clothes and a shining car. We were fortified with a breakfast of excellent coffee, toast, and honey, and it was one of those dry, blue mornings for going up into the mountains. When we stopped on a mountainside to fill the Chianti bottle from a spring the air was rare and *apéritif,* full of aromatic scents from the carpets of thyme and lavender that covered the rocky ground. I picked two enormous bunches of thyme bushes and hung them on the roof of the car, and the boys joyfully picked their hands full of anemones, tiny blue dwarf irises, and wild tulips to adorn the dashboard. I filled two of the wine cups at the spring for this purpose, thus pleasing Billy who hates to see his flowers wilt.

Everything went like a good dream. We had lunch at Aix-en-Provence in the hot sun: puréed vegetable soup, mushrooms with chopped garlic and parsley, warm, crusty bread, and Cassis wine, the color of the sunlight. The taste of garlic on the tongue and the drowsy feeling induced by wine and sun were part of the Frenchness, the full-flavored life we were living. We drove into those silvery Provençal cities where the warmth of spring lay

163

in a blue mist under the plane trees, and we were curiously at home in all of them.

It was as though the French in their wisdom had discovered exactly the combinations of line and color most sympathetic to the senses. The angles of the streets, the tiny shops, the tall pale-colored houses, shuttered and secret, the café life on the pavements, the very taste and texture of the bread and wine, satisfied something deep within one, at least in me. I loved every single thing about this part of France and it seemed to act beneficently on us all.

This route, planned to the last inch by me after weeks of research, was, unlike the Riviera section, a great success. Also we had perfected our system of making hotel accommodations. We would first drive around a town and look at the hotels, consulting Michelin the while. Michelin, that incomparable guide to France, tells you all you need to know about a hotel right down to the last details, although it contains so many hieroglyphics of bathtubs, faucets, bidets, tiny cars, and telephones, as well as stars, daggers, circles, heavy print, and colored dots that it's like translating the Rosetta Stone to read it. However, we finally learned the code.

I alone would go inside and lay my Michelin open on the desk to show that I knew their listed prices. I then announced crisply (I didn't *ask*) that I wanted two rooms with accommodations for three in each. If necessary, I said, put in a *"lit pliant"* (folding bed). Sometimes the concierge objected and said that he was not accustomed to putting three in a room.

"Eh, bien," I said, closing Michelin. *"Au revoir, monsieur, et merci."*

This almost always worked, and in no time everything was arranged. Of course, this system, economical though it was, had its drawbacks. The worst one was being unable to retire peacefully with Bob and close the door on the young for the night. Under the System each of us was simply headed for more Togetherness.

The second drawback, which underlined the first, was the inevitable argument about who should sleep in which bed. In France there was always a large double bed, one single, and possibly one inferior pallet which might be a folding canvas cot, a trundle bed one inch off the floor, or even a crib. If there was a crib all hell broke loose.

We would streak upstairs like people doing a hundred-yard dash and the porter would be nearly trampled to death in the efforts of various individuals to case the rooms first. I used to sprint up the stairs three at a time, in order to beat the children, thus courting a heart attack, for I insisted on Fascist government where bed-assignments were concerned. No democratic methods here, no voting or peaceful settlements—just pure totalitarian domination by Bob and me, especially me. The minute we had tumbled into the rooms there would be screams of "I choose the single!" "My turn on the left side," etc. They never learned that all this had absolutely no effect on my relentless rule. Above the caterwauling, I would roar, *"Quiet!"* then after subduing the peevish squeaks, shovings, and whimpers of "He hit me," "Quit punching," etc., I would then dictate as follows:

"Daddy in the double bed. *Quiet!* He's the driver and this is the best bed. Pete in cot, Billy in that thing."

If there was no third bed I had to assign sides to the boys in the double bed and give Bob the single, but as Pete and Billy kicked and fought half the night when in the double beds, we bent every effort to secure a third piece of furniture. But no matter what it was, nobody ever wanted to sleep in this third number and, frankly, I can see why. If it was a crib there was a universal groan of anguish above which Billy's voice screeched in guinea-hen tones.

"I won't sleep in the rotten thing!"

Then came the treatment: "Hey, that's a neat crib." "Gee, can I sleep in it?" "This is more comfortable than that old double *bed,*" etc. During the treatment Billy exploded periodically and yelled, "Go ahead, sleep in it, I won't," "I'd rather sleep on the floor," *"Shut up,"* and so forth. Yet he always took the crib, there being no choice, and unless some evil-minded sibling giggled and said, "Little baby Billy, idda wadda woo," all went calmly and he retired to bed with a sense of being deeply privileged.

In the girls' bedroom things were more civilized. I autocratically took the single, assigning other quarters to the young. I had to do the assignments in both rooms because Bob was too easily driven mad by arguments and was apt to say in a senile voice, "Oh, I'll take the army cot."

Except for these rather exhausting aspects of the system, it was wonderful. True, Bob and I may have spent the money saved fortifying ourselves at a nearby bistro.

We never had the slightest difficulty getting good accommodations, and in every case these were superior to those we had made ahead in our days of innocence and caution. I don't know whether this would be possible in the summer, but it was in the spring, which is the tourist off-season.

We had driven out of summer and back into spring, and the mornings were clear and silvery rose, the noons warm and gold, and in the evenings a violet haze filled the squares of the little towns, muffling to a romantic murmur the sounds of footsteps and the rush of traffic. We used to look out over our curly iron balconies into the tops of plane trees where the late sunlight was caught in the sticky baby leaves, and when we woke up there would be blackbirds warbling above the brisk, early noises of the new day. In spring everyone wants to be on the road living the gypsy life, and for once we were doing it, the only idle people in a busy world.

We developed the picnic to a fine art, stopping to buy food just before the stores closed at twelve for the noon siesta and choosing our picnic place carefully to provide shelter from wind, back rests, sunlight, a view, and if possible a carpet of flowers. We ate on cushions of wild thyme on mountain sides and in green hollows warm in the sun.

If it rained we ate in the car on a board across the backs of the seats. We were in such a mellow state that we rather liked the rain, and the sound of it on the slate roofs was nice at night.

It rained in Cahors but the sun came out the following day as we ran into the valley of the Dordogne. Here the river wound in silver loops through green fields, and the classic spires of poplars stood above their long shadows. There were little peach trees blooming in walled gardens and as we drove through the deep lanes we would see castles rising into the sky above red-roofed villages. That day we saw the caves at Lascaux and by nightfall were in Angoulême. Time seemed to have stopped and we moved from one kind of landscape and weather into another with a magical leisure. Without any apparent effort we were seeing a great deal of France. From the old red-tiled roofs of the Dordogne we came to the limestone towns of the Loire, where all the roofs were of slate, blue-black in the sun, with the pointed turrets and gilded weather vanes of the towns in illuminated manuscripts.

Those days in the Loire Valley seemed to mark a new phase in the development of the journey. A hundred forces and counterforces working in innumerable ways achieved there a miraculous equilibrium. For one thing, weather as clear and shining as the pale gold wines we drank filled the valley to the brim. Willows were clouds of gold on the river bank, the grass glowed with a hot emerald flame. I remember the whole world seemed a dizzy blur of green and gold where at intervals we came upon a château with fairy-tale towers, mirrored in water, spun over with the quivering lines of reflected sunlight.

A comparable serenity reigned in the car. Group-dynamically speaking, we had reached the ideal state of integration, and, if one is to believe the psychologists, were so interwoven with each other that any outsider would have been regarded with suspicion and hostility. Anyway we were delighted with ourselves. We thought we were killingly funny and were in perpetual fits of admiring laughter. It is useless to tell what we did or what we

167

laughed at since no one else ever understands this kind of family autointoxication. It is best described as the exact opposite of loneliness. Nothing said goes very deep, in fact most of the time the only exchanges are idiotic to make the others laugh. They are often improper and earthy, they are usually incomprehensible to outsiders because families have their own language.

I had stopped feeling like a mother or even a parent, except during bed-assignments, and I think Bob had also. We had stopped feeling like Americans or members of society. What, you may ask, did we feel like? Well, I for one felt the way I used to when I read Robin Hood—like one of those merry beggars who sit under a hedge drinking nut-brown ale and eating pasties while in the distance rise the fragile pinnacles of improbable castles. Maybe the raggle-taggle gypsies felt the way we did—tribal, self-sufficient, belonging to the whole earth rather than one place or country.

We lay on our backs in the new grass watching brown and orange butterflies opening their wings on the plum blossom. We saw the blinking silver of the river through screens of poplars. Every noon while I was setting out the picnic, Bob played soccer with the boys, and once they kicked the ball into the Loire.

We made up games to play in the car and I taught them a word game invented by my brothers and myself while driving through Wales. The game was simply a kind of contest to see who could make up the funniest alliterative name. It sounds dull but it isn't, although to enjoy it everyone has to be in a state of helpless idiocy. Only a family with a lifetime of common allusion can play it properly, or, rather, improperly. It is a very improper game, and used to reduce us all to jelly from laughter. My father, a man of the cloth, had made up some of the best combinations and Bob now contributed others which made it necessary for him to stop the car and collapse over the wheel.

At Chenonceaux I so far forget my position as to tell Pete about a very basic dance which had been a specialty of my oldest brother. This dance was about a milkmaid with an overdeveloped torso and involved all kinds of juggling, staggering, and overbalancing. My brother had once broken a valuable victrola record in his gyrations and Pete, like a true artist, invented a completely new interpretation, in French Donald Duck language with songs.

Kathy and I, who were the audience, laughed so much that Bob had to come upstairs from the bar to quiet us. Pete was lying backwards over the foot of the bed yelling, *"Au secours! Au secours!"* in Donald Duck at the time.

"Godalmighty," said Bob, "what's going on up here?"

"Show Daddy," I squeaked, mopping my eyes.

Pete did so, a magnificent display. Bob laughed wildly and then said suddenly, "Who taught you *that?*"

"Mum," said Pete, leering at me.

"It isn't really very bad," I said.

"Your mother is a coarse woman," said Bob.

"Ho!" I said. "Who made up that thing in the game today? Who laughed so much at his own coarse, crude joke that he had to stop the car?"

Bob looked smug.

You can see how far out in left field we were as parents, but I must say the rapport between us and our young had never been so good. Gesell, Spock, all of them would have danced for joy at the results, but what about the methods?

We found in Chenonceaux the kind of castle portrayed in illuminated manuscripts where in the foreground peasants are plowing or nobles hunting a boar. It had the airy look of the castles the beggar under the hedge would have seen.

We came upon it, walking down a wide avenue in the spring woods—tall French woods as formal as an etching. At the end of this dreamlike vista, framed in clouds of tiny leaves, was a château that might have been carved out of ivory, with clustering pepper-pot turrets which caught the blue of the sky on their slates. As we approached it through beds of box and lavender, we saw that it was built out over a little river in a series of arches where the reflected sunlight perpetually quivered. The same watery light ran and wavered over the creamy walls so that the whole fantastic building seemed to be a mirage from an age sunk below time's horizon. It is curious how moods and places fit each other, or do they cause each other? I could almost believe that Chenonceaux had been created by our enchanted state of mind.

All the next day the magic held. Again the spring world lay under a spell of sunlight and in the motionless air the blossoming fruit trees were translucent, the young green leaves like candle flames going straight up. We visited three more châteaux—Azay-le-Rideau, Ussé, and Chinon. At Azay I saw a chaffinch singing so close to the path that every feather was clear. Rose and slate-blue, plump and sleek he sat, his whole body puffed up with song. On that day we ate lunch in a field full of the rare guinea-hen flower, the checkered lily, and all through the hedgerows were primroses and white violets. The field had a limestone wall on one side, overgrown with ivy, and here we cut our bread and cheese and drank a red Médoc.

The rest of the way was through ancient villages with lichened sway-backed roofs and tiny fruit gardens, beautifully neat in their frame of stone walls. We were to sleep in a cathedral town near the Breton border and it just happened that about a million salesmen were having a convention there that night. Well.

At first the change was almost imperceptible, as though someone had fallen out of step in a procession. The rhythm was off. Still it was a blue evening, and in Brittany the primroses filled the ditches like spilled cream. There were bowl-shaped meadows framed in ivy-covered dikes and pollard willows where primroses grew in delicious round nosegays, but it didn't do any good. Slowly but steadily the virtue was draining out of us like air out of a pricked beach ball, and with its going the magic went out of the world. It began to look perfectly awful.

We passed sinister little thatched cottages that I still hate to think about. Then we went through a huge town next to the great air base and the entire place was dreadful. The modern

170

buildings had a hideous, plastic gloss. Then we came to one of those European resorts lined from end to end with stucco villas and hotels, with the usual highway separating their front porches from the beach. This, too, was perfectly terrible and there we stayed the night. When Bob took out the suitcases he dropped a bottle of wine and my *scaldino* and they broke into a thousand pieces on the road.

"Where did that thing come from?" he asked, as we picked up the bits out of a pool of wine.

"Oh, I bought it once," I said. "It was only about a quarter."

"Exactly what did you intend to do with a *scaldino?*" he asked.

"Put bulbs in it," I said quickly, having never thought of it until that moment.

"Those jugs——" began Bob.

"Now let's not talk about jugs," I said.

We crawled into the bar and had some brandy. If this journey seems to be punctuated with references to liquor, it is only because I am determined to give the total picture. We did not drink much, however, at any one time and in any case could not have afforded it. The only time we exceeded our usual single *apéritif* was when we had to persuade Billy to sleep in a Victorian crib made of carved rosewood. This was also the only time we drank whiskey, but so would you.

The next day we drove to Concarneau and although it was a day of the most jewel-like brilliance most of us were apathetic. The colored sails on the fishing boats that I had described so rapturously were all gone. The boats ran on Diesel engines. I was stricken by some nameless germ and huddled in our bedroom and ate bananas. There's simply no use trying when the luck turns on one of these journeys, and the next day even God gave up and the wind blew cold and raw, freezing us to the marrow.

We drove to Saint-Michel under a sagging gray sky and I knew that we shouldn't go there. For years I had longed to see the lovely Mount, but I knew it would be somehow spoiled, since the fates were against us. For a few minutes we saw it, medieval and exquisite above the pearly sands. Gulls were flying over the causeway and all the colors were gray, white, and silver. Then we trudged across in the chilly sea-wind and were nearly seized bodily by the buzzing swarm of concierges and souvenir vendors. The place was like a wasps' nest. Nobody seemed to think of anything but omelets and copper. The omelets were because of Mère Poulard, who had made her hotel on the Mount famous for her brand of fluffy omelet.

After dinner, which I need hardly say was omelet, it began to rain and Bob and I went up the street to find a *bistro* and shore up our spirits. We found one, empty and cold, and watched from its window the famous tide come in, a boiling soup of garbage. Now I am almost willing to believe that if we had been in our golden mood at Saint-Michel the tide would not have been full of garbage.

The next day the rain came down in buckets and Bob was carried out to the causeway on the shoulders of a fisherman. This, the only incident of our visit that I would have given anything to see, I missed, because I forced myself to climb up to the cathedral again and, once inside, was mysteriously impelled to join the guided tour which took forever. In my wet, cold state I couldn't understand French and also didn't really want to see anything. One more deterrent to complete enjoyment was the appearance at intervals of one of the children saying, "Daddy says for Pete's sake hurry *up!*" These hissing exchanges made everybody look at us and somebody always said "Ssh!" which angered me.

Once more on the road we hacked along in driving rain until we reached Chartres, the most perfect cathedral there is, in my mind, and one about which I had been lecturing for some time. Things went as we might have expected.

We chose an inferior hotel which smelled of wet laundry.

As we shambled over to the cathedral the rain drove into our faces.

Inside the cathedral, for one moment the sun came out, which seemed almost like a wink from God saying, "How am I doing?"

The children insisted that we light some candles before the shrine of Saint Christopher, the patron of travelers. This seemed a sensible move, but then they went off and lighted a lot more without paying.

"You can't do that," we said.

"Why not?" asked Margie.

"You have to pay every time," we said, nervously looking over our shoulders.

"Well, I didn't pay and I lighted a whole bunch," said Billy.

"Sh, sh," we hissed.

"Let's get out of here," I said, pushing them ahead of me.

"But why——?"

"Sh!" I said angrily.

Bob tactfully led us out and into the small park in front of the cathedral. I said we must go down and see the old town by the river.

"It's going to rain," said Bob.

"Who wants to see any old town?" asked Pete. "I want to get ice cream."

"Hey, yah!" cried all in chorus.

"First let's see the old town," I said, glaring about me.

Bob helped me to herd our whining little band towards the river but somehow I couldn't remember the way.

"It's around this corner," I said, or "Down that street," but it never was.

When we were miles away from everything the rain came boiling, hissing, roaring down upon us. The roads were ankle-deep, and in two seconds we were soaked to the skin.

This was our visit to Chartres, and there followed a fevered night during which Bob walked in his sleep, because, he said, wild animals were trying to get in the window. He also tore his bed apart and I had to get up and remake it.

The next day we drove up to Paris.

It hardly seemed possible to live through the last miles but we made it and, without reservations, hungry, angry, and exhausted, stopped the car on a side street down by Saint Sulpice. Then we just sat there while the rain sluiced against the windshield and ran down the street toward us in black rivers. People splashed by under umbrellas and above us I saw the blessed shuttered fronts of Paris, the curly balconies, the familiar signs in French.

Every now and then in the midst of one of these briar patches of life, one is given the power to detach oneself, to look down and evaluate. That morning it happened, and I suddenly saw, as if from above through the rain, the chubby form of Tom Thumb sitting in the heart of Paris and inside *us*—squalling and scratching like a basket of kittens. My God, I thought, we're in *Paris* and look at us!

"Come on, men," I said. "We're going to find a place to live." After all, the trip was over.

When I look back on the afternoon of that day, I remember the blue gleam of the pavements, polished by rain, and the marvelous blaze of light as the sun opened out like a great, yellow flower over the roofs of the city. The light shone through the transparent new leaves on the plane trees along the river, the Seine glittered under its ivory bridges, and the sky was Wedgewood blue with thistledown tufts of cloud. I remember sitting in one of those little wire chairs on the quay across from Notre Dame, looking through a sheaf of butterfly prints, and I remember exactly the quality of the spring sunshine that warmed my back, the smell of wood smoke in the air, the look of the bookstalls where the colored prints fluttered, and all around me the enormous murmur of Paris, deep and drowsy in the soft afternoon. The reason, I believe, that this moment remains so vivid is that I was living in the exact center of it, looking forward to nothing, looking back at nothing, but totally aware of the present.

It had taken us about one minute (after getting out of the car) to forget all about the horrors of the journey's end. As travelers we had grown up.

"This Precious Stone Set
in the Silver Sea"

Our second visit to Paris was supposed to last a week, but Bob, who was—rightly—worried about money, insisted that we leave the second day. I was the only one who minded this and I minded so strongly that I left nothing unsaid that might have prolonged our stay.

At dinner the night after we arrived I delivered a speech on the subject of England. We were eating a Basque dish called *paella,* containing every known crustacean and shellfish as well as chicken and a large fish, and I told Bob that English food was horrible. There would be no wine, I said, nothing but ginger beer, and all you ever had to eat there was boiled meat, boiled greens, boiled potatoes and tarts. Not only that, I said, it would be freezing cold and rain every day.

Bob said that it had rained in Brittany, Saint-Michel, Chartres, and Paris. I said the English never spoke to Americans. When during my childhood our family of seven had entered the lounges of the hotels, the inmates had never opened their traps. Bob replied that no one when in the presence of my entire family ever had a chance to open his trap, and anyway he knew that we had not been allowed into bar parlors where all right-thinking Britishers spent their time. Nobody ever sat in lounges, he said, except angry retired army officers and old ladies who complained about drafts. I never thought of this angle, and of course it explains a lot about that earlier visit.

All my pleading was in vain because Bob was determined to get to England as soon as possible. He seemed to think that once there we would somehow have more money. This was true, in a way, as an unknown relative's bequest, announced out of the blue, was awaiting him in a place called Pinner.

"Not that the money will hold out until June," he said gloomily, "but if we're going to starve we might as well do it in our own language."

I said I'd rather starve in French, but it was decided. We would leave in the morning.

Of course, it rained in torrents or was gray and cold all the way up to Boulogne, but the minute we came in sight of England the sun burst out in regal splendor. Across the dark blue of the channel, the white cliffs shone like snow. Gulls clamored over the boat as we sidled into the dock. High and small against the sky, two men and a dog watched us from the curve of the downs. We shuffled off the boat and all around us people were speaking our own language. It's hard to describe how miraculous this sounded after all these months.

My first personal encounter with the voice of England was in a telephone booth where I was trying to stop thinking,

"There are bluebirds over
The white cliffs of Dover."

177

I was also trying to decipher coins and read the elaborate and almost endless directions about Buttons A and B, when a voice spoke at my elbow, "Want 'elp, lidy?" it said.

I said, "Yes, I do," backing up so as to focus my eyes.

A red face was practically on my shoulder and it said for me to hand over the coins and it would itself push Buttons A and B at the proper time. The affair proceeded correctly. A male operator responded to Button A, and I gave the number of an inn in Canterbury. "Righty-oh," he said, "haold on, now." My Cockney friend put in the correct number of coins, the operator said, "When your party answers push Button B." Eventually a cold female voice articulated the name of the inn in Canterbury. My assistant then pushed Button A, and with a clatter and clanging of bells all the coins cascaded into the cup below. Our eyes met.

"Oh, Gawd," he said, "now ah've done it. No use trying this one again. It'll be arf a day strightening 'im aht." We moved to the next booth and started afresh, my friend perspiring and breathing heavily. This time we were successful and parted with words of esteem on both sides. However, the cold-voiced female on hearing that we were a party of six said they were full up.

"No luck, eh?" said the operator. "Just landed, what? Got the kiddies with you, eh?"

"Yes," I said. "Well, let's see. Try this number." We did and they were full up, too. This went on for some time and finally I said, "Oh, damn, I've got to go back and get some more change."

"You do that, dearie," said the male operator, now a close friend. "I'll be waiting."

When I returned he gave me a warm welcome.

"I say," he said, "you haven't been telling these blokes abaout the kiddies, have you?"

"Why, yes," I said, surprised.

"Ow, that's it," he said. "Never get anywhere telling the treuth, girlie. Just ask for what you want and don't let on abaout the kiddies."

Following this course, I instantly secured reservations at the Flying Horse in Kent and thanked the operator effusively afterwards.

We drove up from Dover through the delectable Kentish country: apple-green fields full of new lambs, ditches and hedge bottoms bunched and garlanded with primroses the color of fresh butter, and all the cottage gardens gay with daffodils and wall flowers. Fruit trees were just bursting into puffs of blossom, and out of the froth of petals and delicate new leaves the tiled roofs and smoking chimneys rose like symbols of home. Villages hidden in folds of quilted landscape seemed to hold out the promise of nursery comforts, the remembered coziness of childhood. Having been so long in Italy, a country where the concept of coziness is unknown, this aspect of England affected us powerfully. We had all been brought up on Beatrix Potter, *Winnie The Pooh,* and *Wind in the Willows,* and the villages we saw were exactly like those inhabited by anxious mice in dimity, bright-eyed hedgehogs, and comfortable mother rabbits. The feeling of recognition, which so many people notice on their first visit to England, is a poignant thing, all tied up with these childhood associations as well as the adult hodgepodge of Dickens, Merrie England Christmas cards, poetry about primroses and nightingales, and those innumerable country houses in detective stories.

The Flying Horse embodied everything one had ever heard, read, or imagined about English inns. It was made of old brick with sharp tiled gables the color of apricots. Inside were black-beamed ceilings, snow-white walls and a leaping fire that shone on copper warming pans and brass jugs. Pots of blue primroses stood on the window sills and the late sun poured through open casements.

There was a jolly bar parlor, paneled in black oak, where a lot of merry people were drinking. While Bob was signing the register I distinctly heard several "cheerios," two "jolly goods" and several "old chaps." I was enchanted and thought I had never seen such delightful looking individuals: the men handsome and tweedy, the ladies fresh and pretty with black curls and appleblossom complexions.

We had a superb dinner with French wine, thus disproving another of my generalizations about England, and still another was demolished when the inmates of the bar parlor engaged us in a conversation which only terminated when we went up to bed. I later suspected that as nonresidents of the inn they felt themselves safe from any closer association with those frightful creatures, Ameddican children. However, I may wrong them.

The morning was sunny and full of bird song, cock crow, and country noises. Out the bathroom window I could see the wavy tiled roofs, mellow with lichens, and clustering chimneys smoking upward in blue corkscrews. Down below in the richly dug garden, primroses and daffodils grew in fat clumps with wallflowers of brown velvet. A thrush ran like our robins on the grass cocking his neat head. I saw a chaffinch warbling in a plum tree and a yellow-billed blackbird sang garrulously and sweetly from the top of the wall.

The enormous English breakfast of bacon and eggs was just the sort of breakfast people in English novels eat before going on a journey. The drive up to Canterbury through the mists of early morning was so easy and gay that we were deceived into thinking that we had overcome the usual difficulties of the final phase in a trip and were at last in total command of the situation. This happy state of ignorance lasted until after lunch, so that we were able to enjoy Canterbury to the full. As we entered the town, the silvery towers of the cathedral dodged us in the little streets, appearing between gables, over chimney pots and roof tops.

We walked toward the cathedral close and everything— *everything*—was enchanting to us: the churchmen in black bowling along on bicycles, the red post boxes, the bow windows full of spring flowers, the signs saying *Tea and Hovis,* the little boys in shorts and blazers who spoke with the accent of earls. Our children were overcome by the speech of the English and from that moment began to imitate it, only returning to normal to fight and argue. They were also overcome by the appearance of the English males.

"Jeeze," Pete would say, "what's the matter with these guys? Why don't they cut their hair?"

Months of living in foreign countries had made us careless, and during the first days in England we were continually forgetting that everyone around understood what we said.

We spent a long time in the cathedral and then, still in a daze of English history, went to Woolworth's and bought a "spirit stove," a saucepan, and six steel spoons. Then we bought some tins of soup and a loaf of very dull bread which we ate by the road near a place called Old Wives Lees. It was not a good picnic.

I have described more than once the kind of thing that makes family driving an exquisite form of torture during the last stages of a trip. I will not, therefore, enlarge upon the horrors of our progress up to London except to say that we went a great many miles out of our way following signs saying

SLOUGH

THE WEST

because Bob said they meant "Bypass the West (of London)." I said I remembered the old Kent Road went straight up, but no, we had to slough the west. Well, the truth is that Slough is a place (pronounced "Slaow") and the signs merely pointed the way to Slough and the west of England.

This kind of thing is all very amusing a year later but when we came to the outskirts of Slough it wasn't amusing at all. Also, the luggage began to work loose inside the car and things kept falling on people. Two bunches of thyme fell on Margie and one of my copper jugs dealt Pete a stunning blow on the back of the head.

"Hey, *Jeeze!*" he yelled. "All this junk of yours is killing me, Maw."

I told him that when I was driving through England with my family a pair of seven-point antlers kept falling on me. Now

181

that, I said, was really painful. Also, I went on virtuously, there were seven of us in a much smaller car with twenty-eight pieces of luggage.

"When I was your age I walked *two miles* to school through *deep snow*," chanted Pete.

"Anyway we've got a giant sword in here," said Margie, "and all these rotten bushes and jugs."

"Everybody be *quiet!*" said Bob.

"We had a sword, too," I said.

"*Quiet!*" roared the master who was still acting Italian.

"What's wrong with *you?*" I asked him in revenge for sloughing the west.

After this our arrival in London was apathetic. The Houses of Parliament, hitherto known to the children only on bottles of a sauce for fish (HP), caused a mild sensation, but otherwise the atmosphere in Tom Thumb was so dense with mutual hostility that no one even looked out the windows. I was so tired that for two cents I would have tossed a hand grenade into the back seats and shot Bob through the head.

Evening found us assembled in the vast front bedroom of our rooming house off the Bayswater Road. In this bedroom were the four beds where Bob and I and the two boys were to sleep, a lot of fumed-oak furniture, a gas grate, and every single piece of luggage we owned. The result was perfectly appalling and induced in me a kind of paralysis, a merciful numbing of all sensation.

I had finally forced Bob to dismantle his precious structure on the roof of the car. When this was done, we discovered that all three duffel bags were soaked through and in one of them everything was dyed pink from the red ribbon on Margie's fuzzy dog. This disaster, on top of the drive to Slough, was too overwhelming to take in and hardly seemed to matter.

We draped the wet and musty-smelling clothing around the room, which, with the two naked bulbs hanging from the ceiling, created the usual George Price atmosphere always such a feature of our homes-away-from-home. There was a sofa piled with suitcases, Florentine baskets, swords, and book boxes, and the table was buried under the Paris-London haul of mail, Kathy's music, two recorders, the school books, some new lead soldiers, and my bunches of French thyme.

In the center of the shambles Bob was washing a dacron shirt in the fixed basin; on the floor by the gas fire, Kathy crouched in her slip drying her hair. I sat in an arm chair stripping a bush of thyme into a newspaper. The younger children poked about in the mounds of possessions, saying at intervals, "Hey, somebody's stolen my box of Argos" or "That's not yours, it's *mine*," etc.

In spite of the disorder and confusion, everyone was perfectly at home. This ability to adjust, this blessed resilience, we had acquired at the cost of considerable suffering, but it was finally ours. We all knew that everything would be fine as soon as we left London and in the meantime set our teeth and prepared to see it through.

In order to build morale we had to spend money, of course, so we used to eat in an Italian restaurant in Soho, where the chef and his copper pans, as well as all the food, were cheerfully visible. Thus we continued to retain a slight feeling of being in Italy instead of in London, which was cowardly but pleasant.

There are those who will take issue with our attitude toward London; there are those who *have*, saying, "Do you mean you didn't go to one play?" and "Didn't you do anything but watch the change of guard?" The answer is, no. Well, some of us went to the old bookstores and we all went to the Tower and lost Pete for an hour. Otherwise we spent most of the mornings in front of Buckingham Palace, our foreheads crushed against the railings, watching the scarlet coats and the kilts, drunk with the squealing of bagpipes and the roll of drums.

We used to walk through Kensington Gardens and Hyde Park, and up The Mall to the palace, nearly getting run over every day at Hyde Park Corner. In the park there were a great many ducks, rabbits, and horseback riders, which gave con-

183

siderable pleasure to all. Then there were the sentries and the mounted police who kept shoving us back. Then the sound of martial music would approach from the direction of the barracks. After the change of guard was over, we always went to the American Express.

It rained most of the time we were in London, and weather is an important factor in the creation of mood or atmosphere. Modern London is far more crowded than it was twenty years ago, and as all the traffic comes at you on the wrong (to us) side, your instinctive reactions are wrong. We escaped death by inches on several occasions, and this hazard, combined with rain, dulled the perception.

Once as I was going into the American Express an elderly American lady, clutching an umbrella, gave me a sharp look.

"You're an American," she said. "If you have any sense you'll get out of this place. I am. What a climate!"

She then vanished into the rain.

We knew we were missing all the charm of London. It was rather like being outside a marvelous restaurant and smelling the savory dinners cooking. However, we were borne down and defeated by exhaustion, overabundance of children, and lack of money. Bob went out to Pinner where the unknown relative had left the money. Why the u. r. left it in Pinner when he lived in Manchester no one knew, but anyway it was there.

However, this addition to our finances was insufficient and Bob said we must find a cottage somewhere. Even with the rent this would cost far less than a hotel. So I called The Universal Aunts, a magnificent organization which had already provided us with a first-rate baby sitter. They promptly gave me the address and telephone number of a Miss Emily Price with a cottage to rent in a village on the Thames. After amassing quantities of sixpences and shillings, I called Miss Price from the telephone in the lower hall. The landlady, obviously eavesdropping, made me feel nervous, as did the sharp voice of La Price when she answered. I explained our wishes and identified us as

184

well as I could, but Miss P seemed depressed, in fact hostile to the idea of renting.

"You do have a cottage?" I asked.

"Oh, mercy yes. Elizabethan cottage—really charming but you wouldn't like it."

I resented this. "Why not?" I said. "It sounds perfect."

"It's too small," she said, "and, oh dear, I just thought of something."

"What?" I asked, now fairly sure I was speaking to a true eccentric.

"The plum tree. Your children would pick the buds off it, I'm sure."

"No, they wouldn't," I said. "I have a garden and they know all about fruit trees."

"Well—I don't know—" said Miss P vaguely. "Oh, dear, there's another thing, an awful thing."

"What's that?"

"One of the upstairs bedspreads has coffee spilt on it. Do you know how to get out coffee stains?"

"Well," I said, "it's either cold water or hot, can't remember which, but—"

This vacillating attitude seemed to confirm Miss P's worst fears.

"Oh, no," she said. "I'm afraid it won't do. And anyway there is another family of Americans who want it." I was sure this was untrue.

"Will you let us look at it?" I asked, taking a firm line.

Miss P finally agreed rather hopelessly that she could not prevent our looking at it and then went into a long garbled account of how to get to the village. At last we parted and I stumbled upstairs to report. Bob then went into a happy dream of how much money we could save, even suggesting that we might make a profit by the time we reached the boat.

We set forth two days later for the village on the Thames to see Miss Price's cottage. It was a dreamy spring morning when we drove out of London through the Thames Valley. All was pale green and silver, and the enchanting villages were buried in fruit blossom. Our village was on the other side of a humped bridge from another village—both made of old brick and flint with mossy russet roofs of tile. The lawns and gardens ran down to the river, which was full brimming silver sliding softly under the willows.

We could hardly believe our luck and had no difficulty in finding Miss P's cottage, a half-timbered one right on the main street and the smallest human habitation I have ever seen. We got the key in the next house and after unlocking the door fell into a tiny square room. Bob's head was up among the beams and I hit my forehead a stinging blow on the door into what passed for a kitchen. There was a two-burner oil stove and a few pots in a cupboard, also a miniature sink. Up a flight of stairs as steep as a ladder were two bedrooms where we crouched under the roof beams and counted beds. Four were up there, and a kind of broken-down couch in a small cell off the kitchen.

We went out the back door into a tiny square of garden where all the American children (who lived next door) were playing tent under an old sheet. One little girl stuck out her tongue at Pete and the others regarded our children with hostile eyes. Bob and I exchanged glances of revulsion.

"Well, we'll have to take it if we can," said Bob. "Call her up—and ask her. It's cheaper than a hotel anyway."

The telephone was working and I called Miss P's number. She was there.

"Oh, dear," she said instantly.

"We'll take it," I said, "if it's all right with you. Of course, we'll have to get another bed somewhere."

"Oh, my," said Miss P. "I didn't know you'd rush me like this. How do I know I want you to rent it?"

"Shall we come and see you?" I asked.

"Oh, dear, no," she said. "Oh, my, this is all so sudden."

"Well, what would you like us to do?" I asked as politely as I could.

"I'm sure I don't see how I can decide this now," she said frantically. "No, you can't have it. I've decided."

A great wave of relief surged over me.

"Fine," I said. "Well, goodbye." I hung up thinking I'd let her pay for the call.

"The hell with her and this," said Bob. "Let's go up to Oxford."

As we drove across the bridge I looked down at the river and saw a long black-and-white building with a wavy roof and boats drawn up level with the grass. A sign with a swan on it hung beside the gate, and people were having tea on the terrace.

"Hey, look at that," I said to Bob. "Why not check up on prices just to see?"

We did this, but although the price was reasonable we were mysteriously impelled to go up to Oxford and torture ourselves by looking at hideous rooming houses on back streets. All were full. Everybody began to get cross and even the sight of Magdalen Tower and the High didn't help.

"This is the end," I said to Bob. "Let's get out of here and go back to the Swan."

There are times when it seems as though the batterings of fate, unpleasant though they are, serve to drive one into making the correct turn. So after being harried and broke in London, after being foiled by Miss Price and frustrated in Oxford, we arrived at the place above all others to spend spring in England. For this very stretch of river was the setting for *The Wind in the Willows,* which to us had been the essence of spring and England, since we were small.

The Barbarians and the Swan

If you were to draw a circle with the point of the compass on the Swan Inn and the radius extending just to Oxford, you would have the perfect little world in which we lived for the next month.

The greater part of the area was rolling country criss-crossed by hedgerows, so that it was rather like a quilt of velvet in all shades of green and brown. On the tops of some hills were woods, at this time hazy and golden with new leaves; in the folds and hollows were villages hardly changed for hundreds of years, each with its church tower and red or thatched roofs the very sign and symbol of peace.

Through the middle of this delectable circle ran the river, the "Sweet Thames" of Edmund Spenser, hardly a river at all compared to our Hudson and Mississippi. It was narrow and domestic, controlled by locks and weirs, bordered by gardens. On little islands swans nested, and kingfishers, electric blue and noisy, lived in holes in the banks, as did the water rats. From our bridge downstream ran the towpath, where on Sundays all the world congregated to picnic, make love, drink ginger beer, or fish.

The Swan Inn was a very old building and had, I believe, been an inn in the days of the Tudors or some period nearly as remote. It was long and rambling, half-timbered with several gables and a roof, rippled by the centuries, its old tiles covered with lichens and moss. In front of it were beds planted with daffodils and wallflowers and then a panel of lawn running down to the river. There were tables with umbrellas over them where one could have tea in the afternoons and watch the swans fighting the ducks. Beyond the tea lawn was the boathouse containing a selection of rowboats, punts, and canoes. Beyond the boathouse was the vegetable garden and some dwarf apples and pears and beyond that those fat, swampy fields called in England water meadows, where there were cows and horses grazing. The river ran along the edge of the water meadows, so smooth and polished that it hardly seemed to flow at all, and a bit below the Swan was a weir and right across from it a lock, tended by the husband of our chambermaid.

The village on our side of the bridge was simply two rows of bewitching cottages, a great house, a church, and at the top of the street a white pub with *The Bull* in gold letters across the front. The village on the other side of the river included a post office, a church, a shop with glass jars of "humbugs" and striped peppermints in the window, a fruiterer, a greengrocer, a purveyor of wines and spirits, a chemist, a cleanser, a butcher, and a fishmonger.

The Swan's Annex, which we had almost to ourselves, was an ancient mill right on the edge of the river and just below the humpbacked bridge. Inside, the oak beams were black as coal with age, setting off the white plaster walls and ceilings. Across these snowy surfaces ran the rippling reflections from the water just outside. It was rather like living in a boat, and through the open casements came the constant, rushing murmur of the weir.

Every morning at seven o'clock, the chambermaid knocked

189

on our door with my early tea. She would pull back the pale blue curtains, saying "Good morning, madam dear!" just the way chambermaids do in English novels, and then leave me to half an hour of the purest bliss. Bob, for some reason, preferred sleep to tea so I would begin each day with thirty minutes of precious solitude. No one but a wife and mother knows just how precious such solitude is, especially on a trip abroad, and I used to savor every second of it.

While I drank my tea I read Trevelyan's *History of England*. The effects of tea and Trevelyan were the exact opposite of wine and Italy and I became possessed to learn Everything about England. I began with its geological structure, and got fearfully confused during the Barbarian Invasions. Farther on all those kings called Troth or Ethelbreath or whatever drove me nearly mad, so I skipped to 1066. I used to lecture the family at breakfast saying things like: "Did you know that all the polite words for food are French and all the vulgar ones Anglo-Saxon?"

Bob said that there were certainly a lot of vulgar Anglo-Saxon words, mostly in four letters. That ended that cultural discussion.

I told the children all about Henry the Eighth and they said, "Oh, yah, we saw him on television. He was awful."

After a bit I accepted the fact that the children were totally apathetic about history and culture although Kathy, having taken a course in Italian painting, wanted to see the Uccello in the gallery at Oxford. The other three were interested in just one thing: the river. From morning until night they pursued relentlessly one idea: Could they rent a boat or the kayak? When they couldn't they played in the boats anyway. However, being made only of frail human stuff, we usually broke down after the third "no" and rented boats. Bob had figured out how much money we had spent on the trip, and the total was so colossal that he said it no longer mattered how much more we spent, since we were already ruined. Also when you are dealing in five figures a sum like six shillings for a boat is just plain silly.

Unless you think this way you might as well forget about going abroad with children.

The safety of the English village was marvelous after Italy. I went alone anywhere I wished and the tall, bronzed blue-eyed men in tweeds whom I met on back roads simply averted their eyes and passed me. No gestures here, no leers or throwing of kisses. At the Swan our fellow inmates acted as though we didn't exist, although sometimes I caught them watching us, as though we were ticking bombs. If we were having tea in the lounge they would stop dead in the doorway and those behind would pile up against the backs of the first arrivals, their faces craning over shoulders and around corners to get a good look at the horrid scene. Then with a murmur of "those Ameddican children" they would retire, the last ones looking back over their shoulders with ill-concealed distaste.

"See what I mean?" I said to Bob. "Just the way it was before. You'd think we were lepers."

We sat in the bar, we sat in the lounge, we sat on the terrace, but nobody approached us. We might have been invisible except to members of the staff. We were not invisible however, to countrymen in the fields, storekeepers, or boatmen—only to The Upper Classes. The children couldn't have cared less and took to the back premises.

Here they were welcomed royally and as a result spent most of their time in the boathouse or around the kitchen being treated to cups of tea and other privileges not available to the public. They knew the story of everyone's life, who was married to whom, where so-and-so had come from in Scotland and why someone else was planning to "skip." We never shared this mysterious inner life of the Swan, and I imagined it all taking place in a large Pickwickian kitchen full of Sam Wellers and other vivid personalities.

Our co-inmates of the Swan stayed at arm's length for several reasons: one is the English temperament, which is naturally cautious and restrained; another is that most upper-class English

191

people hold a fixed belief that American children are barbarians; the third reason is, most regrettably, that a great many American children *and* their parents behave like barbarians when abroad. We were often horrified to hear our fellow countrymen refer to Frenchmen as "frogs," Italians as "these wops." In England we met several servicemen stationed in the country who not only knew nothing about England but criticized the qualities of the English in an unforgivable manner.

As far as children go, a large number of American children have the manners of Attila the Hun. The Permissive School seems to allow the little ones to climb all over the guests, interrupt adult conversation, and say things like "Your nose is funny" to complete strangers. This doesn't go down well even in the States and naturally prejudices a race whose children behave like a cross between Basil Rathbone and a Duke. The result is that in England a large family of children is a liability, whereas in the more relaxed Latin countries it is a distinct asset.

During our probationary period we were avoided but carefully watched from a distance. The issue was whether the children were Well Brought Up or whether they were Barbarians. We warned them that the honor of our country, to say nothing of ourselves as parents, was at stake, and they did not let us down. This was not too difficult because the English are surprised if American children do not destroy property, throw food at the table, and attack human beings. After a few days we were accepted, and several charming ladies approached us separately with congratulations.

"My dear," they said, "your children are darlings! So well behaved. We have always believed, you know, that Ameddican children are barbarians."

"Ours are quite average," we said, modestly.

"Oh, no, my dear, I assure you they are not," said one elderly lady in a hat made of violets. "I have seen many Ameddican children. Absolutely gahstly, you know. Parents let them do anything they wish."

"But they really *don't*," I began.

192

It's no use. The English are a tough race and the mere sight of American children in the flesh who are behaving well does not shake their conviction that All American Children are Barbarians and are allowed to Run Wild. When faced by this kind of thing my brothers used to say calmly, "Oh, in New York there are flagpole sitters on every building now," or "We don't dare go out on the streets after dark because of gangsters." The English victims would exclaim, "Oh, I say, how frightful," and "Not rahlly!" looking pleasantly horrified.

England has almost graduated from the idea of Indians in our back yards, but we ourselves were in a peculiarly fortunate position since we do have Indians in our back yard—at least in the summer—on our island in Canada. This gave us a magnificent opportunity to say things like, "Oh, at home our Indian does all the heavy work."

Once we were accepted by the Swan's residents we were overwhelmed with kindness and only the new arrivals or tea-time customers had to be dealt with. This we took care of by providing the boys with a pair of secondhand bowlers, acquired at an auction. From that moment they wore them constantly. Their appearance was so dreadful—rather like two depraved dwarfs—that the tea drinkers could hardly contain their curiosity and horror. Several gentlemen took furtive pictures of them from behind bushes and I suspect that they now believed All American Children wore derby hats. I thought of all the damage that would follow, "My dear, they wear bowlers, actually. I saw it myself," and some helpless American mother like me saying, "But they *don't!*"

There was only one inhabitant of the inn who never recognized our existence and he was a crimson man in a Cambridge blazer who was the other occupant of the Annex. He was the absolute prototype of the American's idea of an Englishman and was the kind of man for whom Sir Henry Newbolt wrote, "Play up! Play up and play the game!"

He was a valuable addition to our collection of Types and we were sure he said, "Oh, good show," and "Right-ho," but he

193

never spoke, never smiled, and looked right through us. Anyone could have told him how it would be. The children, who would otherwise not have given him a second's thought, focused on him an X-ray scrutiny. They watched his every move and presently invented a motif which, as in operas by Wagner, heralded his appearance. It was the television commercial for Smith Brothers Wild Cherry Cough Drops. This is a hideous chant interspersed with a rhythmic theme on the tuba and/or bass drum which was currently on television at home. Pete sang it constantly in Donald Duck, rendering the accompaniment as "bump-bump." He began humming this song whenever the crimson man appeared and after a while we called him Bump-Bump. We saw Bump-Bump for the most part at meals and his entry into the dining room was rather like a royal progress. It was always accompanied by the barely audible Cough Drop commercial.

"This has got to stop," Bob said sternly one day. "It's rude, and he might notice. No more singing or humming that tune in here!"

After that they tapped it out on the table or with knives on the water glasses or with their toes on the floor or simply by sniffing. These subterfuges put them all, and I'm sorry to say ourselves as well, into helpless fits of laughter and several times we came dangerously near death by suffocation.

Bump-Bump, however, who sometimes stole quick glances at us when he thought we weren't looking, did not appear like a shy man whose feelings are hurt, but more like a Cambridge man who suspects others of mental derangement.

One day Pete reported in ecstasy that he had overheard Bump-Bump drumming out the Smith Brothers Commercial on the wall while waiting for a telephone call to come through. This was the nearest we came to communication but our attitude toward Bump-Bump changed completely almost overnight. Kathy who happened to be sitting in the lounge overheard him telling someone how he used to pick bluebells in these woods. Apparently he had come to the Swan in order to revisit the happy country of his childhood. This revelation seemed to us so touching that we could hardly bear it. From then on Bump-Bump could do no wrong and we watched him with affectionate tolerance. Kathy even took a picture of him through our bedroom window but it was so small that you had to look at it through a magnifying glass.

Aside from these minor difficulties, being in England was curiously like being at home, only in someone else's life by mistake. I thought of this one day walking alone on the towpath on a glittery green-and-silver Sunday afternoon. The bell-ringers were practicing, ringing the changes from the square gray church tower and bowling the round notes one on top of the other over the trees. The sweet smell of some unfamiliar shrub filled the sunlight but it was all familiar, nevertheless. It was where I belonged but it wasn't.

We were at first quite ignorant of our location in the English landscape but I continued to have this feeling of recognition which grew almost uncanny. The curve of the river bank, the feathery pollard willows, the weir—all were familiar. When we went out in the boats they too were exactly like some other boats—the little seats with arms, the rudder-ropes, the cushions. Once when we were floating by the bank a water rat plopped from his hole into the stream and I said to Bob, "Hey, I know, this is like *Wind in the Willows*. There's Ratty."

"That's what it is," said Bob, "I was trying to think."

Back at the Swan I asked the manageress if she had ever read Kenneth Grahame.

"Oh, of course," she said. "You know he wrote *Wind in the Willows,* right on this stretch of river."

We were overwhelmed with delight. The children were tolerant of our transports but obviously believed that Ratty's River Bank had been correctly portrayed in Disney's *Toad of Toad Hall.*

When Bob discovered that the name of our first lock was Cleeve Lock he gave a cry of ecstasy.

"Three Men in a Boat!" he said. "They were here too."

195

Three Men in a Boat is a book of Victorian humor by Jerome K. Jerome.

The children allowed us to point out moorhens, dabchicks, Toad Hall, and other sentimental landmarks, but were themselves interested only in whose turn it was to row or steer, whose turn it was in the bow, and whether the lock keeper would let them turn the wheels *this* time.

We would usually go on the river after breakfast and in the radiant spring weather "boating" was the perfect way to get to the heart of a day. On those mornings a blackbird sang in the pear trees; the water was polished as quicksilver, brimming up full against the fat green banks. On the far shore the willows made golden clouds, their trailing branches pulled downstream by the current. The swans cruised along beside us, puffed out like peonies, their milk-white reflections inverted below their breasts. Some carried a black webbed foot over one wing, like a man with a pencil behind his ear. The King Swan, an enormous bird with a lumpy orange bill and great curved wings, swept royally through the water setting up a considerable bow wave.

There were two locks, one operated by our chambermaid's husband who allowed the boys to turn the wheels; the other by a speechless man in a peaked cap who did not permit this at first but did eventually. On the islands where the lock keepers lived were neat Victorian houses with window boxes. The one upstream had a garden full of primroses, a blossoming apple tree, and lilacs.

We would row into the lock and grab a chain, then the lock keeper or the boys would spin the two big wheels that closed the gates. Then the water boiled in the sluices, and our boats rose feather-light to the level of the gardens. A bit above one lock was a stretch of river bank, close cropped by cattle and soft as green plush. Here we used to eat our picnics which were provided by the Swan and usually composed of enormous numbers of flannel sandwiches filled with dry chicken or rubbery Spam.

Sometimes our picnics were unsuccessful to an almost spectacular extent. Once we had to eat with a large horse chumping grass in our midst. He smelled for some reason like a skunk and kept switching us with his tail. But we were afraid to chase him away, as even the offer of grass by Billy had caused him to charge us, nostrils dilated. We had tried to move to an island, but here we were attacked and chased by a nesting swan. Everybody was too tired to row any farther so we simply stayed there with the horse looming above us and the Spam turning to ashes in our mouths.

There were days, soft with rain, when the countryside seemed swollen with sap, saturated with a moisture which burst out in giant succulent weeds, dock and cow parsley with its round lace flowerheads tilted every which way by the weight of water. On such days I could hardly believe that a few weeks before we had been on the Amalfi Drive where the Bay of Naples glittered like a floor of jewels and in the dry burning sunlight the terraced gardens smelled of lemons and honey. Had we really climbed the narrow streets of Amalfi and bought sponges?

Now through air like milk, smelling of cut grass and lilac, we walked in our mackintoshes between cottage gardens, and all that violent beauty, that brilliant light which had been like our natural element, seemed incredible. We had drunk Falernian wine in Italy and the only possible philosophy had been eat, drink, and be merry for tomorrow we die. Here we drank tea and worried about whether the English would think our children were Well Brought Up.

Maybe the Romans had felt this way, exiled from their sun-baked villas and their olive trees, when they saw the cold primroses in the rain. In Italy one is really closer to the fundamentals. The only important things seem to be birth, love, and death, whereas in England we were back in the complicated structure of a far more cerebral, far more inhibited, far more idealistic society.

The children, to whom apparently adjustment was a thing of

the past, now made it known that the Swan was the neatest place since Austria. For the first time everyone was completely content and completely comfortable. We were also completely broke but this didn't seem to mean that we had no money. Bob said that we were in the process of spending our July and August salary checks but we continued to buy books, hire boats, and order wine for dinner. I had said so often, "One never regrets one's extravagance, only one's economies" that we began to feel actually proud of being improvident and reckless.

One of our barbarians—Pete—now discovered two boys of his own age, both of whom were dressed like Christopher Robin in gray flannel shorts and jerseys with long socks. Their hair was cut English fashion—rather like Audrey Hepburn's—and their speech and manners were so charming and polished that I myself felt like a barbarian beside them. Still, I was uneasy about the reactions of our two boys, who had been in long pants since the age of five and had crew cuts from the time they had hair. I need not have worried, because the Christopher Robin façade was the only difference between ours and the English. Merry and mischievous, they were a godsend to Pete, who now led an entirely independent life, checking in only for meals, if then. The boys were having their holidays, which luckily lasted most of our remaining time at the Swan.

The parents of one of the boys came down to the bar to meet us one evening and proved to be amazingly good looking and a great deal of fun. After the usual formalities had been disposed of—Pete so delightful, had always thought American children barbarians, ours not, etc.—we were asked to come to dinner and play bridge.

"I can't play bridge," I said quickly.

"Yes you can," said Bob traitorously.

"I can play bridge only when we're up skiing," I said.

"The only thing she does wrong," said Bob, "is to play out of turn, and then start laughing and saying they're just a lot of pieces of cardboard."

198

The two looked shocked at this, but said nobly that they were sure I was a wonderful player.

"I can't bid either," I said, "and I don't know what slams are."

They laughed heartily and said we *must* come and I was probably magnificent.

"For Pete's sake," I said to Bob after they'd gone, "now see what you've done. You know I can't play bridge."

"Just don't say they're only pieces of cardboard," said Bob, "and don't start laughing and playing out of turn."

It was exactly as I feared. Our hosts were the kind of people who throw down their hands after a couple of plays and say, "The rest are mine." Also they and Bob were constantly remarking that if I had finessed the Queen of Spades, So-and-So's ten would have been good, or words to that effect. However, they were very kind to me and subsequently lent us their motor launch, so I did not apparently destroy our friendship by my frightful mistakes.

Now that we had the use of a boat and had found delightful people to talk to, there seemed to be no real reason ever to move again. If it hadn't been for early tea and Trevelyan I would have deteriorated completely, but these two stimulants made me drive untold miles hunting for somebody's tomb. Bob also wanted to see things, especially Roman remains, and we once drove all day, with people fighting in the car, to see the Roman town of Silchester which was dug up and then reburied under a wheat field. This trip was a failure and discouraged us from further efforts *en famille*.

Day after day of perfect weather brought on the apple blossoms and the lilacs, unpleated the new leaves on the beech trees, and poured lakes of bluebells between their silvery trunks. In those serene mornings the sun struck gold into deep trees. The horse chestnuts by the bridge were in full leaf and flower and the distant woods had a brooding, heavy look. Through the long, dreaming afternoons the wood pigeons cooed sleepily,

199

and the monotonous voices of the cuckoos answered each other across the whole soft landscape. The river, especially on weekends, was as busy as a city street and the towpath swarmed with people. There were picnics on the grass, rowboats, kayaks, single shells, and motor boats waiting at the locks, and launches moored along the banks with brown, merry families drinking ginger beer on the cabin tops.

It was a great temptation to spend these days like gypsies, doing nothing but enjoying the sun and watching the endless changes of light and color on the river. "All paths lead to water," says Melville at the beginning of *Moby Dick*. "There is magic in it . . . meditation and water are wedded forever." This is perfectly true and the river all but hypnotized us so that we had to make a painful effort to leave it and explore the rest of England.

Bucolic Adventures

We began our *en famille* exploration of England gradually, the way people get accustomed to taking arsenic. At first we went for short drives, then we made expeditions with some special treat as a goal. The most successful of these was the trip to Windsor where we discovered the Royal Horse Show in progress. We were even able to get tickets and after a picnic on the field of Runnymede spent an enchanted afternoon in an atmosphere of crushed grass and horses. The crowd was England at its best—tweedy squires, red-faced farmers, elegant lords and ladies, and a liberal sprinkling of Eton scholars. The sight of these, in their swallowtail coats and top hats, nearly killed Pete and Billy.

"My Gawd!" said Pete. "I can't believe it. Jeeze, they must be nuts!"

"They have to wear them," we said.

"Boy, that must be *some* school," said Billy with deep disgust.

201

Our next move was to tackle the one-inch ordnance map of our area, and we became connoisseurs of villages. The names Nutbane, Nether Wallop, Buckleberry, and the like led us down tiny lanes where the layered hawthorne hedges nearly touched the car doors, over high commons where plovers cried, and through the green undersea light of beech woods ankle-deep in bluebells. Some of the villages were neat, whitewashed rows of houses flush with the street; others had pink and pale blue Tudor cottages set at all angles in a maze of paths and lanes; still others were brick and flint like ours, hidden away in the quilted landscape.

English villages are not like New England villages; they still bear the mark of the feudal or manorial systems. In nearly every one is the Great House or the Castle, and in the little churches you find noblemen lying in effigy on their tombs with their dogs at their feet, their wives at their side. They are often famous men whose names resound through history, and you see warriors in armor like those in the Bayeux tapestry, crusaders in chain mail with their elegant legs crossed to show they had been to Jerusalem. The Elizabethans are often painted in the colors of life, and in the dimness of a country church we would be startled by a recumbent figure in a scarlet cloak, slashed doublet, and ruff.

I had read so much Trevelyan that the discovery of one of my historical friends would simply bowl me over.

"Look," I would cry. "Alice Chaucer! Imagine!"

"So?" one of the children would say.

The churches often had living Englishmen inside them as well, and once we met the bell-ringers who were practicing ringing the changes. At the foot of the tower, a group of men and girls stood with the ropes in their hands bobbing up and down in turn. One man was resting and, much against my family's will, I asked him to explain what they were doing. He was delighted.

"Now watch!" he said. "That's the Treble starting. See, here in the book. 'Over' means 'after,' 'under' means 'before.' These numbers show the mathematical progression. A 'hunt' is a diagonal or jump across to an opposite number, a 'dodge' is a hunt and back (written like this > in the score). A 'bob' is a special insert to get the full number of changes out of seven bells. The head ringer calls it in a particular place where he feels it should come in. A 'peal' is the full number of changes and a full peal for seven bells takes three hours. A touch is part of a peal. Now he's one over fours, now three over fives, now he's dodging five and back to one. Now he's six, then he hunts back down to one [this was the Treble's progress]. Now they're calling a bob."

While we were there the bell-ringers played something called "Cambridge Surprise" and another called "London." It was wonderful to watch, and the clashing, tumbling bells seemed to be not only all around one but inside as well. My friend told me that most bells have names like Great Tom or Big Ben. I wish I could remember some of the unfamiliar ones—names like Dilly and The Old Bull. One ringer came over wiping his brow and spoke affectionately of his bell as "she."

These excursions very seldom included the whole family. Pete spent most of his time with his friends on the river or the golf course. Billy and Margie lived out in the kitchen or in the boathouse, and I gradually stopped picturing them drowning. There was a scummy stagnant brook behind the boathouse and here they poled about in an old punt. The thick tangles of cow parsley and burdock and the long silky grass curved over their heads, and in this perfect hide-out you could hear them giggling and splashing.

Kathy enjoyed picking names off the ordnance map at random, and she and I drove for hours through fat lanes and echoing beech woods chasing a Drunken Bottom or a Charlsy.

The end of each day was the same. We went through the dark garden to the Annex. In our rooms the curtains would be drawn, the beds turned back, and a little oil stove threw spinning wheel-like patterns on the white ceiling. There were hot-water bottles between the sheets, and after reading peacefully for a while we went to sleep to the sound of the weir.

Finally the time arrived when we all went off for a whole weekend. We chose as our destination the Cotswolds, an area in the west of England famous for its beauty. An overpowering old man at the Swan firmly insisted that we make reservations ahead and gave us the R.A.C. and A.A. guides. He recommended to us the Trust Houses, which are old coaching inns, private estates, or famous buildings taken over by the nation and run as hotels. They are relatively inexpensive and quite reliable. Most of them have cream paneling, chintz curtains and chairs, paintings of apprehensive race horses, mahogany, blue china soup tureens, and the eternal copper warming pans polished like gold. There are open fires and bowls of spring flowers; the bedrooms are down miles of creaking corridors with red Turkey carpets; the doors don't latch very well, and the bathrooms have elderly fixtures, but the general effect is a Pickwickian comfort, cozy and spotless. (If you are lugging a family around England, the Trust House List and a book called *Good Eating* are essential baggage.)

Our first Trust House was in the Cotswolds, and it was a coaching inn called the White Hart. We were extremely fortunate here because the bar parlor was also the local pub. It was small and square, with one whole side taken up by a roaring wood fire and another side by a mahogany bar. Bob and I, somewhat attenuated by a long day of driving with children, went in there for a beer. Bob settled me by the fire and edged his way up to the bar. Here was a perfect vignette of English village life, and I had the feeling that we had met the people there a hundred times before in *Punch*. They were as follows: a large old gentleman in russet tweed with a bunch of primroses in his buttonhole and a voice like a bull; an octogenarian with a wispy moustache and no teeth who sat in the corner with a "pint o' bitter"; a round, rosy ancient in a shapeless gray hat who talked about crops; a square tweed female; a droopy damp female in a mackintosh; and a small pink cockney in leather gaiters. They all knew each other and exchanged news of weather and local gossip.

It was obvious that American women were rare birds in that pub, and our presence caused a sensation. I was interested, if slightly embarrassed, to note that every eye in the place was on me. The gigantic man with the primroses told a long story, ostensibly to the bartender but really at me, and pretty soon they all did this, the octogenarian even going so far as to wink at me occasionally. The cockney edged his way over until he was leaning against the mantelpiece. Then, giving up the empty pretense of telling the story of his life to the primrose man, he simply drew up a chair beside me. This came as a relief to several who now moved over and stood looking down at me. Bob crawled in beside me, and all the people in chairs hitched them over until we were almost crowded into the fire.

"Will you let me buy you a drink, lidy?" asked the cockney politely.

I said I had one but thanked him.

"Ow much do you suppose a glarse o' whiskey cost when oi was a nipper?" he said.

"How much?" I said.

"Tuppence," he said, drawing back to get the effect on me.

"Aye," said the octogenarian, "I mind when my old father brought me in here the year X won the Derby."

A long argument followed about who had won the Derby in 1898, and then the cockney, leaning so close to my ear that I had to back away to see him at all, told me in merciless detail every moment of his career as a trainer of horses and something about his life as, or with, the South American Dempsey. The others said, "Aye, that's right," or "So ye did," and "I mind that," in the nicest way, but occasionally the strain was too great and one would interrupt with an anecdote from his own experience.

At one point I noticed that Pete was sitting among us, thus breaking the law. However, after a while Bob made him go away. Then the two small ones came in saying they wanted a coke and why couldn't they stay, etc. After this we left amid the hearty farewells of all our new friends.

205

This weekend in the Cotswolds was one of our great triumphs. Everything we did succeeded. We drove through one golden stone village after another, each with its tall square church tower and its row of shops bow-windowed and appealing. The gardens were full of daffodils and primroses, gay as confetti, and often there were fruit trees espaliered on the walls of houses. In the village of Broadway there was a great pear tree covering the whole gable end of a house with its pattern of white blossom.

We had, it is true, a slight contretemps at tea when Billy put an entire cupcake into his mouth and sat with bulging cheeks hoping to convulse the company. In this he was entirely successful; his ultimate explosion, which sprayed crumbs all over the table, caused Margie to choke in her tea. I led the two out whooping and crowing while the other members of the family abandoned the tea table in fury, cursing Billy in hissing whispers.

It was in the Cotswolds that we christened Tom Thumb in a ford at a place called Upper Slaughter. The day was bright and cold, with immense cloud shadows running over the checkered landscape. The oak woods were swarming with leaves of pink and cream, and the green fields were full of furry red cows. The ford or font was simply a paved place over which the shallow stream ran, and right next to it, somehow giving the whole thing extra charm, was a field containing hundreds of pink piglets.

It was also in the Cotswolds that we saw the lady who had met God. This occurred, appropriately enough, on a Sunday afternoon when Bob and I were taking a walk in order to escape from our children, or more correctly to be alone together, which is quite different. In the quiet, sleepy street of the little town nothing stirred; the sun lay warmly on the golden stone, and we amused ourselves by looking in windows. In one window of a shop were hundreds of excellent photographs of the town showing the Hunt meeting in front of the inn, market day, and so forth. The only queer note was that they were all taken back in the Nineties.

The shop was open, and we decided to ask about this. To enter we went through an entry way papered from floor to ceiling with what looked like children's paintings. Inside was an old lady, who launched at once into the story of her life—early years, father a photographer, her marriage, death of husband, only son wanted paint box. Here she paused dramatically and Bob attempted to escape, but was foiled by her holding up her hand and saying, "I was One Hour from Death."

"One Hour from Death," continued the old lady, running her hand through her doll-like head of curls, "and what did I do?"

"What?" I asked obediently.

"I spoke to God and then I saw Him."

"Oh, *what* did He look like?" I asked, almost adding, "Does He have a beard or not?"

Our friend ignored this tactless question.

"I saw God," she said, "and asked Him to help me. I had no money, no hope and I was One Hour from Death, I said, and if He would only give me one sign, one little bit of hope, I would ask no more."

At this point my eyes filled with tears. "What did God do then?" I croaked.

"Well," she said, "I woke up. There was the paint box. I picked it up and then I had a vision." She closed her eyes and put her hand up for silence. Bob and I waited for quite a long time.

"I painted the vision just as I saw it. The colors were told to me and now—" she made a sweeping gesture toward the entry. "Look! They call me a second Grandma Moses! An American gentleman did," she added in a matter-of-fact voice.

Bob and I then, naturally, went out into the hall and looked at the paintings and in spite of their childishness we were rather impressed. Either they were no good at all, I thought, or they were real primitives.

"How much do you charge?" Bob asked.

"Two for ten shillings," she said, briskly.

We then picked out two of life in the village, done in, I

207

thought, delightful soft colors, and bore them off to our hotel.

"What if they *were* good?" I said.

"We might make money on them," said Bob, who right then would have gladly sold his wife and children if he could have made a profit on the deal.

"Maybe we ought to buy them all," I said.

"And if she was like Grandma Moses we'd make a fortune," said Bob.

We showed them to the children.

"Good God," said Kathy.

"Gee, *I* can draw much better than that," said Billy with contempt. "That dog looks like a horse."

"It is a horse," I said stiffly.

I still think, though, that they are charming, and after all how many people have two pictures painted by someone who has met God? The only thing I don't understand is why on earth she didn't paint His portrait when she had the chance.

When we returned to the Swan there were two new residents, a charming couple who had bought a cottage in the village. They told us that there would be an auction at the cottage to clear out the possessions of the former owners. Pete, who was with us, saw several bags of golf clubs among the loot to be auctioned and from then on gave us no peace.

"Do you think I can get those clubs?" he would say at breakfast, lunch, tea, dinner, and between meals.

At first I said, "How should I know?" and Bob said, "No, there's no room in the car and no money," and finally we were both saying, "If you mention those golf clubs again you won't even go to the auction," all of which had absolutely no effect on Pete, who knows we're weak and easily broken down.

It poured on the day of the auction and Bob had a raging sore throat and shut himself up in the lounge with a book on Greek criticism written in German. Pete and I found our way into the tent where the entire population of the area was squashed together in mackintoshes. I saw a stuffed gannet in a glass case who seemed to me extremely appealing and I bid on him at once. Pete, who had moved over to be near the golf clubs, looked alarmed and shook his head at me. I bid again and he squeezed over until he was close beside me.

"Hey, Maw," he said, "you can't buy that thing!"

"Why not?" I said. "I like him."

"Daddy would kill you," he said simply.

"He probably will kill you if you get all those golf clubs," I said.

"That's different," said Pete loftily. "I *need them* and you don't need any stuffed bird. Why that thing's as big as I am."

"O.K. O.K.," I said.

As a gesture of independence I then bid sixpence on a gigantic stack of books, and since nobody else bid anything I got it.

"That's a lot of books for sixpence," said the auctioneer, "and look how big they are." He held up a volume about two feet square. There were fourteen of these and twenty volumes of a deluxe set of *The History of Science* printed in 1902. The first set was on World War I and was called naively *The History of the War*. Altogether the lot must have weighed more than a refrigerator and was about the same size.

"Oh, *boy,*" said Pete, almost admiringly. "Wait till Daddy sees that!"

After this I bid on two ginger jars, a pitcher, a rug, twelve suit cases, and a lot containing a dressmaker's dummy, a strawberry net, and a small lawnmower. Fortunately, I was outbid throughout.

By this time we were out in the garden and the golf clubs were put up in a lot with seven trunks, a hat box, and some old horse collars.

A large orange-colored man in a hairy orange tweed suit bid against us, and I was up to seventeen shillings and sixpence when Bob appeared. By certain dilations of his eyes and nostrils (a gift of his) he mysteriously made me stop bidding at nineteen shillings and the lot was knocked down to the orange man.

"Now look what you've done!" I said to Bob as Pete cast us a glance of anguish. I went over to the orange man and said bravely that my little boy wanted the golf clubs and the orange man, whose name I would make immortal if I knew it, sold them to me for seven shillings, throwing in free two derby hats that were in the hat box.

Bob was relieved not to be the villain of the piece but said curiously, "Where are you going to put them in the car?"

"Hey, wait till you see what Mum bought!" said Pete, grinning evilly.

Bob had to get the car to carry off my library, but soon became fascinated with *The History of the War* and spent the entire evening reading it.

Every afternoon we would all meet in the bay window of the lounge for tea, and the various parties would report on the day's activities. Bob would stoke up the coal fire to white heat and Kathy would count the Gentlemen's Relish sandwiches so that each child would get the same number. The children then picked out which cupcakes they would take and we would say that nobody could choose food in advance.

As the days grew warmer we took our tea on the terrace and watched the people pretending not to watch the ducks mating just offshore. At intervals the King Swan, whose name was George, used to try to drown one of his sons and Bob once went out in a boat with a man in a handlebar mustache and beat off George with oars.

In such simple and bucolic adventures, our days passed, and at last the time came for us to go up to Scotland. All of us were desolate, and the children spent the last evening in the back premises saying goodbye to their friends in the kitchen. In a fit of inspiration I gave *The History of Science* to the chambermaid, who said it was just the thing for a long evening and staggered off loaded to the eyes.

Bob, now convinced that *The History of the War* was worth Money, took it up to Blackwell's in Oxford along with four large boxes of other books to be shipped home. I spent that day washing clothes and hanging them out on the Swan's clothesline, a ten-foot string between the coal bin and incinerator.

After this, I folded things, discarded as many of the worn-out underpants as I dared, lay down on the floors of all the bedrooms and fished stuff out from under the beds, tried unsuccessfully to clean my gray suit with water, washed and hung on a hedge twenty-nine socks, and secretly packed several interesting hunks of flint I had picked up in the garden.

Under one bed I found a letter written by Billy to a friend saying,

Dear Davey,
The ducks hear keep getting on each others baks all the time [vivid drawing of mating ducks inserted here]. The King Swan tried to kil his baby.
Love, Bill

Sentimental Journeys

Sentimental journeys are dangerous things, but so is life itself and practically everything worth doing. There are several kinds of sentimental journeys: attempting to repeat experience; hunting down the settings for favorite books; visiting ancestral homes, or duplicating some pilgrimage described in literature. There are probably many more, but in every case reality is waiting there ready to deal you a stinging blow or present you with a fulfillment of wonder and delight.

Inside everyone's head is a private landscape as romantic and satisfactory as those old maps where the seas are full of dolphins and high-sterned galleons and the land abounds with leopards, castles, and peacocks. Bob and I had entered successfully into one area of our imagined landscape when we lived on the river bank of *The Wind in the Willows*. It is a tribute to Kenneth Grahame's style that we both had the same picture, and were able to meet in one of these dreamlike places.

This triumph gave us appetite for more of the same, and with the map of England before us and our own maps in our heads we planned our final journey. England, Scotland and Wales were all ours and we had two weeks left. We were like people forced to abandon a banquet after the soup. Panic-stricken, we licked our lips and began to choose. We had trained for the ordeal over a long period. The car was stripped to the bone of all but essentials; we had driven all the heavy baggage down to Salisbury and stored it at the Rose and Crown, an inn that represented the last link in the chain.

Leaving the Swan was very hard, and to ease the wrench we worked the children into a frenzy over Scotland.

On the trip up the Great North Road they said nothing but "Hurray for Bonnie Sco'land!" and "Oh, good show!" They addressed us as Pater and Mater and said, "Oh, right-ho!" for yes. They refused to get out of the car to see anything and sprawled in the seats leafing through old comic books.

"What *do* you want to see?" I asked, looking at them and the comic books with maternal distaste.

"I want to see Bonnie Sco'land, Mater," said Pete cheerfully. "Hurray for Bonnie Sco'land!"

"I want to see our ancestors," said Billy.

"You can't see ancestors, dope," said Pete.

My ancestors were relatives of Sir Walter Scott and the ancestral mansion was near Abbotsford, Scott's home. It was called Synton.

My grandmother's country house in Massachusetts was also called Synton and was full of treasures from Scotland. Much of the furniture there seemed to belong to dead people—"Aunt So-and-So's chair, Great-Grandmother's table"—and a large part of it came from the original Synton in Scotland. My grandmother was always saying "the mate to" this or that was at Synton. A print of Synton hung in the drawing room and showed a gaunt, high house among trees, and in the foreground a tiny man in a tight suit and a tiny woman in hoop skirt and bonnet. These were our tiny ancestors.

213

Fortunately Bob knew all about Scots ancestry. If you have Scottish ancestors it's much easier to marry someone who has them too.

In Northumberland it began to rain. Black clouds boiled up ahead of us and on both sides of the road the moors rolled away in endless waves of heather and bracken, swept by rain. A few sheep and lambs cried thinly over the noise of the wind but the only other sign of life was an occasional stone sheep pen or a wall. This was the Border, dividing England from Scotland.

We were to cross into Scotland at Carter Bar but by late afternoon we were still driving through the rain and presently passed a stone house with "Teas" on a little board outside. We stopped and had a real Scottish high tea with scones, oatcake, bramble jelly, toasted crumpets, currant tea cake, and boiled eggs. I tried to explain The Family to the children but after a minute or two found that I only knew for certain that the blue fruit dish we have came from Synton and that the portraits known as The Ancestors didn't live there.

"Who did?" asked Kathy.

"That one with the brown curls over the oil heater," I said, feeling that this was not perhaps the best way of describing the cousin of Sir Walter Scott.

On this fascinating note the discussion closed and we went back to the car.

We passed a sign saying *Beware of Sheep* and followed a road that wound upwards through purple-brown drifts of heather to the crest of a hill. As we came to the top the sun slid out from under the black roof of cloud and there below us lay Scotland in dazzling sunshine, a sight to stop the breath.

The Lammamuirs were blue and violet, the near hills velvet-green. Shadows of amethyst moved over slopes bronze with old bracken. In the center of this vastness was a pastoral country of golden fields, crisscrossed with walls, bunched with trees. The bleakness of the Border moorland was at our backs but down in the valley the chimneys were smoking cozily. There were white lambs in green pastures; the hawthorn bursting into bloom in the hedgerows. The view was one of Scott's favorites and all this country is Scott country where he wrote *The Minstrelsy of the Scottish Border*. These are the Lowlands.

We spent the night in Hawick, a gray stone town made immortal by cashmere sweaters. When we asked the bartender the way to Synton, he recognized the name at once.

"Turrn right by the wee loch," he said. "Ye canna miss it."

We found it—a blue saucer reflecting the morning sky—and turned right down a narrow country road. There on our left was a small shining valley with horses grazing in neat pastures and fields and clumps of trees rolling away to distant hills, the color of blue grapes. At the head of the valley, four tall chimneys rose out of a cloud of leaves. Bob stopped the car.

"I'll bet that's it," he said.

A shepherd carrying a crook, with a collie at his heels, came abreast of us, his glance stern and incurious. He looked rather like a Presbyterian God and I asked him timidly where Synton was.

"Why, yon's Synton," he said, pointing with his crook. It was incredible to hear that familiar name spoken by a strange man on a lonely road in Scotland.

We drove down the lane and up a slope where thousands of primroses bloomed under beech trees. Synton, instantly recognizable from the print, rose bleak and forbidding at the top of the rise. In front of it was a pickup truck containing two people.

"Oh, dear," I said, "what shall we do?"

Bob drove right up beside the truck so there was nothing to do but get out. This I did and approaching the truck saw an extremely pretty person of about my own age looking out at me.

"I'm sorry," I said, "but I think we're cousins."

"Oh, from Australia?" she said.

"From the States."

"Oh, lovely," she said, and climbed out of the truck. In two minutes she had somehow cleared up all the names, informed us that her husband was away, and mysteriously spirited Bob into

215

the driver's seat of the truck with instructions to water the calves. The children piled into the back of the truck, obviously charmed with the whole thing, and the pretty cousin and I went into the house.

A country house that has been in one family for several centuries has a dense, rich atmosphere like a Christmas cake in which all kinds of colored fruits and nuts are imbedded. Synton was a honeycomb of rooms with high ceilings, crooked corridors, doorways, closets, corners of shadow, sudden sunlight through tall windows, and air that smelled of beeswax, smoke, carpets, roast beef, geraniums, and leather. In the large hall were some paintings of the hunt showing pink coats and galloping horses. There was a billiard room on the right, a drawing room on the left full of chintz in faded colors, old oriental rugs, mirrors reflecting the rows of miniatures on the mantel, and the backs of many books.

I waited there while my hostess went up to change from her garden clothes and looked about me with a curious feeling of having been there before. The reason was that much of the furniture was from sets that I had grown up with. There was the lyre-backed mahogany chair that no one but guests ever sat in. There was "the mate to" the clock; there was the desk chair and the chair that had a broken leg. The two Syntons seemed to telescope and that room so full of detail, so complicated with interwoven lives, its old soft colors dimmed by layer upon layer of time, was at once enchanting and disturbing. What a curious organism a family is, I thought, and how many eyes have looked out those windows at the primroses.

The pretty cousin came up behind me and said, "It's a pity the snowdrops are past. They are thick along that path and are a famous sight in March. There's a watercolor somewhere by someone done long ago."

The past made a late-afternoon feeling in the room, even the morning sunlight seemed gently sad as we looked at old pictures: delicate miniatures and sepia photographs of the house in its prime with stiff little groups of ancestors arrested in the act of drinking tea. At last we said goodbye and set out for the King's House on the edge of the Highlands where I had stayed with my family twenty years before. On that earlier visit I had spent half the time crouched over a gas fire in winter tweeds and the rest of the time squelching around in the rain. I had always pictured Scotland as a wet sponge of heather with a purple sky sagging so low that you could almost touch it. That had been in July.

Now in May the transparent sunlight seemed to hold all objects motionless in its amber depths. The new leaves on the birches hung breathlessly—drops of honey too heavy to fall. We passed fish-shaped lochs, silver smooth, reflecting the unmoving hills in exact reverse. Fishermen stood with uplifted rods, transfixed on the shores.

I remembered every inch of the road but was unprepared for the bluebells on the banks and the great bonfires of gorse that blazed against the sky.

"We're almost there," I said every few minutes. "Oh, I remember that stream."

These rhapsodies were greeted with dead silence. We had been "almost there" for an hour. But presently we saw the white-washed farmhouse with the slope of grouse moor behind it. Someone had added a hideous porch on the front and I felt a deep, personal resentment.

"That porch shouldn't be there," I said angrily.

"Let's go tear it down," suggested Bob.

When we climbed out of the car it was into sweet, summery air. I looked down the glen to the mountains and it was as though the whole green valley were under a bell glass. In the stillness we could hear the lambs crying on the hills.

The same family who had run the King's House twenty years before was still there, only this time the son was in charge. He remembered me well and was outside waiting to give us a royal welcome. I introduced the children and explained to Billy and Margie that Ian (our host) used to take my small brother and sister to see the cows every day. We went upstairs to the same rooms and looking down the glen from my window I felt distinctly strange, as though not a moment had elapsed since that day when I was nearly as young as Kathy.

We had tea and scones with black currant jam by a wood fire and I kept saying, "This is exactly the same," until everybody told me to stop. The two younger children then went off with Ian to the cow barn. Pete took his golf clubs over to a field to teach Kathy how to play, and Bob and I walked up the glen in the low, rich sunlight. The hills on each side and ahead were purple and velvety but the glen itself was brilliant green and secret. Everywhere was the sound of running water and the bleating of lambs, and down by the river the curlews tumbled, never ceasing their curious whinnying cry.

"Do you suppose those are 'whaups'?" I asked Bob. Books by John Buchan or Maurice Walsh are always full of "whaups." Bob didn't know. These birds with their black and white somersaulting flight had a cry which a velvet doorbell might make. There was a shivery quality to it like the lament of a lost spirit.

We followed the road that led up the glen, between stone walls and banks where the fiddleheads of springing bracken were sticky as barley sugar. Wild pink rhododendron and holly leaned over the walls, the gorse was egg-yolk yellow on the slopes above us. We passed low white crofts smoking dreamily in their bright fields and stopped to watch a shepherd collie nosing some sheep up from the river pastures. His master directed him with whistles and gestures of his crook. The quick, darting efficiency of the little dog was miraculous.

The walk up the glen always ended at the ancient churchyard where Rob Roy is buried. I took Bob there and we stood in the spring sunlight and read the wonderful name Rob Roy MacGregor. The names of chieftains are like battlecries, more royal-sounding than the names of kings: Fraser of Lovat, The MacNeill of Barra, The MacNab, The MacDonald of the Isles, The MacLeod.

There were other gravestones tilting together in the tender green enclosure, and several had Bob's family name upon them. This seemed exciting to me and I suggested that we should find out about relatives in this area.

"There might be an empty castle waiting for you," I said. "Or money."

"Unlikely," said Bob. "These characters were probably raiders who got killed stealing cattle."

In honor of our arrival we had for dessert that night something called American Foam. When it was brought in, the other diners and the waitress watched expectantly as though the sight of our national dish would send us into transports of joy. As none of us had ever seen or heard of American Foam before, I'm afraid our reactions were disappointing. I would be interested to know what Americans, if any, eat this Foam.

At the King's House we were so far north that the twilight lasted until nearly eleven o'clock and the sun rose at four in the morning. I would wake and see the far mountains dark blue and snow-veined at the end of the glen and then go back to sleep until early tea arrived at eight.

The children, entranced with the country, the inn, the cows and the people, refused to go anywhere in the car. They spent their time feeding calves, playing golf, or sitting in the heather making twig brooms. Their speech was a mixture of all the languages so far encountered.

"Oh, bun," they would say. "That's frightfully bun. Mamma mia!"

"Oo, aye. Pass me the wee branch wull ye? Merci beaucoup, mein Herr," and similar flights of nonsense.

On some days, the sky was pearl gray with a pale sun, and in the hazy atmosphere the odors of dried bracken, wood smoke, and pine needles were heavy and sweet. On other days the heather turned wine color under a bruised purple sky; the mountain streams tumbled in coffee-brown and gold between granite boulders and in the wild glens skimmers with orange bills fled

219

across the road. On the moors the highland sheep, ragged as great mops, stood up to their bellies in the heather and watched us go by. The whole world was full of the sad crying of lambs.

On one of the last days, Bob bribed Margie to go with him to Loch Lomond. The other children were playing golf as usual, and I went off alone to climb the moor opposite the inn. Twenty years before, my brother and I had tried to run up it after tea but foundered on the first slope.

Today I'll do it, I thought, swinging along in the warm delicious air. I went under a fence, over a wall, stepped into a bog, and ran from a barking dog. Finally I was in the hill pastures where the ground had the quivering sogginess of a soaked sponge. The gorse thickets were full of sheep, who started up ahead of me, each with its lamb. Their silly blatting accompanied my progress. From that height the glen seemed to lie at the bottom of a clear sea of sunlight, and in the green fields below, the smoke from the white crofts spiralled upward in blue corkscrews like cigarettes abandoned in a quiet room. The hot sun brought out the heavy almond scent of the gorse. I sat on a rock near one of the little streams and looked back at the King's House. The years dissolved and I almost believed my father and mother were waiting there for me.

When you are up high on a warm spring day you are made free. You have climbed out of time and the complications of people and for a little while this freedom makes you feel weightless, ageless, and merry. I ran all the way down the hill bouncing on the feather-bed of grass and moss. My sneakers were soaked, I was covered with mud and damp with heat, when I slid out onto the road. Rolling up my gloves in my sweater, I tied them on the end of a stick and swaggered back down the valley, solitary as a tramp. I was nobody's wife, nobody's mother, until I came to the knoll where the golfers were still flailing.

"Hi, men," I said.

"Why, hello, Parint," they said.

We allowed one day to go from the King's House in Balquhidder to Grasmere in the Lake District, where we had reservations. As Balquhidder is on the edge of the Highlands and the Lakes deep in England, this entailed driving like a bat out of hell through the worst country in Scotland, the area between Edinburgh and Glasgow. Bob took one of his "short cuts"—we drove around and around the town of Airdrie and went through a village called Clarkson five times.

"Watcher languidge, dahlin'," said Kathy as we saw the sign on the fifth round. There were slag heaps like nightmare mountains and signs saying *Beware Subsidence*.

"All we need now is to end up in a coal mine," I said.

The spring was rampant over the land and in the sheets of bluebells, the acres of apple blossom, there was a look of elegance, of fancy dress that shocked the eye as autumn foliage does. Pink and white trees stormed the road with petals; in the bluebell woods the ground was the color of a summer sky.

We came down into the Lakes in the late afternoon, stopping at last in Grasmere. Wordsworth's cottage is here, but somehow he had no place in our sentimental map. There was, however, an enormous section of all our maps that belonged to Beatrix Potter, the creator of Peter Rabbit. Her delicate water colors, so dear to all who know her books, had made the Lake country vivid to us before we knew England existed. Our childhood was between the covers of the little green books: *Peter Rabbit, The Flopsy Bunnies, Jemima Puddleduck, Tom Kitten,* and all the rest. This was one place that simply had to be the way we pictured it. If it wasn't—well, it would take years of hard work to blot out the reality and we might never regain the enchanted country.

The day was the most perfect of our entire journey, and this seemed propitious. We drove over roads that wound up through pastures and oak woods, down into steep valleys full of cherry blossom and through corkscrew lanes where bluebells made a soft haze under the trees. We passed small snow-white farmhouses with rows of currant bushes beside them and beehives under apple trees. Hawthorn brushed both sides of the car, showering petals in the windows. Then a high upland. A green field with a horse beside a blue lake. Great trees. Then, around a corner, the small village square of Sawrey where whitewashed cottages stood at odd angles and chimney pots were buried in apple blossoms. It was the exact street where the Puddleducks walked off in Tom Kitten's clothes and there was the wall that the kittens sat on. There was the gate and presently we were walking up the path in Tabitha Twitchet's garden.

Everything was exactly right; the farmyard was the one in *Jemima Puddleduck* and there was the green hill where she had gone to find her own nest. Inside the house Bob and I pointed out the doll's house in the *Three Bad Mice,* the cups in *The Tailor of Gloucester.* We recognized every piece of furniture, the very rooms themselves. We had climbed these stairs when we were three.

The children were pleased but not completely bewitched as we were. They said, "Oh, yah" and "Yup," and "Hey, that's right!" but it was plain that Bob and I were the only ones under the spell. To us it was really magic, like walking through a mirror or seeing a painting come to life. Then I remembered that the children had been almost wild with excitement when they saw Roy Rogers and his horse Trigger at the Boston Rodeo. Would Disneyland have for them the same enchantment that this place had for us?

We found a bluebell wood for our picnic and ate bread, cheese, and wine sitting in the warm bracken with the sappy fragrance of bluebells all about us. The light filtered through young oak leaves was pale green and cool, but beyond the wood's edge the whole radiant landscape simmered in the May sun. A small soft owl, the size of a beer mug and the color of cinnamon, caused me to say, "There's Old Brown." I suppose our children may feel the same way about Donald Duck.

222

We were on the way from Bath to the Devonshire coast when I found Exmoor in the atlas.

"Lorna Doone!" I cried. "Here's Dulverton. It's only a bit out of the way."

This was an extremely romantic piece of territory in our imaginary map and here we had wandered in our teens. Even the names in the atlas made me feel young and dreamy-eyed. Bob and my father have always said that Lorna Doone is the most beautiful woman in all literature so he was as eager as I.

"We could follow the route John Ridd took from his school the first time he saw the Doones," said Bob.

I rooted in the luggage until I found the book of *Lorna Doone* and as we drove I read aloud directions. Presently we found ourselves in front of the school in Dulverton. The road then turned into a stony track winding through treeless uplands. From the lush valleys of fruit blossom and hedgerows we had come in an hour into moors as wild as those in the Highlands of Scotland. We were on Exmoor. The sky grew overcast and the air had a cool, peaty scent. Plovers cried over the dark heather and sheep ran bleating away from the road.

"Look," said Bob, "that must be Dunkery Beacon." It was certainly something where the Beacon should be, and we stopped the car in a high stretch of moor to let the children have a run. According to the book it was about here that J. Ridd lay on his stomach in the heather and watched the Doones ride by below on the Doone Track.

Pretty soon we were following the edge of the sea which shone like a steel floor far below us. Then we dove down a perpendicular track between bristling hawthorn bushes and entered a narrow, hidden valley with a stream running through it. Sheep jostled each other in the road ahead of us. A soft rain was falling when we found John Ridd's farm, the village, the church, and, farther on, Doone Valley itself, green and deep.

All was exactly as described; we were charmed with everything but as far as I was concerned it wasn't John Ridd's house

223

nor was it Doone Valley. *My* Doone Valley was based on a picture of the Swiss Alps. And Bob admitted that his idea of the waterfall had been nearer Niagara Falls than the reality. The house was all wrong, too. To please me it would have had to resemble in every detail a house in Massachusetts where I had played as a child. This house, vaguely Tudor in design, to me was the scene of every book about England. P. G. Wodehouse, Galsworthy, Trollope—it made no difference. As John Ridd's house it reached a new high because I had to work in Doone Valley, Exmoor, and various streams, precipices, and woods not actually present.

In spite of these faults, the reality was so much more probable and so much better that I was able to exorcise my own version. The children, having seen *Lorna Doone* in the movies, were disappointed at the pitiful proportions of the falls and the valley. Apparently Hollywood had also used the Swiss Alps and Niagara for models.

It was tea time when we left Doone Valley, and we had spent quite a day, beginning with a tour of the city of Bath, a visit to Wells Cathedral to see the swans ring the bell for food (not a swan went near the bell), a stop at Glastonbury, and in between driving furiously to catch up with our reservations. As we hacked along toward Barnstaple I said to Bob that we must stop and have a cream tea at a farmhouse. (Devonshire specializes in clotted cream which is eaten with jam on warm split scones.) Bob said that we had to keep going.

My head ached and I was annoyed with Bob who had not said that I was like Lorna Doone when I said he was like John Ridd.

We finally stopped at a gigantic hotel in Barnstaple for a late tea. Only Kathy was allowed to participate because the other three had behaved so abominably. Why *I* was permitted to have tea I can't say. The maid said there was "only a bit" of clotted cream left and the boys chased a small dog outside and were reprimanded by the manager. Saturation point had now been reached.

We still had before us the visit to Clovelly and the night at Hartland Quay—where I had been on the earlier visit. Unfortunately, we had almost nothing left to appreciate with. Glutted with sentiment, memories, architecture, and literature we returned to the primitive pleasures. It was enough that food and lodging awaited us.

There was also sunlight, but not in Clovelly, which was in the cliff's shadow. Still, it was a perfect afternoon. The hedged fields were apple green, the woods silvery. Larks rose quivering into the sun; magpies flared black and white across our path. The roadsides were like flower prints in pink, blue, and white. The sea was at the end of every lane, its color filled the chinks in the hills, its diamond light illumined the valleys. Just at dinner time we came to the blind plunge where the road goes over the edge of the downs to the hotel.

After we had eaten, Bob and I climbed the spongy moorland above the hotel chimneys and lay down in the long grass among sea pinks and campion. The scent of honey came from the pinks where bees murmured drowsily above the rustle of the sea. Far below, the waves creamed around tilted black rocks and we looked down on the backs of gulls.

I tried, for Bob's sake, to be as much like Lorna Doone as possible, but he didn't seem to notice. The top-heavy structure I had been building all day now avalanched. Rain, not being like Lorna Doone, "only a bit of" clotted cream for tea, leaving England, nostalgia for my youth—these bore me to earth in a confused mass.

"Do you still like any of us?" I asked Bob, who was lying on his back in the sea pinks.

"Now what?" he said. "Come on, let's go down and play darts in the bar. Stop hunting for something to fuss about."

So instead of weeping for everything and nothing, I went down and we played darts.

Last Lap

The psychology of the Last Lap is very curious and very different from the psychology of departure. They have, however, some things in common: butterflies in the stomach and a debilitating inertia.

Every time I thought about going home I felt as though I were dropping eighty floors in a fast elevator and apparently Bob and the children felt this way too. In our last drive across the south of England, we all examined the idea of home from different angles, like people unwrapping a wedding present.

"Hey!" Pete said, "we'll be seeing the dogs."

"Maybe Mollie's going to have puppies," I said.

"Cluny's her son!" said Billy, shocked.

"Oh, that's right," I said.

"We'll see our friends," said Margie reverently.

"The piano!" cried Kathy. "Gosh, I can't wait!"

"Boy, the minute I'm home I'm going to get out my bike," said Billy.

"The old car!" I said lovingly.

"I hope nothing's gone wrong with the furnace," said Bob. "I'll bet nobody checked it."

"Don't be silly," I said. "Somebody would have noticed if the house had burned down."

"Maybe the pipes froze," said Bob.

"Hey!" said Pete. "It'll be summer vacation, practically. There'll only be two more weeks of school."

"Do we have to go?" they all said.

"Yes," we said.

"Oh, jeeze," they moaned.

Outside the car, the whole of England had the dreamlike, remote quality of places that you are about to leave. It was already in the past, and the light over the fields and trees was nostalgic and afternoonish. We drove into Salisbury after tea and presently trundled through the archway into the courtyard of the Rose and Crown. This hostelry, though far beyond our means, was too good to miss. It was a long, black and white thirteenth-century coaching inn, flush with the sidewalk on one side, but the rear faced the river and the famous view of the cathedral spire.

The walls of the main hallway were panelled in black oak and hung with huge fish in glass cases and a number of ancient sinister man traps. The children spent hours examining the teeth and wanted to know exactly how they caught men.

The first evening the manageress, a dead ringer for Becky Sharp, took me aside and told me that the boys had broken some fixtures in their room. This scared me a good deal and I hated to announce that we had decided to eat our dinner in town to save money.

"You tell her," I said to Bob. "You're a man."

"You tell her," said Bob. "You're a woman."

I told her. She was not pleased.

227

The next day I felt the way I did when I had gone to the hospital on a false alarm and was taken home with no baby. In the Rose and Crown the feverish mood of the drive from Devon was replaced by complete calm. We all acted as though we had four months instead of four days in which to enjoy England and moved in an atmosphere of spacious leisure. No one made the slightest attempt to pack, check the baggage stored in the stables, or deal in any way with our impending departure.

Ever since Italy we had been tutoring the children in their studies and each morning they had sat scowling over their books. Now my role as teacher to the small ones collapsed and Bob turned all the force of his professional mind on Pete. This unfortunate was soon to take his entrance exams for Exeter in the Consul's office at Southampton. For once he did not have to be urged to study, and he and Bob worked with a common passion.

I felt as though my brain had been ironed smooth so that any thoughts I had slipped off. Rather than pack or be efficient, I hunted for pieces of broken china in the garden, an imbecile pastime to which I became addicted. I infected the children, and we used to poke around the inn's vegetable garden while the other guests and the staff watched us apprehensively. I accumulated masses of old blue china in pieces up to three inches across, and the children specialized in bits of church-warden pipes which must have dated from the eighteenth century and before.

I also collected whole moments of a day by writing down lists of everything I saw, heard or smelled. Here, for posterity, is the hour of 4 P.M. on May 28th, as it came to me in the garden of the Rose and Crown in Salisbury, England.

SOUNDS

Birds—blackbird warbling in apple tree
Coot clucking from reeds by river
Wood pigeons cooing in woods
Cuckoos calling each other
Swallows twittering over the water

228

Chaffinch bubbling in nearby bush
Click of hoe in garden when gardener is at work
Rustle of leaves over head and all over the land in different
    degrees of sibilance
Chuckle and gurgle of river against the bank
Distant swish of traffic
Voices calling
Cathedral bells
Harsh sound of two men scraping down a punt across the
    water

SMELLS

Mealy, heavy sweetness of hawthorn
Cut grass
River mud and rushes (a rank smell but nice)

SIGHTS

Curve of river upstream, polished like glass except where
    rising fish make dimples
Willows in bunched, feathery masses along the river bank
Trunks looped in dark ivy
Vertical strokes of rushes
Seaweed weaving in current just below garden wall
Inverted reflections of willows, puffed white clouds, rushes,
    hawthorn bloom, and in the center the cathedral spire
Cathedral spire itself across green and gold water meadows
Flowers—buttercups, English daisies, sorrel, clover, moon
    daisies (like ours)
Long, silky, silvery grasses
Five-arched bridge downstream with small children trotting
    across it, only heads visible
Garden downstream of small cottage where men are scrap-
    ing punt, two girls are gardening, and two black angora
    cats are up in a pear tree
Man upstream in punt fishing
Swan cruising by, all puffed out
Goldfinches fluttering over grass tips

Thrush running on lawn
Children in garden hunting for pieces of clay pipes
Back of half-timbered inn and stable yard
Cows up to their stomachs in buttercups in the water
    meadow across the way
Elderly lady in a violet sweater having her tea nearby

By the time I finished this list Bob and Pete returned from Southampton, relaxed at last and now able to think of other things. Pete went off to hunt for more pipe fragments in the garden. Bob sat down and said I must realize that we might not have enough money to last until the boat.

"You can't buy *anything*," he said.

"Can't I even get my hair done?" I asked piteously.

"Godalmighty, no," he said. "The *only* thing we can buy is food. That's *all*."

The last day began badly. The night before I had dreamed that Bob was in love with a large-eyed female in an office at home. Although to my certain knowledge he had never exchanged two words with the woman, if indeed he had noticed her at all, I still felt abused.

"You were *awful* in my dream," I said indignantly.

"Whassat?" he said hoarsely.

"You behaved terribly," I said. "You were in love with that pop-eyed woman in Jack's office."

"What pop-eyed woman?" he said.

"You know perfectly well," I said. "That bulbous one. How men can find her attractive I'll never understand."

"Who said I found her attractive? I don't even know which one you *mean*," said Bob, yawning loudly.

"Well, you certainly knew in my dream," I said. "Really, it was repulsive—"

"Look," said Bob, "I refuse to be blamed for something I did in a dream. Now get up and relax."

Although the atmosphere was that of a Turkish bath and everybody was cross, we decided to have a final picnic, and in this elfin mood set out for Stonehenge. Everybody was cross at lunch. Billy spilled milk in the back seat, but it was sour anyway so nobody cared.

In the afternoon, though, things mysteriously improved. We went to the open-air market and bought a mustard-yellow tin trunk for six shillings. I reminded Bob that I could have bought *seven* trunks for the same price at the auction.

"We don't need seven trunks," he said simply.

Back at the Rose and Crown, Kathy and I washed out the last laundry and hung bras and panties rather frivolously on the casement windows where they twirled in full view of the people having tea below (we were unable to join them because of lack of funds). In a moment of reckless abandon, I washed my own hair, something I never do because I can't set it properly. It dried wonderfully in the sun when I hung my head out the window and it felt so good and clean and smelled so sweetly of soap that I felt noble and pure.

However, one look in the mirror nearly cost me my reason. My face was almost invisible in the center of a gigantic ball of blond fuzz. With twitching fingers I ransacked Kathy's effects until I found her box of bobby pins, and with a damp comb and these wretched little instruments managed to torture the front of my head into an irregular and lumpy mass of hair and metal. Then my arms became numb to the shoulder and ached terribly, and in a rage I tore out all my work. I now looked exactly like Medusa with the snake hairdo, and, wrapping my head in a towel, I called to Kathy from the window. She looked up and said, "Oh, jeepers, did you wash it?" I said, yes, and would she please come right away or I might kill myself. When she arrived and saw me without the towel she became hysterical but finally recovered enough to start work with the pins.

"Gosh, Maw," she said finally, "I can't do this. You've got about twice too much hair."

"I know," I said. "Well, do the best you can or they'll never let me on the boat."

She struggled for about an hour and we both nearly died

231

laughing. While it was setting I packed and put aside a large pile of stuff to use instead of money for tips. Then by mending and doing some ineffectual dry cleaning with the methylated spirits for the stove, Kathy and I managed to get the boys one set of near-respectable clothes. Bob's overcoat was hopeless and had only one buttton, but he refused to let me spend money even on buttons. Presently my hair was dry again so we took out the bobby pins. Every curl seemed to go in a different direction and the general effect was that of an insane Fiji Islander.

"Well—" I said, and then we both howled with laughter.

"Thanks anyway," I said, mopping my eyes. "Now you see why I can't set it myself."

When I had subdued the corkscrew effect somewhat by brushing and flattening, we went down to the garden.

"Mummy!" shrieked Margie.

"Jeeze!" said Pete, almost reverently.

Billy seemed to be stricken dumb with horror and only stared at me, but Bob, of course, remained unmoved.

"What's the matter with all of you?" he asked.

"Do you mean you don't notice anything?" I asked.

"Anything about what?" said Bob, puzzled.

"My *hair!*" I said. *"Look at it!"*

"I don't see anything wrong with it," said Bob.

"Oh, Daddy," moaned Kathy.

"Never mind," I said. "He wouldn't notice the difference if I cut off my head. As long as there's some sort of human figure with my voice he just goes along as usual."

"Your mother's annoyed," said Bob, grinning.

Just then George, the Boots, seeing us all in the garden, came bobbing out in his striped apron. He looked like a cross between a cockney Figaro and Sam Weller and had a pointed elfish face with black wispy hair. He walked with a kind of hobbling roll and had a merry and fantastical turn of mind.

"Ready for your tea?" he asked.

"Not today," said Bob, who never explains anything.

232

"Wot? No tea for the kiddies?" said George.

"We can't, George," I said. "We haven't any money left."

"You leave it to ole George," he said. "Just see wot ole George will bring you."

In a moment he was back with a bowl of apples and oranges—apparently emergency rations to sustain us until the actual tea arrived. Then, after a bit, he staggered out under an enormous tray. On this was the biggest tea we had ever had—scones, cakes, cookies, toasted currant buns, and more apples.

"Oh, George!" we said.

"That's all roight, that's all roight," said George, holding up his hand. "Nobody's going to starve around ole George."

We finished our tea gratefully—and I went back upstairs to continue my fatal work among the Car-pacs. The manageress was waiting for me at the top of the stairs.

"Why didn't you *tell* me?" she asked, almost in tears. "I would have taken care of everything. George told me," she added.

"Please, it's all right," I said. "We are so much obliged to you for the tea and George was so sweet. We'll manage."

"I'm sending you up a picnic dinner," she said. "I can't feed you free in the dining room because I don't own the inn, but I'll provide dinner tonight upstairs and a picnic for your lunch tomorrow."

I had a hard time persuading her to let us go into town for a hot meal. Even then she must have feared that we were about to eat grass or chew shoe leather, because she sent up the sandwich dinner anyway—hundreds of sandwiches, fruit, cakes, candy. The children were delighted and ate a great deal, undeterred, as far as I could see, by the fact that they had just consumed a gigantic tea and were about to have dinner.

When we came back from dinner in town—a repast which they merely poked at—we found that the manageress had left a box of chocolates outside the girls' door. It was really very touching—this generous solicitude—and I at once sought her out and, nearly in tears myself, told her how kind she was and how deeply we appreciated it. I offered her some of my American nylons, still in their Peck and Peck envelope, which she refused, saying, "I didn't do it *for* anything. I just wanted to."

"I know you did," I said, "but I would really be very happy if you would let me give you these for the same reason." She finally accepted and we parted both in a highly emotional state.

On our last walk through the Cathedral close we all felt maudlin about leaving England. The close was deep in late sunlight, and the level lawns, freckled with daisies, stretched away into the long shadows of trees. The cathedral's marvelous spire seemed to move across the evening sky, carrying with it a flock of daws and their creaking voices. We went inside, into the enormous hush, the whispering stone silence, and saw the knights and nobles lying asleep with folded hands.

The next morning I felt as though I had no insides at all and couldn't eat. We were served a regal breakfast and loaded with sandwiches and other delicacies for our picnic lunch. I stayed upstairs finishing the packing while Bob and Pete struggled with the loading of Tom Thumb. George circulated, reporting the progress below and keeping an eye on the pile of discarded possessions.

He had confided to Bob that he had seen a small case of French cognac in the stable where our luggage was stored. Would Bob be willing to sell it to him to give as a birthday present to his old mother? Bob said he certainly would, but insisted on *giving* George half the case in place of a tip, a deal which pleased everyone. We had some doubts as to how much of the cognac the aged mother would see, but possibly we wronged George in this. Anyway we wanted him to have the best of everything, as we absolutely adored him.

While we were packing he said to the children, "Oim coming to visit you, you knaow!"

"Oh, yes, come *on*, George," cried Billy, his face radiant. "Mum, George is coming to visit us!"

"You come," I said, "and stay forever."

"Naow wen you're in the middle of the ocean," said George, shaking his forefinger like Sam Weller, "you'll look aht the winder and wot will you see? Ole George peddling by on 'is bicycle fahst as anything. Ole George'll come peddling, peddling roight into Noo York, 'ee will. 'Aow's that, Bill?"

Billy giggled in homage to this delightful picture and we all urged George to come somehow, sometime. Then I gave him the R.A.C. and A.A. Guides, the Berlitz German phrase book, a copy of *David Copperfield,* the aluminum soup saucepan, the bottle of methylated spirits, one half a pound of butter, a can of soup, an empty tin candy box with a pretty girl on it, and some old comic books. I gave the chambermaid Kathy's broken Brownie camera, but George was depressed by this faithlessness and said he could have used it. He then hid all his loot in an ash can and went on to help load the car. I couldn't imagine what he would do with the Berlitz phrase book and guides but he said he loved reading and especially liked to look up things in the R.A.C.

"Learn a lot that way," he said.

"Yes, indeed," I said, dubiously.

"My mother likes to read, too," said George.

Dressing the family for the boat was a terrible problem. Bob was dressed as usual, but his flannels had been dry cleaned back in Italy, so he was relatively respectable. His mackintosh was filthy, but they are supposed to be, and a good English friend of ours once showed my brothers how to take the crease out of flannels so Bob was actually in high style.

I, on the contrary, was wearing a brown corduroy suit purchased for seventy-five cents at the Episcopal Church rummage sale five years before. Some fatalistic instinct caused me to pack it for just such an emergency. My hair seemed to have grown longer and fuzzier during the night and practically obscured my face. This was for the best because at this point I didn't want anyone to recognize me.

Kathy was wearing a suit which hadn't been cleaned since we left but somehow she managed to give an impression of spotlessness, partly because of her hair. It was very well set, which depressed and pleased me simultaneously. Pete and Billy, having been forced into the clothes we prepared for them, had decent shirts and pants, but their tweed jackets looked very strange. Our dry-cleaning operations did not remove the spots; they created much larger ones. Margie had clean hair but her plaid skirt was dirty even through the plaid.

Europeans must get their clothes dry cleaned somehow, so perhaps our informants were wrong about the lethal effects of dry cleaning abroad. Still if we'd spent money on cleaning we might never have arrived in Southampton.

This, then, was the shabby but gallant little group that gathered about Tom Thumb and said goodbye to the Rose and Crown and all its inhabitants. We were saying goodbye in fact to England, to Europe, and to our free and roving life, to infinite leisure and infinite diversion, but we were not thinking along these lines. Bob thought of money. The children thought of whose turn it was for which seat. My mind was a total blank.

A Study in Homecoming

Southampton in the low afternoon sunlight looked unusually revolting. The hotel looked revolting. *We* looked revolting. Tom Thumb smelled of hard-boiled eggs and the children peered fretfully out between piles of dirty duffel bags, like mice in a rubbish heap.

Bob, too far gone to hear their peevish cries, drove steadily through the town and parked on a grimy street down by the docks. He then disappeared into a block of offices and I sat in the car with the children and read all the signs in the area two hundred times.

"Kin we get out of the car?" they asked.

"No," I said.

"Kin we buy comic books?"

"No," I said.

"Kin we get Cokes at that drugstore?"

"No," I said.

"Kin we get out of the car, please?"

"Oh, *all right!*" I said.

"Then kin we get comic books and Cokes?"

"Oh, all right," I said.

"Oh, boy," they said. I read the signs again.

After what seemed like several weeks, Bob came back, looking gray, and said that we had to take every single thing out of Tom Thumb because he had to be fumigated.

"Oh, *no,*" I shrieked. We had used the bus as a kind of giant trunk, and it was one solid mass of objects all fitted in and around us like a Chinese puzzle.

Bob explained in dead tones that they had to expose T. Thumb to some fearful temperature in the form of steam to kill possible potato-blight bacteria.

"Potato blight!" I said scornfully. "Are they going to boil us, too? What about our shoes?"

"Say," said Bob, "that's true. I wonder whether anyone's thought of that?"

"Well, for the love of heaven don't suggest it to them," I said, "and go tell them T. Thumb hasn't been near any potatoes and that I refuse to unpack him."

"We *have* to," said Bob. "It's the law."

Just to show the poor dumb law, I toyed with the idea of smuggling a blighted potato out in my pocket, but I hadn't time to comb Southampton for diseased vegetables.

We unloaded in front of the hotel and the manager stood by with bulging eyes as the pavement filled up with a squalid array of jugs, swords, balls, baskets, golf clubs, crates, duffel bags, Car-pacs, and picture-tubes, all salted down with orange peel, egg shells, and bread crumbs. I used my favorite swear word so many times that Bob said it would be a wonder if the children were ever again acceptable members of society.

"Your mother's a crazy woman," he said.

"Your father's an old hide-bound law-abiding Britisher," I said.

We went to a cheap Italian restaurant, escaping momentarily

from the junk-shop atmosphere of our bedrooms. From there we could see the steamer looking enormous and divinely beautiful, with the American flag flying from her stern. I felt the customary lump in the throat at the sight of the flag. Bob seemed unaffected by anything. He just kept saying over and over that he hadn't allowed for the cost of sterilizing Tom Thumb and that we now had barely enough money left to pay the hotel bill and buy gas in New York. Tips were impossible. We would probably be stoned out of the hotel.

"Who cares?" I said. "We've got our tickets so they can't stop us going home."

Bob muttered something about Extra Expenses.

Our rooms were filled from wall to wall with luggage, but after rooting around we found the beds and made an abortive attempt to sleep. The children kept coming in to say that they were boiling, could they order a Coke, and imagine, we'll be on the *boat* tomorrow!

The next morning, bleary-eyed but unexpectedly relaxed and cheerful, I helped the family drag our possessions down to the car. Bob, now isolated from us all in a tower of gloom and worry, drove off to the boat and we followed later in a taxi. Down at the docks we joined him by the mountain of luggage and sat around on it until we were driven into line to have our passports checked. Bob once more disappeared, grimly determined that our bus must be the first car aboard.

After this we went and visited the Thumb, who had a large sticker on his window proving his sterility.

The ship's photographer, standing by the gangplank, started violently as our sordid little company straggled into view. Bob led the procession, his face set, with the crated Della Robbia in one hand and a bouquet of suitcases in the other. I followed, much impeded by all the pictures rolled up in tubes, various coats, and our tickets. The children—carrying baskets, swords, soccer balls, golf clubs, and other bric-a-brac—surged up in my wake, and the photographer, snapping madly, immortalized us for posterity. Below in Tourist Class the red and gray corridors

239

and their smell were unchanged. Five months fell from us.

While they were loading the baggage, I trespassed on the First Class sports deck and overhead against the blue June sky the Flag snapped and unrolled its marvelous folds. In a great burst of joy like the breaking of a dam, the fact of Home poured over me and in typical maudlin fashion I began to weep with emotion. Home, Home, Home! I thought incoherently. Oh, blessed, crass, overabundant America! Oh superhighways! Oh, Esso stations! Oh, Howard Johnson and his repulsive orange roofs! Oh, New York! Oh, New England and the white houses by the summer sea! We had been wanderers for so long that I thought we had outgrown nationality, outlived homesickness, but now it seemed this was not so. I loved every stick, stone, and clod of earth in America, and I suppose this is why people fight wars. Kathy came up and said, "When we land I'm going to kneel down and kiss the ground."

Kisses were in the air. Everybody on the dock was kissing. The ship's foghorn split the blue day in half and tears filled my eyes as the boat began to swing out into the harbor. A young man far below on the tug threw kisses up to Kathy and me (or just Kathy?) and we returned them with abandon. Then Bob appeared and I hugged him but was not allowed to go so far as kiss because were In Public.

"We did it!" I said.

"Just," said Bob. "We have seven shillings left, and ten dollars for the drive home."

"For heaven's sake stop talking about money!" I said.

"Well," he said, evidently hard pressed for another topic, "Tom Thumb was the first car aboard. I saw to that."

"Is that supposed to be a good idea?" I asked.

"Of *course* it's a good idea," said Bob suddenly looking as though it weren't.

．　．　．　．　．

Eight days later I stood on the upper-deck companionway between two Czechoslovakians and we were all in tears. New York

240

rose out of the morning mists, out of crimson and violet waters, like a mirage. There was the famous sky line and all around us swarmed the traffic of the river, busy and noisy after days of wide and empty sea.

"Eet is so beautiful," said the female Czech, sobbing, "so veree, veree beautiful."

"Like fairy story," said the male, frankly wiping his eyes.

"Yes, it is," I croaked, wiping mine.

Entering the dining room I looked with distaste at my family, phlegmatically eating breakfast.

"Dopes," I said. "Clods. You should have seen it. It was wonderful. How *could* you sit here eating?"

"Pack," said Bob, as though I hadn't spoken. "That steward isn't around, so he can go without a tip."

"Your suitcase's at the bottom of the whole pile of tourist luggage, Ma," said Billy with relish. "It's squashed flat."

"I can't wait to see Tom Thumb come off on the crane," said Billy.

. . . . .

Hours and hours later he and we were still waiting for the bus to come off on the crane.

"Well, anyway, we can get our stuff inspected," I said. "Watch this." A customs inspector was standing by the railing with his hat on the back of his head. I moved in on him with Billy and Margie as props.

"Do they ever drop those cars?" I asked, innocently batting my eyelashes.

"Oh, no, dear," he said, leering at me.

"I suppose you're very busy," I said. "Do you often catch people smuggling things?"

(Brief résumé of his life followed.)

"Where's your luggage, dear?" he asked, after a while. Past groups of envious waiting passengers I proudly conducted him to our mountain of junk and motioned to Bob to join us. At this point a terrible thing happened. Bob revealed that we had paid

241

for the Volkswagen *over here*. The customs man threw up his hands.

"That does it," he said. "Now you have to pay duty."

"Duty?" we cried in unison.

"Yes," he said. "It's an import, see? That should be about a hundred dollars."

"What?" we bleated.

"No way around it," said the man, sadly. "God, I'm sorry, but it's the Law."

"But we haven't got a hundred dollars," said Bob. "We only have about ten."

"God," said the man. "Well, let's see."

After a dreadful period, we persuaded someone (against regulations) to accept a check. The inspector then asked if we had anything else to declare and when Bob mentioned our few items he said, "Either you're a teacher or a thief."

"I'm a teacher," said Bob.

Then we were abandoned by everyone and waited and waited and waited.

The customs sheds were slowly emptied; car after car loaded its baggage and drove away. The customs inspectors went off to lunch and so did almost all the dock personnel. After a while I saw some stevedores buying hamburgers at a window by the door, and we spent some of our precious money for one very thin hamburger apiece.

I stared out of the shed door at New York and many of the cars seemed to be stretched out to grotesque lengths. They were also most peculiar colors—fuchsia pink and purple, orange and yellow—and some of them had unbelievable fins like sharks.

"Hey, *look!*" I said.

Then there was a wild shriek from Billy.

"There's Tom!" he yelled.

There indeed was Tom Thumb suspended in space above our heads, slowly twirling.

When we finally rolled out into New York I waited for the shooting-star ecstasy to begin. There were the skyscrapers honeycombed with windows leaning toward each other high overhead; there were the crawling, beetle lines of traffic stretching into a purple haze of exhaust smoke. The yellow taxis darted about us as usual, drivers in black peaked caps swore at each other, and one shouted, "Whereya thinkya goin', Mac?" as Bob swerved past. Traffic lights, street signs, great stores, little stores, hamburg joints, places just going out of business, places selling Armenian embroideries, bars, bowling alleys, and above, around, below, and even inside, the enormous orchestration of sound, like a chord prolonged. It was all there as we had left it.

The surprising and disappointing thing was that I felt as though we had been there the day before. It was the same with the parkways, the superhighways, the toll roads, and even our own exit with the name of our town. We might have been down to Boston for the day. The truth is we had come home mentally two weeks earlier, on the drive across England to Salisbury.

I felt that somehow, somewhere I had been robbed.

We passed the electric company's truck. Gilbert Bean was standing at the foot of a pole looking up. He waved casually as we went by. Mr. Babcock was out clipping his hedge. He jerked his chin in greeting. The laundry truck was parked outside of the Brown's, and our driver was taking the clean packages out of the back.

"That's right. It's Thursday," I said.

"What?" said Bob.

Piercing screams rose from the back seat as the end of our street came into view. It looked exactly as it always did in June, and when we made the turn we saw all the children sitting in the gutters playing marbles, bobbing around hop-scotch designs in the center, and jumping rope on the sidewalk. Two tiny ones in red-and-blue sweaters tricycled ahead of us, and we slowed down to a crawl. They all looked up and a high thin screech answered the roar from our back seat. Small running figures converged upon us from all sides. Screen doors burst open. Dogs barked.

"They're back! Hey, look, they're back!"

"We're home! Hey, Davy, we're *home!* Hey, kids, we're home! Hi! Hi!"

With a galloping herd in our wake we rolled down to our driveway. Dogs yelped and attacked each other in sheer hysteria on the fringes of the mob.

"We're *home!"* screamed our children, tumbling from the car. Like a flock of starlings they flashed away chattering. Two dogs remained behind fighting horribly on the lawn.

"First unpack the car!" shouted Bob. *"First unpack the car!"*

But we were alone at last.

THE AUTHOR

JANET GILLESPIE spent her childhood years in Holyoke, Massachusetts, where her father, Robert Russell Wicks, was minister of a large church. When he became Dean of Princeton University Chapel, she moved to Princeton and attended Miss Fine's School. After four years at Mt. Holyoke College (class of '36) she became an apprentice teacher at Shady Hill School in Cambridge, Massachusetts. She then went back to Princeton, where she taught English and History at Miss Fine's and became engaged to William Ernest Gillespie, Princeton '33, whom she married in '38. When Mr. Gillespie accepted a teaching job at his old school, Phillips Exeter Academy, they moved to Exeter, New Hampshire, and built the house and garden she described in her two garden books, *The Joy of a Small Garden* and *Peacock Manure and Marigolds*. In 1956 they took their four children to Europe—a trip Mrs. Gillespie made into her first book, *Bedlam in the Backseat*. Mr. Gillespie was Dean of the Faculty and Vice-Principal of Exeter when he died in '67. At this time Mrs. Gillespie wrote *A Joyful Noise* about the happy summers of her youth and the family summer place in Westport Point, Massachusetts. In '69 she married Robert F. Grindley, formerly of Detroit. They lived year round at Westport Point, doing over an old house and making a new garden until his death in '95. Mrs. Gillespie still lives in Westport Point, and from '91 to '98, she wrote a gardening column for the New Bedford Standard Times. Mrs. Gillespie says she loves Westport Point as much today as she did in childhood.

Printed in the United States
16905LVS00002B/61-204